FOUNDATIONS OF REAL-TIME COMPUTING:
COMPUTING:
Formal Specifications and Methods

THE KLUWER INTERNATIONAL SERIES IN ENGINEERING AND COMPUTER SCIENCE

REAL-TIME SYSTEMS

Consulting Editor

John A. Stankovic

REAL-TIME UNIX SYSTEMS: *Design and Application Guide,*
B. Furht, D. Grostick, D. Gluch, G. Rabbat, J. Parker, M. McRoberts,
ISBN: 0-7923-9099-7

FOUNDATIONS OF REAL-TIME COMPUTING: *Scheduling and Resource Management,* A. M. van Tilborg, G. M. Koob
ISBN: 0-7923-9166-7

FOUNDATIONS OF REAL-TIME COMPUTING:
Formal Specifications and Methods

Edited by

André M. van Tilborg
Gary M. Koob
Office of Naval Research

KLUWER ACADEMIC PUBLISHERS
Boston/Dordrecht/London

Distributors for North America:
Kluwer Academic Publishers
101 Philip Drive
Assinippi Park
Norwell, Massachusetts 02061 USA

Distributors for all other countries:
Kluwer Academic Publishers Group
Distribution Centre
Post Office Box 322
3300 AH Dordrecht, THE NETHERLANDS

Library of Congress Cataloging-in-Publication Data
Foundations of Real-Time Computing: Formal Specifications and Methods
    edited by André M. van Tilborg, Gary M. Koob.
        p. cm. -- (The Kluwer International Series in Engineering and
Computer Science ; 142. Real-Time Systems)
        "Preliminary versions of these papers were presented at a workshop
...sponsored by the Office of Naval Research in October 1990 in
Washington, D. C." -- Foreword.
        Includes bibliographical references and index.
        ISBN: 0-7923-9167-5
        1. Real-Time data processing. I. van Tilborg, André M., 1953-
    II. Koob, Gary M., 1958- . III. United States. Office of
Naval Research. IV. Series: Kluwer International Series in
Engineering and Computer Science ; SECS 142. V. Series: Kluwer
International Series in Engineering and Computer Science. Real-Time
Systems.
    QA76.54.F678 1991   91-17472
    004'.33--dc20   CIP

Printed on acid-free paper.

Printed in the United States of America

Contents

FOREWORD

This volume contains a selection of papers that focus on the state-of-the-art in formal specification and verification of real-time computing systems. Preliminary versions of these papers were presented at a workshop on the foundations of real-time computing sponsored by the Office of Naval Research in October, 1990 in Washington, D.C. A companion volume by the title *Foundations of Real-Time Computing: Scheduling and Resource Management* complements this book by addressing many of the recently devised techniques and approaches for scheduling tasks and managing resources in real-time systems. Together, these two texts provide a comprehensive snapshot of current insights into the process of designing and building real-time computing systems on a scientific basis.

The notion of *real-time system* has alternative interpretations, not all of which are intended usages in this collection of papers. Different communities of researchers variously use the term *real-time* to refer to either *very fast* computing, or *immediate* on-line data acquisition, or *deadline-driven* computing. This text is concerned with the formal specification and verification of computer software and systems whose correct performance is dependent on carefully orchestrated interactions with *time*, e.g., meeting deadlines and synchronizing with clocks. Such systems have been enabled for a rapidly increasing set of diverse end-uses by the unremitting advances in computing power per constant-dollar cost and per constant-unit-volume of space. End-use applications of real-time computers span a spectrum that includes transportation systems, robotics and manufacturing, aerospace and defense, industrial process control, and telecommunications.

As real-time computers become responsible for managing increasingly sensitive applications, particularly those in which failures to satisfy timing constraints can lead to serious or even catastrophic consequences, it has become more important than ever to develop the theoretical foundations to ensure that the designs and implementations of time-dependent systems are verifiably correct and predictable. The papers in this volume offer a vivid portrayal of the cutting-edge research in this topic being pursued by ONR investigators, the exciting advances that have been achieved within the last few years, and the important unresolved issues that remain.

There is still a surprising amount of diversity in the models and notational systems that are intended to allow faithful representation and analysis of real-time systems. Indeed, not just a few of the key open research issues in this discipline turn on the question of how properly to arrange the formal structure required to enable robust specification and verification of real-time systems. Many of the papers in this book can be viewed as describing *hypotheses* of appropriate formal systems, rather than as convincing validated solutions. In these papers, the rich, creative genius of the researchers in this discipline is starkly evident as they try to uncover the still-murky roots of formal methods for real-time systems.

The chapters in this volume are each written by different sets of researchers and are mostly self-contained. Although each chapter can be profitably studied without prior familiarity with previous chapters, a serious student of this discipline would do well to examine each chapter carefully because only then do many of the important, and sometimes subtle, differences in approach become evident. Chapter 1 sets the stage for what follows by carefully laying a groundwork of intuition regarding real-time computing systems and the need for formal methods to represent them. Chapters 2-6 then provide detailed descriptions of alternative formal structures for modeling and reasoning about real-time systems. Chapters 7 and 8 follow with a close look at formal approaches for modeling real-time concurrency. In Chapters 9 and 10, the implications of timing properties on programming language structure and features are explored, while finally in Chapter 11 a rare example of the practical application of formal methods to real-world problems is presented.

This book is suitable for graduate or advanced undergraduate course use when supplemented by additional readings that place the material contained herein in fuller context. Most of the techniques and notations described in this book are not yet ready for widespread use in commercial settings, although some have been exercised in relatively realistic circumstances. A true opportunity exists for devising practical mechanisms to exploit the theoretical results reported in this volume.

Provable correctness and formal verification of real-time systems involves research that cuts to the core of fundamental questions at the foundations of computer science. It is likely to be a long, difficult process to extract key illuminating insights that can effectively contribute to practical real-time system development approaches. This volume can claim to settle no more than a fraction of the puzzling questions involving real-time system specification and verification. It is our hope that this book will convey not only the hard-won nuggets of important ideas and results about real-time formal methods to a wide audience, but also the excitement of discoveries still to be made at the foundations of real-time computing.

André M. van Tilborg
Gary M. Koob

Arlington, Virginia

FOUNDATIONS OF REAL-TIME COMPUTING:
Formal Specifications and Methods

CHAPTER 1

Towards Mechanization of Real-Time System Design

Aloysius K. Mok[†]

Department of Computer Sciences
University of Texas at Austin
Austin, Texas 78712

Abstract

Real-time software is used to control external devices (e.g., in automobiles, robotics, telephone switches) subject to stringent timing constraints. As the requirements of real-time systems become more complex, the design of real-time software will require formal techniques and automated design tools. In this paper, we shall discuss some of the major issues in mechanizing the specification, validation/verification, and synthesis of the control structure for real-time software. Our goal is to provide a foundation for the systematic design of real-time software. Such a foundation is needed before we can justify the integrity of the large real-time software systems of the future.

INTRODUCTION

As computers are increasingly used to monitor and control machinery, e.g., in automobiles, robotics, telephone switches, the systematic design of real-time systems has become an important issue, especially when safety-critical functions are involved. Real-time software must satisfy not only functional correctness requirements, but also timeliness requirements. In this paper, we shall discuss some of the major issues in mechanizing the specification, validation/verification, and synthesis of the control structure for real-time software.

[†] Supported by a research grant from the Office of Naval Research under ONR contract number N00014-89-J-1472.

The Role of Timing Constraints in System Design

The design of real-time systems is difficult inasmuch as implementation dependencies such as hardware speed and resource sharing policies are essential in determining whether it is possible to meet stringent timing requirements. In conventional software design, such dependencies are deliberately hidden for robustness reasons. The imposition of timing constraints reintroduces these dependencies, and one should have good reasons for doing so. The following are important purposes for introducing timing constraints.

• *Timing constraints are an explicit requirement in ensuring system integrity in some applications.* For example, the control surfaces of some modern aircrafts must be adjusted at a high rate to prevent catastrophic destruction. This places an upper bound on the response time of the avionics software system. Lower bounds are also needed, as in the case of an operating system which requires a potential intruder to wait for some minimum time before retyping a password that has been entered incorrectly. In these cases, the "physics" of the application dictates the timing requirements. From the computer science point of view, real-time software design may indeed be thought of as solving synchronization problems with processes whose progress cannot be dictated by the programmer.

• *Some forms of timing constraints are an essential synchronization mechanism for solving many reliability problems.* An example is the well-known Byzantine Generals problem in distributed systems in which non-faulty processors (generals) must arrive at a correct consensus even though faulty processors can exhibit arbitrary faulty behavior. It is well known that there is no asynchronous solution for this problem. However, a solution is possible if the generals adopt the synchronous protocol of voting in rounds. In each round of voting, the good generals must observe a timing constraint of the form: complete a set of actions within a deadline (a reference to real time). This timing constraint is needed to introduce partial synchrony in a distributed system so that an otherwise unsolvable reliability problem can be solved.

• *Timing constraints are a powerful control mechanism which can be exploited to achieve performance goals.* An example can be found in communication protocols which use rate control to improve throughput, e.g., the NETBLT protocol. In these protocols, the receiver guarantees the sender that it will be able to process incoming packets at a certain rate, or alternatively, it will meet the deadline associated with each packet. Since the sender does not need to wait for an acknowledge from the receiver, network throughput can be significantly improved, especially for networks where the round-trip transmission time is long compared with the width of a packet, e.g., fiber optics communication systems.

It should be noted that the development of highly distributed and massively parallel systems will likely increase the role of timing constraints in system design. Fault tolerance is a major concern in these systems. Timing constraints in various forms are fundamental to the solution of many otherwise provably unsolvable fault-tolerance synchronization problems. The basic reason is that it is in general impossible to tell a slow process(or) from a faulty one, and some form of time-out is required. This imposes a dual requirement on the nonfaulty processes. In order for the system to make progress, the nonfaulty processes must avoid missing a deadline (respond before the other process times out). In general, timing constraints may not be just simple time-outs and may in fact be implicitly required in the implementation of some higher-level synchronization primitives.

In practice, distributed systems are unlikely to be completely synchronous or completely asynchronous because of engineering considerations. Partial synchrony is needed to achieve reliability and efficiency goals. Timing constraints are a useful means for introducing partial synchrony to systems. Undisciplined use of timing constraints, however, may exact an unacceptably heavy implementation and maintenance cost. How to impose timing constraints in a structured fashion is still a major problem in real-time computing research.

The Need for Design Automation: a Systems Engineering Perspective

Computer-controlled real-time systems have been in use for a number of years, often as replacements for analog controllers. For current real-time applications, the fundamental software engineering problem is not so much in our ability to field them, but rather in the costly and often *ad hoc* way in which they are designed, and the resulting difficulty in maintaining them. Timing assumptions, in particular, are often implicitly embedded in the software, and subsequent modifications must take them into account. This is a highly labor-intensive, error-prone effort and raises two major concerns.

Firstly, the lack of a theoretical foundation in current design methods makes it impossible to predict the behavior of systems under all operating conditions. System validation has depended almost entirely on testing. This is an expensive procedure, and more importantly, it does not permit us to characterize the design limits of complex systems. Thus we are liable to be surprised by unexpected failure modes under stress conditions that testing may not have uncovered. This is a problem even with the relatively simple real-time systems today.

Secondly, today's *ad hoc* design methods will not scale up well to deal with the complexity of future systems. This increased complexity may be due to the sheer size of future systems or to more complicated interactions among subsystem, especially in a distributed environment. While it is possible to hand-tune the performance of a small system to meet a few simple timing constraints, it is unlikely that *ad hoc* methods will suffice for the highly distributed and massively parallel real-time systems of the future.

The difficulties in predicting system behavior and in scaling up are serious bottlenecks in the design of future real-time systems. There is a way to resolve these difficulties: by maintaining a separation of concerns in meeting the functional and real-time requirements of a system, and by mechanizing the timing-related design chores, we allow the real-time system designer to make timing constraint assertions about the system and leave the complex problems of resource allocation to meet timing constraints as much as possible to automation. The predictability of system behavior should follow logically from the chosen timing assertions; the satisfaction of timing constraints should follow from the mechanical application of resource allocation procedures and the adherence to design disciplines for managing the complexity of the resource allocation problem as system size scales up.

The ultimate goal of this design paradigm is to allow the application engineer to specify the structure of the target system in a domain-specific language for real-time systems, provide appropriate tools for the engineer to understand (through logical deduction) the real-time behavior of the specified system, and to generate the control structure of the real-time software from the system specification, with the engineer supplying only the high level design decisions. The question is whether this high level of automation is possible for real-time system design.

Design Automation - Domain Specificity

In general, a high level of design automation requires domain specificity (i.e., a sufficiently focussed characterization of the application domain to permit precise definition of design problems) and the availability of sufficiently efficient design tools. For real-time systems, we must answer the following questions.

(1) Can we identify a general model for large classes of real-time programs?
(2) Can we mechanize the analysis of real-time properties?
(3) Can we mechanize the allocation of resources to meet stringent timing requirements?
(4) Can we build automated design tools which are sufficiently efficient in practice?

For traditional real-time applications, an answer to the first question can be succintly captured by the following "equation":

$$Real\text{-}Time\ System = State\ Machine + Timing\ Assertions$$
$$+ Dataflow\ Model$$

The control structure of many real-time applications seems to be naturally given by state machines. However, the state transitions are governed not only by the state of the system and the occurrence of events, but also by their time of occurrence. State machines may also be hierarchically and modularly composed, with state transitions triggering complicated interactions among the state machine components. This creates some additional subtleties in defining the semantics of state transitions.

The control structure of a real-time system determines what computation to perform and the set of timing constraints in effect at any time. Real-time computation can be modelled by a directed graph, where the nodes denote transformations to be performed on the data and the edges denote data flow. We shall elaborate on the dataflow model and discuss some related real-time scheduling problems in a later section.

In recent years, there has been a significant amount of research in resolving questions (2) and (3). With regard to question (4), some design tools based on earlier research results have been built and tested for restricted types of timing constraints. Work is ongoing to define an integrated set of tools to help mechanize the industrial design of real-time systems. A satisfactory answer to question (4) still needs considerably more theoretical and practical work and tremendous efforts in technology transfer.

The rest of this paper discusses the major technical issues in mechanizing the specification, validation/verification, and the synthesis of the control structure of real-time software. In order to provide a unified framework, we shall use the logic **RTL** (Real Time Logic, see [2]) as a notation to relate the different technical issues together. Since real-time systems are usually required to be highly reliable and fault-tolerant, we shall also discuss a design approach that integrates real-time performance with reliability/fault-tolerance considerations.

MAJOR ISSUES IN DESIGN AUTOMATION FOR REAL-TIME SYS-TEMS

Before we can mechanize the design chores of real-time systems, we must have a precise way to specify the constraints that the design chores are to maintain. The *specification problem* concerns the selection of appropriate formal notations (models) for specifying real-time properties. After a real-time system has been specified, we may want to ensure that the specification indeed prescribes the correct behavior such that any implementation meeting the specification will not exhibit undesirable timing behavior and lead to unsafe operation. We call this the *validation problem*. An acceptable specification must eventually be implemented. The problem of ensuring that an implementation meets the timing specification is called the *verification* problem. Both validation and verification may be performed by applying formal methods and decision procedures to reason about timing properties in the chosen notation. The *synthesis problem* is the construction of the control structure that allocates resources to meet the real-time specification. This requires the scheduling of events to satisfy a set of stringent timing constraints.

The intent of the following discussion is to provide a framework for exploring the major technical problems and to introduce one, our own, approach to tackle these problems. This paper is not a survey and does not provide comprehensive cross references. We ask the reader to study other approaches elsewhere in this book series.

Specification of Real-Time Properties

As a result of the tremendous amount of work in programming semantics in the last twenty five years, a great deal is known about how to specify and reason about properties of sequential programs. For example, Floyd-Hoare logic was invented to axiomatize the effect of executing a statement by means of pre and post conditions. The advent of distributed systems likewise spawned significant work in specifying and verifying concurrent programs. The standard way to bridge between sequential programs and concurrent programs is via the interleaving model of computation, e.g., Pneuli's temporal logic of concurrent programs. The idea is to think of a run of a concurrent program as a run of one in a set of sequential programs. Suppose two statements, S1 and S2 in a concurrent program P can be executed concurrently. Then a run of the program P is a sequence of statements in P in which either S1 precedes S2 or S2 precedes S1 (assuming both S1 and S2 get executed in the run). An assertion A holds for program P if and only if A holds for every allowable interleaving of the statements in P in any run of P. In effect, we are reasoning about a set of sequential programs when we reason about a concurrent program in the interleaving model. The interleaving model has been very effective for specifying the behavior of concurrent programs. However, it has problems in specifying the behavior of real-time programs.

True Parallelism. In a real-time system, the outcome of a computation may be specified explicitly as a function of the time of occurrence of events, e.g., whether a booster rocket can put a satellite into geosynchronous orbit from a lower orbit depends on whether it is fired within a specified time window. By its nature, the interleaving model determines the outcome of a computation by the relative position of the events in some total order, and not by their time of occurrence. When two events happen at the same time in a computation, it is possible that the intended outcome may not be the same as in either of the two ways to order the two events.

Consider the following example. Two contestants in a game show, A and B are each provided with a button which they are supposed to hit if they want to answer a question. A light in front of the contestant will be lit if the contestant hits the button first. In the case both A and B hit their buttons *at the same time* (this happen if the two interrupt lines connected to the buttons are raised high in the same machine cycle of the computer that acts as the arbiter), then both A and B's lights should be lit to signal a draw. Typical of real-time systems, we can use a state machine with two parallel components (A and B) to specify this game show protocol, as shown in figure 1. Notice that A remains in state A1 (light not lit) before the event e (A hitting button) occurs and will make a transition to A2 (light lit) only if B is in state B1 when e occurs. The same holds for B with e' denoting the event B hitting the button. We may represent the state of the system by the pair (x,y) where x ∈

{A1, A2} and y ∈ {B1, B2}. Initially, the system is in the state (A1,B1).

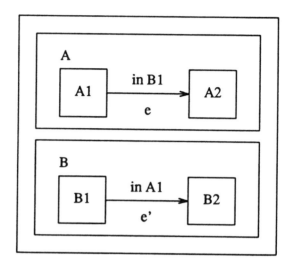

Figure 1. True parallelism of events in a state machine

In the interleaving model, the simultaneous occurrence of the events e and e' is captured by the two state transition sequences:

(A1,B1) → (A2,B1)   if e occurs before e'

(A1,B1) → (A1,B2)   if e' occurs before e

However, this does not allow for the possibility of a tie in which case the transition sequence (A1,B1) → (A2,B2) should be considered instead. If this state machine specification is given to a programmer for implementation, with no other information about the intended semantics of the state machine, then the programmer might implement the machine to unfairly favor A (or B) when there is a tie, depending on the relative priorities of the interrupt lines from A and B. Misinterpretation of specifications is a major source of errors. The importance of precise semantics cannot be overemphasized.

While temporal logic may be extended to allow true parallelism (e.g., by introducing the so-called maximal parallelism model where events that can happen simultaneously will happen simultaneously), the semantics of a real-time system specification obviously depends on the underlying concurrency model. There is a whole range of possible models between the interleaving model and the maximal parallelism model, depending on the amount of parallelism mandated by the run-time environment, e.g., in a two-processor system, exactly two events will happen simultaneously when two or more events can be scheduled, assuming that processors do not unnecessarily idle. Regardless of the model used, it is unwise to tie the semantics of a specification language to the resource availability of a run-time environment that may not even have been decided. In our approach, we resolve this difficulty by allowing events to happen in a partial order in our concurrency model. In our logic RTL, a computation is a sequence of event sets; events in the same set occur truly in parallel. Whether events occur simultaneously is constrained only by the timing specification of a system. Implementation constraints which limit parallelism can be represented by additional axioms.

Faux States. Another problem in using the interleaving model for specifying real-time system behavior is the existence of *faux states*. Most temporal logics for reasoning about concurrency are based on transition systems. In a transition system, the behavior of the system is represented by a state trajectory, i.e., a sequence of states. Time passes in states, and transitions between them are instantaneous. Activities that take non-zero time to complete may span two or more states and are called actions. If two actions begin and end at the same time, however, transition systems may introduce faux-states in which one action has completed and the other has not. Consider the following scenario.

There are two sensors, X and Y, in a certain distributed system. Sensor X (Y) is activated to respectively update a variable x (y). Both x and y are set to 0 initially. Each sensor takes 1 second to complete an update. A timing constraint has been specified to activate both sensors at time=0 and update the variables x and y by time=1. Obviously, both x and y must be updated in parallel. At time=1, x (y) is respectively updated to a new value x' (y'). In the interleaving model, the parallel execution of X and Y is equivalent to the two execution sequences: (1) X; Y. (2) Y; X. We characterize the state of the system by the vector (clock,x,y). The trajectories of the system state corresponding to the two execution sequences are:

(1) $(0,0,0) \rightarrow (?,x',0) \rightarrow (1,x',y')$
(2) $(0,0,0) \rightarrow (?,0,y') \rightarrow (1,x',y')$

There are two obvious choices: 0 or 1 in assigning a value to the clock variable "?" in the second state in both trajectories. Neither one makes sense because we know that both x and y are 0 when clock=0, and both x and y are 1 when clock=1. The second states in both trajectories are faux-states.

To avoid faux-states in the interleaving model, one could use a very fine time scale and insist that only one transition can occur at any instant of time, and revise the timing constraints so that the sensors take not one time unit, but between 0.9 and 1.0 time units. Thus, for example, sensor X might complete updating at time=0.9 and sensor Y at time=1.0, the basic time unit being revised downwards to 0.1 second. However, this approach puts a bound on the number of event occurrences in a finite interval, and this bound is on the number of events in the entire system, not just the sensor subsystem. The 0.1 second precision will not be sufficient if there are 100 instead of 2 sensors, or more importantly, if the number of events per second increases in some other part of the system. This would severely inhibit modularity of both design and analysis.

An alternative approach for avoiding faux states is to insist that events that happen simultaneouly must be grouped into a single event. However, a combinatorial explosion in the number of joint events may result from this approach, since a single event may not be sufficient because a specification may require two events to happen simultaneously some of the time but not all of the time. Therefore, in the worst case, we might have to consider all comibinations of potentially simultaneous events.

The problem of faux states may yet be avoided if one selects a dense representation of time, e.g., use the real numbers to model time instead of assuming a smallest time unit. This makes it possible for every event occurrence to be mapped to a unique time value so that no two events can happen at the same time. However, there is also no *a priori* bound on the number of event occurrences in a finite interval. Such a computation model can be dangerously powerful, for it is possible to solve the halting problem in a model that permits an infinite number of computational events to occur in bounded time. Realistically, digital computers run in clock cycles and are discrete-time devices. If one is interested in specifying the behavior of discrete-time systems, it seems more appropriate to use a discrete-time model. As will be seen, by its very nature, RTL avoids this difficulty.

The Logic RTL. RTL (Real Time Logic) is a multi-sorted first-order logic. A computation in RTL is a sequence of event sets. Time passes between sets of events, and the actual sets of events are instantaneous. In RTL, we reason about individual occurrences of events where an event occurrence marks a point in time which is of significance to the behavior of the system. There is an important distinction between an action and an event in RTL. An action is an activity which requires a non-zero but bounded amount of system resources. However, events serve only as temporal markers. An occurrence of an event defines a time value, namely its time of occurrence, and imposes no requirement on system resources. The execution of an action is represented by two events: one denoting its initiation and the other denoting its completion.

Events have unique names. Two classes of events are of particular interest: (1) start/stop events marking the initiation and completion of an action, and (2) transition events denoting a change in a state variable.

Start and Stop Events: We use the notation $\uparrow$A to represent the event marking the initiation of action A, and $\downarrow$A to denote the event marking the completion of action A. For instance, $\uparrow$SAMPLE and $\downarrow$SAMPLE represent the events corresponding to the start and the stop of action SAMPLE, respectively.

Transition Events: A state variable may describe a physical aspect or a certain property of a system, e.g., an autopilot switch which is either ON or OFF. The execution of an action may cause the value of one or more state variables to change. A state attribute, S is a predicate which asserts that a state variable takes on a certain value in its domain. For example, S may denote the predicate: the autopilot is ON. The corresponding state variable transition events, represented syntactically by (S:=T) and (S:=F), denote respectively the events that mark the turning on and off of the autopilot switch. Whenever it is unambiguous, we shall use state variable and state attribute interchangeably.

In addition to the above two classes, other classes of events can be specified when modeling a real time system. For instance, in [2], the class of external events was introduced to denote the events that cannot be caused to happen by the computer system but can impact system behavior. We use the notation of any name in capital letters prefixed by the special letter Ω (Omega) to denote an external event. For example, ΩBUTTON1 represents the external event associated with pressing button 1.

The *occurrence relation*, denoted by the letter R (Theta), is introduced to capture the notion of real time. The event constants introduced earlier represent the things that can happen in a system. The occurrence relation assigns a time value to each occurrence of an event which happens. Informally, $R(e,i,t)$ denotes that the ith occurrence of an event e happens at time t, where e is an event constant, i is a positive integer term, and t is nonnegative integer term. For instance, $R(\downarrow\text{SAMPLE},1,x)$ denotes that the first occurrence of the event marking the completion of action SAMPLE happens at time x. (In [2], we used an uninterpreted function instead of a relation to capture the notion of real time. The use of a relation has the advantage of not requiring that all occurrence of an event must happen since an event may occur only a finite number of times or even not at all. This avoids some technicalities that come with the use of a partial function in the functional notation. However, the functional notation is more intuitive and easier to use in manipulating the arithmetic inequalities in proofs.)

The notion of an occurrence relation is central to RTL. In particular, a specification of a system and the timing requirements on its behavior are restrictions on the occurrence relation and its arguments.

RTL predicates are formed from the occurrence relation, or from the mathematical relations ($=, <, \leq, >, \geq$) and algebraic expressions allowing integer constants, variables, and addition. Multiplication by constants is used as an abbreviation for addition. One further restriction is that time values cannot be added to or compared with occurrence values. RTL formulas are constructed using the occurrence relation, the equality/inequality predicates, universal and existential quantifiers, and the first-order logical connectives $(\neg,\wedge,\vee,\rightarrow)^\dagger$.

The Syntax and Semantics of RTL. We begin by introducing the language of Real Time Logic. The formulas of RTL are made up of the following symbols:

- The truth symbols *true* and *false*
- A set of time variable symbols **A**.
- A set of occurrence variable symbols **B**.
- A set of constant symbols **C** including the natural numerals
- A set of event constant symbols **D**
- The function symbol $+$
- The predicate symbols $<, \leq, >, \geq, =$

---

† The standard precedence order is assumed for these connectives. $\neg$ has the highest precedence, $\wedge$ and $\vee$ the next highest precedence, and $\rightarrow$ the lowest precedence.

• The occurrence relation symbol R
• The logical connectives $\wedge$, $\vee$, $\neg$ and $\rightarrow$.
• Existential and universal quantifier symbols $\exists$, $\forall$.

The *time terms* of RTL are expressions built up according to the following rules:
  • The constant symbols in C are time terms.
  • The variable symbols in A are time terms.
  • If t_1 and t_2 are time terms, then the function application
    $$t_1 + t_2$$
  is a time term.

The *occurrence terms* of RTL are expressions built up according to the following rules:
  • The constant symbols in C are occurrence terms.
  • The variable symbols in B are occurrence terms.
  • If i and j are occurrence terms, then the function application
    $$i + j$$
  is an occurrence term.

The *propositions* of RTL are constructed according to the following rules:
  • The truth symbols *true* and *false* are propositions.
  • If t_1 and t_2 are time terms and ρ is an inequality/equality predicate symbol, then
    $$t_1 \rho\, t_2$$
  is a proposition.
  • If i and j are occurrence terms and ρ is an inequality/equality predicate symbol, then
    $$i \rho\, j$$
  is a proposition.
  • If i is an occurrence term, t is a time term and e is an event constant, then
    $$R(e, i, t)$$
  is a proposition.

The *formulas* of RTL are constructed from the propositions, logical connectives and quantifiers in the usual fashion.

An interpretation for an RTL formula must assign a meaning to each of the free symbols in the formula. It will assign elements from a domain to the constants, functions (over the domain) to the function symbols, and relations (over the domain) to the predicate symbols.

Let **N** be the set of natural numbers, and **E** be a set of events. Usually **D** and **E** are identical, although this is not necessary. An interpretation **I** over the domain **N**∪**E** assigns values to each of a set of constant, function, and predicate symbols, as follows:

Each element in the set of constant symbols **C** is assigned an element in **N**, with the numerals being assigned to the corresponding natural numbers. Each element in the set of event constant symbols **D** is assigned a distinct element in **E**. The function symbol '+' is integer addition. The predicate symbols <, ≤, >, ≥, and = are assigned the usual equality/inequality binary relations. The predicate symbol R is assigned an *occurrence relation*.

Definition: An *occurrence relation* is any relation on the set
$$\mathbf{E} \times \mathbf{Z}^{+} \times \mathbf{N}$$
where **E** is a set of events, $\mathbf{Z}^{+}$ is the set of positive integers, and **N** is the set of natural numbers, such that the following axioms hold:

Monotonicity Axioms: For each event e in the set **D**,

$$\forall i \, \forall t \, \forall t' \, [\, R(e,i,t) \wedge R(e,i,t') \,] \rightarrow t = t'$$
$$\forall i \, \forall t \, [\, R(e,i,t) \wedge i > 1 \,] \rightarrow [\, \exists t' \, R(e,i-1,t') \wedge t' < t \,]$$

The first axiom requires that at most one time value can be associated with each occurrence i of an event e, i.e., the same occurrence of an event cannot happen at two distinct times. The second axiom expresses the requirement that if the ith occurrence of an event e happens, then the previous occurrences of e must have happened earlier. This axiom also requires that two distinct occurrences of the same event must happen at different times.

Start/Stop Event Axioms: For each pair of start/stop events in the set **D**,

$$\forall i \, \forall t \, R(\downarrow A,i,t) \rightarrow [\, \exists t' \, R(\uparrow A,i,t') \wedge t' < t \,]$$

where $\uparrow A$ and $\downarrow A$ denote the events marking the start and stop of an action

A, respectively. The above axiom requires every occurrence of a stop event to be preceded by a corresponding start event.

Transition Event Axioms: For the transition events in the set **D** corresponding to a state variable S,

$R((S:=T),1,0) \rightarrow$
$(\forall i \, \forall t \; R((S:=F),i,t) \rightarrow [\exists t' \; R((S:=T),i,t') \wedge t' < t] \wedge$
$\forall i \, \forall t \; R((S:=T),i+1,t) \rightarrow [\exists t' \; R((S:=F),i,t') \wedge t' < t])$

$R((S:=F),1,0) \rightarrow$
$(\forall i \, \forall t \; R((S:=T),i,t) \rightarrow [\exists t' \; R((S:=F),i,t') \wedge t' < t] \wedge$
$\forall i \, \forall t \; R((S:=F),i+1,t) \rightarrow [\exists t' \; R((S:=T),i,t') \wedge t' < t])$

The preceding transition event axioms define the order in which two complementary transition events can occur depending on whether S is initially true or false.

The above description constitutes the formal definition of unrestricted RTL. Technically, it is a **subset** of Presburger Arithmetic augmented by an uninterpreted relation. The axioms of unrestricted RTL apply to all real-time systems. Depending on the application, RTL may be further restricted by additional axioms or other syntactic constraints.

RTL has been used to define the formal semantics of an annotation system that can be used to superimpose timing constraints on block-structured high-level languages without recursion [13]. We have also developed a specification language called Modechart [3] by incorporating timing constraints into state machines using RTL.

Validation and Verification of Real-Time Properties

Given the formal specification of a real-time system, the validation problem is to ascertain that the specification is "safe" in the sense that any correct implementation is guaranteed to satisfy certain properties essential to the safe operation of the system. Such properties are usually called safety assertions. The unique issues in ascertaining safety assertions involving time are discussed below.

The Choice of Modality and Quantitative Reasoning. Traditionally, temporal logics used to reason about concurrent systems are concerned with the qualitative behavior of systems. The typical choice of modal operators allows assertions of the form: *some property must always/eventually hold in all/some computations.* In real-time systems, however, eventualities must be bounded. It is not sufficient to know that some property will eventually hold; we often need to know that it will hold within bounded time. While there has been much recent research in introducing a time metric to temporal logic, the usual approach is to retain the usual modalities, and to either parameterize the modal operators (e.g., allow assertions of the form: *some property will hold within k steps*) or to augment the modal operators by explicit time variables. It is not clear, however, that the usual modalities are the right set for asserting the real-time system behavior of practical interest.

For example, it is known that propositional temporal logic cannot express the assertion that the number of times an event happens is congruent to n modulo m for some natural numbers n, m. Such assertions may turn out to be relevant in expressing the quantitative details of certain types of timing constraints. Furthermore, even if the usual temporal modalities are sufficiently expressive to assert certain real-time behavior, they may be extremely cumbersome to use. For example, while it may be possible to express in temporal logic with bounded eventualities the assertion: *some property must hold at least once every 10 steps*, it is at least considerably more cumbersome to express the similar assertion: *some property must hold* **exactly** *once every 10 steps*. This last assertion is in fact quite common in the specification of automatic control systems. It is quite straightforward to express a wide variety of the timing assertions about automatic control systems in RTL. Consider the following example.

A sensor system consists of a sampling device (called Sam), a processor (called Paul) and a single-buffer memory between them. This system operates as follows:

• Sam puts a message in the buffer at exactly every P time units.
• Paul removes a message from the buffer and processes it every P time units.
• Paul takes C time units to process each message.
• Paul's clock is Θ time units behind Sam's. ($\Theta < P$)

A safety assertion for this system is:
• Paul must remove a message from the buffer before Sam puts another one in.

There are three possible outcomes when one attempts to validate a safety assertion against the system specification: (1) The safety assertion is a theorem derivable from the system specification, in which case any correct implementation will be safe. (2) The safety assertion is unsatisfiable with respect to the system specification, in which case every correct implementation will be unsafe. (3) The negation of the safety assertion is satisfiable under certain conditions, in which case it is possible to end up with an unsafe implementation, depending on the choices made by the programmer. Obviously, the system specification must be revised in case (2). In case (3), the system specification may be tightened to restrict the implementation to only those that satisfy the safety assertion.

To validate the safety assertion in the above example in the RTL approach, we first express the informal English specification in a RTL formulas and then invoke a verifier (a semi-decision procedure) to obtain an answer. For this purpose, we shall use the functional notation of RTL. In the functional notation, the term @(e,i) denotes the application of the uninterpreted "@" function to the arguments e, an event and i, an integer which is the instance of the event e. The value of @(e,i) is the time of occurrence of the ith instance of the event e. With this notation, timing constraints can be expressed as restrictions on the @ function. We give below the RTL specification of the sensor example. The symbols ↑P, ↓P denote respectively the events Paul starting/completing processing a message from Sam. The symbol *S* denotes the event: Sam putting a message into the buffer.

• *System specification (SP)*

Sam: $\forall i \ @(S,i) = i*P$

Paul: $\forall i \ @(\uparrow P,i) \geq i*P + \Theta \ \wedge$
                   $@(\downarrow P,i) \leq (i+1)*P + \Theta$

          $\forall i \ @(\downarrow P,i) \geq @(\uparrow P,i) + C$

Paul's clock skew: $\Theta < P$

• *Safety Assertion (SA):* $\forall i \ @(\uparrow P,i) \leq @(S,i+1)$

With this notation, the objective is to show: $SP \rightarrow SA$. Alternatively, we may show that the formula $SP \wedge \neg SA$ is not satisfiable, where $SA = \forall i \ @(\uparrow P,i) \leq @(S,i+1)$ (and so $\neg SA = \exists i \ @(\uparrow P,i) > @(S,i+1)$). This can be done by first removing the quantifiers and skolemization to obtain:

$SP:$ *(1)* $@(S,i) = i * P$
       (2) $@(\uparrow P,i) \geq i * P + \Theta$
       (3) $@(\downarrow P,i) \leq (i+1) * P + \Theta$
       (4) $@(\downarrow P,i) \geq @(\uparrow P,i) + C$
       (5) $\Theta \quad P$

$\neg SA:$ *(6)* $@(\uparrow P,I) > @(S,I+1)$

To show that the above inequalities do not admit a solution, we focus on inequalities (1), (3), (4) and (6).

    $@(S,i) = i * P$ *(1)*
    $@(\downarrow P,i) \leq (i+1) * P + \Theta$ *(3)*
    $@(\downarrow P,i) \geq @(\uparrow P,i) + C$ *(4)*
    $@(\uparrow P,I) > @(S,I+1)$ *(6)*

Rewriting the inequalities, we get:

    $@(S,i+1) = (i+1) * P$ *(1)*
    $(i+1) * P + \Theta \geq @(\downarrow P,i)$ *(3)*
    $@(\downarrow P,i) \geq @(\uparrow P,i) + C$ *(4)*
    $@(\uparrow P,I) > @(S,I+1)$ *(6)*

Finally, we can "chain" the inequalities by observing that the "@" terms on the left and right hand sides cancel each other.

$$@(S,I+1) = (I+1) * P \qquad\qquad (1)$$
$$(I+1) * P + \Theta \geq @(\downarrow P,I) \qquad (3)$$
$$@(\downarrow P,I) \geq @(\uparrow P,I) + C \qquad (4)$$
$$@(\uparrow P,I) > @(S,I+1) \qquad\qquad (6)$$

Obviously, a solution requires: $\Theta > C$. This implies that a sufficient condition for validating the system with respect to the safety assertion is to ensure: $\Theta \leq C$. This is an answer of type case (3) that a verifier may return.

The usual way to automate the validation task is to find a decision procedure for the logic that is used to express the system specification and the safety assertions. Unfortunately, logics of sufficient expressive power are often undecidable and one might have to settle for semi-decision procedures. Unrestricted RTL is in fact undecidable, although there are various decidable subsets. In practice, whether the logic is decidable or not may be a moot question, since the practical question is often to decide whether a class of assertions (certain safety properties) can be derived from the system specification. This is a more restricted decision question and may be a lot easier to solve in practice, if the specification language is complete relative to the set of safety assertions of interest, and there are practical procedures for verifying formulas in the set of safety assertions of interest. This is possible if the syntactic form of the safety assertions of interest is sufficiently restrictive. For example, even though the Modechart language [3] mentioned in an earlier section is undecidable, we can show that there is a decision procedure for answering useful classes of questions about the timing behavior of Modechart programs. Also see [1].

Verifying an Implementation. The task of verifying that an implementation does in fact meet a set of timing constraint assertions is complicated by the fact that the answer depends not only on the application program, but also on the availability and sharing policies of resources in the run-time environment. There are two ways to extend conventional methods to do this.

In the first approach, we customize the proof system to restrict the state trajectories to exactly those allowed by the run-time environment. Thus for the same concurrent program, different sets of proof rules are needed to manipulate the clock variable, depending on the number of processors available. For example, suppose we have two statements S_1, S_2 that can be executed in parallel and each takes one time unit to execute. If the implementation has a separate processor executing each statement, then the post-condition of executing each statement should have the clock value being one time unit greater than in the pre-condition. However, if there is only one processor which is time-shared, then the simple rule above relating the clock value in the pre- and post-conditions will not be appropriate. The strongest assertion one can make then is that the clock value is two time units greater after the execution of both S_1 and S_2, assuming that there are no other statements executed by the single processor. In terms of concurrency models, this approach requires us to first determine from knowledge about the run-time environment the appropriate concurrency model to use and then proceed to apply the proof rules for that concurrency model.

In the second approach, the behavior of the resource scheduler program is explicitly included in the proof. The availability of resources and the sharing policy are encoded in the scheduler program so that the verification task is to show that the timing assertions are satisfied by the application program(s) in parallel with the scheduler program.

The problem with the first approach is that a new set of proof rules must be established for each resource configuration and resource sharing policy. The problem with the second approach is that the interaction between the resource scheduler and the application program is likely to lead to a computational quagmire because the verifier must in effect perform a schedulability analysis (i.e., decide whether a specific scheduling policy can meet a set of timing constraints given a set of resources) for **any** scheduling policy, since the scheduler is now just another program. It is unlikely that a sufficiently efficient verifier based on logical deduction techniques can ever be designed to solve the general schedulability problem; the latter is known to be a hard combinatorial analysis problem that requires specialized solution techniques on a case-by-case basis.

In our approach, we take an indirect way to tackle the verification problem. Since RTL can be used to assert timing requirements independent of the functional requirements, we consider the RTL assertions as constraints on the run-time environment. This way, we can decouple the timing requirements from the functional, logical aspects of the application programs. The verification task is now isolated out to be exactly a schedulability analysis. This decoupling is important since it makes it easy to bring known specialized combinatorial analysis techniques to bear on the problem, thus achieving a separation of concerns. In fact, RTL was intentionally designed to facilitate the synthesis of resource schedulers from timing constraint requirements (as annotations) on programs. In the case the resource scheduler allows customization, our approach also allows the development of a proof by construction. Specifically, we first identify the timing assertions that are needed for maintaining system integrity, and then make sure that the run-time environment satisfies those timing assertions by deriving a scheduler through synthesis techniques. Synthesis is the subject of the next section.

Synthesis of Control Structures

In principle, the problem of control structure synthesis is that of model construction. Given a specification of the real-time behavior of a system in some formal notation, e.g., RTL, a control code generator (also known as an off-line scheduler) is used to generate the control structure (the on-line scheduler) for the application processes. In RTL, the off-line scheduler needs to create a mapping of event occurrences to time values such that the @ function may satisfy the restrictions imposed on it by the RTL formulas. However, the synthesis of the run-time scheduler involves a couple of complications, as explained below.

• Each model (schedule) is an infinite table of tuples of the form (e,i,t) where e is the name of an event, i an integer, and t the time of occurrence of the ith instance of e. Since we cannot store an infinite table in practice, a finite representation (e.g., in the form of a "cyclic executive" which repeats a finite list schedule *ad infinitum*) is needed.

• The time of occurrence of external events is not assigned by the scheduler. Thus a model (schedule) is conceptually needed for every run of the system, one corresponding to a particular set of occurrence times of external events. This means that the off-line scheduler needs to consider a potentially infinite number of models. A finite representation is again needed for the on-line scheduler.

Fortunately, we can show that finite representations of the on-line scheduler do exist for many types of timing constraints. The bad news is that model construction methods in logic usually rely on enumeration techniques and are in general far too slow to be practical. A more realistic approach is to divide the synthesis problem into classes of combinatorial optimization problems according to the types of timing constraints involved. There are two types of timing constraints which are particularly common in today's systems. In the demand-driven type (see [5]), response time is the main concern and deadlines are explicitly given. In the data-driven type (see [4]), throughput is the main concern, and deadlines are implicit, being imposed by the finite availability of buffers. In a combinatorial approach, the synthesis of the on-line scheduler takes two steps. Step 1 generates a finite set of inequalities involving event occurrences from the RTL formulas. Step 2 finds a solution to the inequalities. The form of the inequalities in step 1 is determined by the type of timing constraints involved. As an example, consider the following demand-driven type synthesis problem.

- There are two periodic processes, A and B.
- A must be executed for 2 time units in each of the intervals $[4i, 4(i+1)]$, $i \geq 0$.
- B must be executed for 4 time units in each of the intervals $[8i, 8(i+1)]$, $i \geq 0$.
- A and B are mutually exclusive, i.e., they cannot preempt each other.

The RTL specification of this problem is given by the following formulas: The notations $\uparrow X$, $\downarrow X$ denote respectively the events X starting execution and X finishing execution where X may be A or B.

(P1) $\forall i \geq 1$ $@(\uparrow A, i) \geq 4(i-1) \wedge @(\downarrow A, i) \leq 4i$

(P2) $\forall i \geq 1$ $@(\uparrow B, i) \geq 8(i-1) \wedge @(\downarrow B, i) \leq 8i$

(P3) $\forall i \geq 1, j \geq 1$ $@(\uparrow A, i) \geq @(\downarrow B, j) \vee @(\uparrow B, j) \geq @(\downarrow A, i)$

Step 1 generates the following 5 inequalities where $t1=@(\uparrow A, 1)$, $t2=@(\downarrow A, 1)$, $t3=@(\uparrow A, 2)$, $t4=@(\downarrow A, 2)$, $t5=@(\uparrow B, 1)$, $t6=@(\downarrow B, 1)$.

(1) $t1 \geq 0 \wedge t2 \leq 4$ *from (P1), i = 1*
(2) $t3 \geq 4 \wedge t4 \leq 8$ *from (P1), i = 2*
(3) $t5 \geq 0 \wedge t6 \leq 8$ *from (P2), j = 1*

(4) $t1 \geq t6 \lor t5 \geq t2$ *from (P3), $i = 1, j = 1$*
(5) $t3 \geq t6 \lor t5 \geq t4$ *from (P3), $i = 2, j = 1$*

Step 2 solves the inequalities (1) to (5) by the following assignments: $t1 = 0$, $t2 = 2$, $t3 = 6$, $t4 = 8$, $t5 = 2$, $t6 = 6$.

A finite representation of an on-line scheduler is given recursively by the following equalities:

$$@(\uparrow A, i + 2) = @(\uparrow A, i) + 8 \qquad i \geq 0$$
$$@(\downarrow A, i + 2) = @(\downarrow A, i) + 8 \qquad i \geq 0$$
$$@(\uparrow B, i + 1) = @(\uparrow B, i) + 8 \qquad i \geq 0$$
$$@(\downarrow B, i + 1) = @(\downarrow B, i) + 8 \qquad i \geq 0$$

where

$$@(\uparrow A, 1) = t1 = 0, \qquad @(\downarrow A, 1) = t2 = 2$$
$$@(\uparrow A, 2) = t3 = 6, \qquad @(\downarrow A, 2) = t4 = 8$$
$$@(\uparrow B, 1) = t5 = 2, \qquad @(\downarrow B, 1) = t6 = 6$$

It is easy to verify that this on-line scheduler generates a cyclic schedule which repeats itself every 8 time units.

Even though this approach is much more efficient than an enumerative method, the number of inequalities generated in step 1 may still be too large for practical purposes. A more practical approach is to consider classes of RTL constraints and investigate the related (more restricted) combinatorial optimization problems. There are two common types of timing constraints: demand-driven and data-driven. We shall analyze the scheduling problem for data-driven timing constraints below, since most past research has been devoted to demand-driven constraints which is covered elsewhere in this book series.

Scheduling Data-driven Timing Constraints

Data-driven timing constraints are used to specify the requirement that processing must keep up with the rate of input data in real time. Unlike demand-driven timing constraints, there are no explicitly specified deadlines. A failure to meet this type of timing constraint is manifested by a communication buffer being overwritten. Suppose WRITE and READ are events that denote writing into and reading from a single buffer. Then the data-driven timing constraint which specifies no buffer overwrite can be given by the RTL formula:

$$\forall \; i \geq 1 \quad @(READ,i) > @(WRITE,i) \; \wedge \; @(READ,i) < @(WRITE,i+1)$$

Instead of representing the scheduling problem by a set of RTL formulas, we shall describe a dataflow graph model which is more amenable to our combinatorial analysis. For lack of space, we shall omit the proofs. Interested readers may consult [11].

The Dataflow Graph Model. The dataflow graph model is a triple (G, f, h). $G = (V, E)$ is a directed graph which consists of a finite set of nodes V and a finite set of directed edges E. Each nodes represents a functional element which may be a software module or a hardware device. Functional elements may have local memory but communicate with one another only through data paths which are represented by the edges of G. Without confusion, we shall use the term node and functional element interchangeably.

The set V is composed of two disjoint sets of functional elements: V_I, the set of input elements and V_C, the set of computation elements. An input element is a node with no incoming edges. It only represents the source of periodic data and thus requires no computing resources. Each computation element consumes a bounded amount of computing resources.

The second component of the triple, f is a function mapping each element of V into a list of integer parameters. If a functional element v_i is in V_C, then f maps it onto a nonnegative integer c_i which is its computation time. (With a slight abuse of notation, we shall write $f(v_i) = c_i$ instead of the list (c_i) when there is no confusion.) If v_i is in V_I, f maps it onto a pair of nonnegative integers (θ_i, p_i). The first component of the pair is the lag which is defined to be the time at which v_i can be first executed. The lag of an input element is measured relative to the time at which the system starts running (time = 0). The second component is the period of the input element and is defined to be the length of the time interval between two successive requests for executing the input element. (Each input element can be thought of as a hardware device which will periodically read from the external environment a data item or a message for the processor.)

The third component of the triple is a function h which maps each edge (u, v) in E onto a nonnegative integer which is the size of the data item passing from node u to node v. The h function is important for defining the interprocessor traffic load on a multiprocessor implementation of the model. Since we only deal with the uniprocessor case in this paper, the h function will not be used; it is introduced for the sake of completeness. (We can include the cost of passing data in the computation times of the computation elements.)

The execution rules (assumptions) of the graph model are described as follows.

Input rules :
(I1) Each input element must be executed once every period, i.e., the ith execution of an input element v_j must occur at $\theta_j + (i - 1)p_j$.
(I2) At the beginning of the execution of a computation element, it removes a data item (if any) from every one of its input edge(s).
Output rules:
(O1) The output of each input node or computation node are immediately deposited on all of its outgoing edges, i.e., it behaves like an AND node. (Each edge e acts as a single buffer whose size is h(e).) Any previous output data on the edges which have not been removed by a succeeding computation element will be replaced by more current data. When this happens, we say that *data loss* has occurred. The difference between an input element and a computation element in this regard is the time when their output become available.
(O2) A new data item is output from a computation node at the completion of each of its executions.
(O3) Since each input element takes no computation time to execute, its output is instantaneously deposited on every one of its outgoing edges at the time it is executed.

A (uniprocessor) schedule for a graph model G is a function which maps an integer into either a functional element in G or the special element NULL. If the integer i maps onto the functional element v, then v is being allocated processor time in the interval [i,i+1]; if i maps onto NULL, then the processor is idle.

DEFINITION 1. A schedule of a graph model is said to be valid if and only if:
(1) The execution of the functional elements in it conforms to the execution

rules stated above.

(2) There is no data loss in the execution.

(3) If processor preemption is allowed, no two executions of the same functional element may overlap each other, i.e., once a functional element starts executing, it may not preempt itself by starting another instance of execution of itself.

EXAMPLE 1. Shown in figure 2 is an example of the graph model; the sizes of data items passing from one node to another have been omitted from the figure since they are not relevant to our discussion. The circles denote input elements and the square boxes denote computation elements. The value in each node is its f-value, e.g. $f(v_1) = (0, 3)$. Although this example shows a connected graph, we do not in general require connectedness.

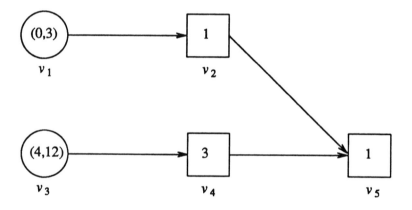

Figure 2. An example of the dataflow graph model

The initial part of a nonpreemptive schedule for the graph in figure 2 is shown in figure 3. The solid up-arrows on the time axis for v_2 and v_4 denote data/message arrivals from v_1 and v_3 respectively. The dash arrows denote data/message passing between the computation elements.

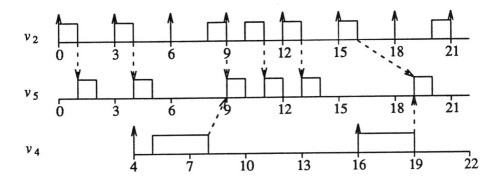

Figure 3. A nonpreemptive schedule of the model in example 1

The Scheduling Problem of the Dataflow Graph. In this section we shall discuss the computational complexity of the scheduling problem which is to determine whether a valid uniprocessor schedule exists for an instance of dataflow graph model.

When preemption is allowed, we impose the restriction that a functional element may be interrupted only at integral boundaries of a basic time unit called a *quantum* which corresponds to the minimum time slice that a processor uses for scheduling. In practice, a quantum may be 1 millisecond or 10 millisecond etc., but the actual size is unimportant to us. We also require that all timing parameters (period, lag, computation time) to be exact multiples of a quantum.

With the above convention, input rule I2 can be interpreted to mean that data on all the input arcs of a functional element are considered removed as soon as the functional element starts receiving its first quantum of processor time. If preemption is not allowed, a functional element will execute to completion with no interruption once it has started receiving processor time. For the case of no preemption, we can show

THEOREM 1. *The scheduling problem of the dataflow graph model is NP-hard when preemption is not allowed.*

EXAMPLE 2. If the value of $f(v_4)$ in example 1 is increased from 3 to 4, then there is no valid nonpreemptive schedule. However a valid preemptive schedule is still possible. The initial part of one such schedule is shown in the figure 4.

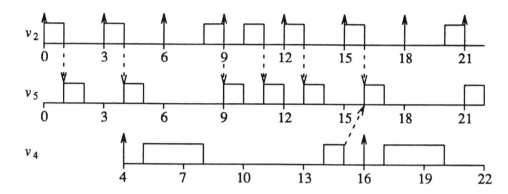

Figure 4. A preemptive schedule of example 2

As might be expected, preemptive scheduling is more efficient (yields more valid schedules) than nonpreemptive scheduling (see example 2). We shall show that when preemption is allowed, there is an efficient on-line scheduler for our graph model. Our strategy is to transform the functional elements of the graph model into a set of independent processes in a process model to be described below. This process model is very similar to the one investigated in the seminal paper of C. L. Liu and J. Layland [9], and later extended in [6]. It will be seen that our transformation is optimal in the sense that an instance of the graph model has a valid schedule if and only if the corresponding process scheduling problem has a valid schedule. This leads us to the definition of the process model.

The Process Model. Formally, a periodic process π_i is a quadruple, $(\theta_i, p_i, c_i, d_i)$ where θ_i is the lag (the instant at which the first request of π_i arrives), p_i is its period, c_i is the computation time and d_i is its deadline. Again, all timing parameters are non-negative integers and are expressed in quantums. An instance of the process model consists of a set of processes, each of which can be scheduled independently, i.e., there are no precedence or other constraints on the execution of the processes. We note that two or more processes in an instance of the process model may have exactly the same quadruple of parameters, i.e., we may have a multiset of processes.

The computation requirement of a process is defined as follows. Each process π_i requests for processor time every p_i quantums starting from time $= \theta_i$. After a request arrives, say at time $= t$, π_i must be allocated c_i quantums of processor time before time $= t + d_i$.

Before discussing the scheduling problem, we want to emphasize the difference between scheduling the graph model and the process model. In particular, the goal of the former is to avoid data loss while the goal of the latter is to avoid missing deadlines. There are no explicit deadlines in the graph model while the process model does not have any constraints imposed by data/message passing. Some notation is in order before we formally define a valid schedule for the process model.

We use the triple (q, k, m) to denote the qth quantum of the kth instance of a process π_m where $1 \leq q \leq c_m$, $k > 0$ and $1 \leq m \leq n$. A special triple $(0, 0, 0)$ denotes the quantum in which the processor is idle. A schedule for the process model is a sequence of these triples. A valid schedule is one which conforms to the execution rules given below.

DEFINITION 2. Let $\Pi = \{\pi_i \mid 1 \leq i \leq n\}$ be a set of periodic real-time processes and T be the set of the triples defined above. A *valid schedule* for Π is a function σ mapping Π onto a sequence $\{s_0, s_1, \ldots\}$, $s_i \in$ T such that

(1) Every triple (q, k, m) satisfying $1 \leq q \leq c_m$, $k > 0$ and $1 \leq m \leq n$ must appear exactly once in the sequence. Furthermore (q, k, m) must appear before $(q', k, m\text{m})$ if $q' > q$.

(2) If $s_i = (q, k, m) \neq (0, 0, 0)$ then i is in the interval $[\theta_m + (k-1)p_m, \theta_m + (k-1)p_m + d_m]$,

(3) If $s_i = (c_m, k, m)$ and $s_j = (1, k+1, m)$ then $i < j$.

The first rule described the uniqueness of the mapping and its range. The second rule specifies that the kth instance of a process π_m must be in the interval $[\theta_i + (k-1)p_i, \theta_i + (k-1)p_i + d_i]$. The third rule prohibits self-preemption.

For our discussion, we identify two submodels of the process model by restricting the values of the lag and deadline parameters. The first submodel, to be called PM_1 is a process model in which the lags of processes are the same and the deadline of each process equals to its period. The second model, to be called PM_2 is the same as PM_1 except that the restriction on the lags is relaxed, i.e., we only require the period of each process to be equal to its deadline. Obviously, $PM_1 \subset PM_2$.

For the PM_1 model, a necessary and sufficient condition for the existence of a valid schedule can be given in terms of a *utilization factor* $U = \Sigma(c_i/p_i)$ where c_i, p_i are respectively the computation time and period of the ith process. In [9], it was shown that a necessary and sufficient condition for the existence of a valid schedule on a uniprocessor is $U \leq 1$.

The Transformation. Our strategy is to map each node in the dataflow graph model to an "equivalent" process in the PM_2 model with appropriate timing parameters. To establish the equivalence, we are guided by the following observations. First, a computation elements reachable from an input element in the dataflow graph model should be executed at least as often as that input element. Therefore the "average period" of a computation element should be at least as short as the shortest average period of its adjacent predecessors. Second, we do not have to start the first execution of a computation element immediately after some or all of its adjacent predecessors (some of which may be input elements whose computation times are zero) finish thier. However we need to make sure that it will certainly get one quantum of processor time (thus removing all the data on its incoming edges) before any of its adjacent predecessors starts its second period since the predecessors which are input elements will produce output immediately when their periods elapse. On the other hand, it is not clear whether setting the period to be the minimum period of the predecessors is sufficient, especially when the periods of the input nodes are almost the same and are relatively prime. Fortunately, this turns out to be not a problem. The formal definition of the transformation is in order.

DEFINITION 3. Let $\mathbf{R} = ((V, E), f, h)$ be a dataflow graph model of a real-time system. The transformation α of $\mathbf{R}$ is a function mapping $\mathbf{R}$ into a set Π of periodic real-time processes such that each functional element $v_i \in V$ is transformed into a process π_i in Π. Initially the period, deadline and lag of all processes are undefined. Each process π_i is created as follows.

(1) If $v_i \in V_I$, let $f(v_i) = (s, p)$. Then the attributes of π_i are $\theta_i = s$, $c_i = 0$, $p_i = p$, and $d_i = 0$.

(2) If $v_i \in V_C$, the process π_i is derived as follow; $c_i = f(v_i)$, $d_i = p_i = \text{MIN}_{(v_k, v_i) \in E}(p_k)$, $\theta_i = \text{MIN}_{(v_k, v_i) \in E}(\theta_k + p_k + c_i - 1 - p_i)$,

(3) Repeat step 2 until there is no further change in the value of the attributes of every process.

The transformation may be performed in some topological order. Notice that the transformation assigns the same value to the deadline as the period, and hence we have a PM_2 process model. For brevity of discussion, we shall say that process x is a predecessor (successor) of process y if the node corresponding to x in the graph model is a predecessor (successor) of the node corresponding to y. The lag is computed to ensure that at least a quantum of processor time is allocated to a process before the second earliest output from any of its predecessors arrives.

EXAMPLE 3. Each functional element in the dataflow graph model in example 1 can be transformed into a PM_2 process model as follows.

$$c_2 = f(v_2) = 1$$
$$c_4 = f(v_4) = 3$$
$$c_5 = f(v_5) = 1$$

$$d_2 = p_2 = p_1 = 3$$
$$d_4 = p_4 = p_3 = 12$$
$$d_5 = p_5 = MIN(p_2, p_4) = 3$$

$$\theta_2 = \theta_1 + p_1 + c_2 - 1 - p_2 = 0 + 3 + 1 - 1 - 3 = 0$$
$$\theta_4 = \theta_3 + p_3 + c_4 - 1 - p_4 = 4 + 12 + 3 - 1 - 12 = 6$$
$$\theta_5 = MIN(\theta_2 + p_2 + c_5 - 1 - p_5, \theta_4 + p_4 + c_5 - 1 - p_5)$$
$$= MIN(0, 15) = 0$$

$$v_1 \Rightarrow \pi_1 = (0, 3, 0, 0)$$
$$v_2 \Rightarrow \pi_2 = (0, 3, 1, 3)$$
$$v_3 \Rightarrow \pi_3 = (4, 12, 0, 0)$$
$$v_4 \Rightarrow \pi_4 = (6, 12, 3, 12)$$
$$v_5 \Rightarrow \pi_5 = (0, 3, 1, 3)$$

The Optimal Scheduler. An optimal scheduler for a set of processes in the PM_2 model is the Earliest Deadline (ED) scheduler which has been shown (see [8]) to yield a valid schedule whenever one exists. (There are in fact more than one such optimal schedulers. See [7].) We say that a process x is active at time = t if there is a request for x for which it has not been executed to completion by time = t. The ED scheduler selects at any time for execution the active process which has the most imminent deadline. If two or more processes have the same deadline at the moment, then ED selects one of these processes by random.

In our case, it can be shown that even if all deadlines are met, the random selection used by the ED scheduler to break ties may cause data loss to occur in the original graph model. To fix this problem, we modify the ED scheduler so that if two processes have the same deadline and one is a predecessor (directly or indirectly) of the other, then the predecessor process has higher priority. Since there is no notion of predecessor and successor in the process model, one way to implement this is to rank the processes in a topological order of their corresponding functional elements in the graph model such that whenever two processes have the same deadline, higher priority is given to the process which appears earlier in the topological ordering. We shall call this modified version of the ED algorithm the ED-PP (Earliest Deadline - Predecessor Priority) scheduler.

EXAMPLE 4. A portion of the earliest deadline schedule of the set of processes in example 3 is given below. In figure 5, we also show the passing of data by the dash arrows. The timing for π_1 and π_3 is shown as solid arrows in the schedule of π_2 and π_4 respectively. Note that no data is lost in the schedule.

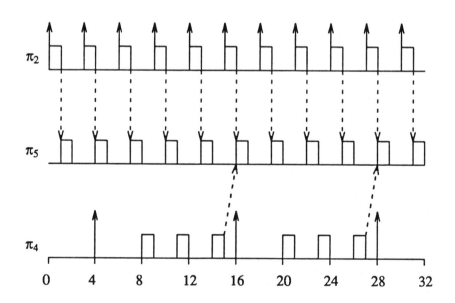

Figure 5. A preemptive schedule for the processes in example 3

Even though the ED-PP scheduler is optimal for the PM_2 model, there is no guarantee that data loss will not occur in the schedule. We can show that the schedule is really free from data loss.

LEMMA 2. *Let* $\mathbf{R}$ = *((V, E), f, h) be an instance of the graph model and let* Π = $\alpha(\mathbf{R})$ *be the set of processes which results from applying the transformation* α *to* $\mathbf{R}$. *If there exists a valid ED-PP schedule* $\sigma(\Pi)$, *then the first quantum of an instance of a process must appear at least once between the first quantum of any two consecutive instances of its predecessors in* $\sigma(\Pi)$.

THEOREM 3. *Let* $\mathbf{R}$ *be an instance of the graph model and let* Π = $\alpha(\mathbf{R})$ *be the set of processes transformed from* $\mathbf{R}$. *If there is a valid ED-PP schedule* $\sigma(\Pi)$, *then there is no data loss in that schedule.*

Given an instance of the graph model, we can transform it into a set of processes and then use the ED-PP algorithm to select a process to execute at run time. However, this does not necessarily give us a polynomial-time decision procedure for deciding whether a valid schedule exists for an instance of the graph model, since in the worst case, we may have to simulate the ED-PP algorithm for an interval whose length is of the order of the least common multiple of the timing parameters of the problem instance (see [6]).

In the following, we show that a necessary and sufficient condition for a valid schedule to exist for the process model PM_2 is $U \leq 1$. The transformation from the graph model to the process model is optimal in the sense that if there is no valid schedule for the process model, then there is no valid schedule for the original graph model. Combining the results, we can obtain a polynomial time solution to the scheduling decision problem.

LEMMA 4. *A necessary condition for the feasibility of* $\sigma(\Pi)$ *where* Π *is a* PM_2 *model, is* $U(\Pi) \leq 1$.

LEMMA 5. *A sufficient condition for the feasibility of* $\sigma(\Pi)$ *where* Π *is a* PM_2 *model, is* $U(\Pi) \leq 1$.

THEOREM 6. *The necessary and sufficient condition for the feasibility of* $\sigma(\Pi)$ *where* Π *is a* PM_2 *model, is* $U(\Pi) \leq 1$.

THEOREM 7. *There is a valid schedule for a graph model* **R** *if and only if there also is a valid schedule for the process model* $\alpha(\mathbf{R})$.

It should be mentioned that the feasibility of an instance of the graph model depends only on the computation times and periodicities of nodes in that graph. The number of buffer on each edge does not play any role in determining the feasibility other than at least one buffer being required for each edge. Thus multiple buffers do not offer any help for the periodic systems in which the arrival rates of data are constant with no deviation. In the sporadic systems or the systems in which the deviations of the data arrivals are presented, multiple buffers would be very useful in regulating the data. The problem of determining the number of buffers needed for such a system has been extensively treated in Queueing Theory, so we will not go into details here.

The scheduling technique described here has been applied to a tactical data communication system of about 4,000 lines of C application code ([12]).

THE MB (MONITORED BASELINE) APPROACH TO SCHEDULING

It should be noted that in our discussion so far, nothing has been said about the reliability of the timing parameters involved in the timing constraint specifications. In reality, a good designer should always prepare for the contingency that the given timing parameters may not be accurate. For example, the execution time of an action may be underestimated, or the separation between two requests from a sporadic task may be shorter than the specified minimum. In other cases, when the worst-case numbers are much bigger/smaller than the average-case numbers, a designer may in fact choose a value which is not the worst-case and is closer to the average-case so as to avoid excessive capacity. When this is done, there is a non-zero probability that the worst-case does occur and a timing constraint may be missed, corresponding to an overload situation. This does not mean that the deterministic scheduling techniques that we have discussed so far are inappropriate. In fact, a deterministic analysis will enable us to provide run-time monitoring so that the system can recover from an overload situation gracefully. This can be achieved by following the **MB** (Monitored Baseline) approach to real-time resource allocation. There are three steps in applying the **MB** approach.

(1) Baseline design parameters determination and justification: Determine

the timing requirements (possibly more than one set if the system has multiple modes of operation) and resource usage bounds. Then perform a hypothesis coverage analysis (an evaluation of the impact of the choice of parameters on system reliability, assuming that a design exists to meet the baseline parameter values.

(2) Deterministic scheduling analysis: Design a system *guaranteed* to meet the baseline parameter values from step (1).

(3) Run-time monitoring and recovery: Provide run-time monitoring for deviation from baseline parameters (e.g., watch out for rare transient in peak request rate, unexpectedly long computation time), and adjust resource allocation to recover from timing exceptions (e.g., frame overrun in a cyclic executive).

The rationale for the **MB** approach is to

(1) provide a way to meet stringent timing constraints when the timing parameters are truly tight.

(2) provide a systematic way to introduce feedback which holds the key to achieving reliability. The fact that we have a baseline allows us to monitor for anomalies.

(3) provide a clear separation of concerns between performance engineering and reliability assessment. This is important from a system integration point of view.

It is important to consider the role of the deterministic scheduling solution in the **MB** approach. Both the hypothesis coverage analysis and the actual resource scheduler depend on the existence of a solution to meet the baseline parameters. The gist is to define a performance trajectory and try to follow it by providing a deterministic solution, monitoring deviation from it, and taking recovery actions.

The **MB** approach will not work if we do not have a good characterization of the tasks in the system (e.g., there is too much unknown about the characteristics of jobs in a university network to use rate control for alleviating "broadcast storms" which tend to paralyze a network). In hard-real-time applications, the characteristics of the tasks are likely to be much better defined.

CONCLUSION

From a computer science point of view, real-time software is unique in that it requires solutions to synchronization problems in which some processes are not programs but physical (external) processes, and the *progress* properties of these processes are not under direct programmer control. The lack of direct control over these processes gives rise to timing constraints. As the requirements of real-time systems become more complex, the design of real-time software will require highly automated design tools. Current methods for dealing with timing constraints are too *ad hoc* for automation. We discussed some of the major research issues that must be resolved in order to provide a rigorous foundation for automating the design chores that deal with timing constraints.

Acknowledgements

This paper derives from some of the work done by the Real-Time Systems Group at the Computer Science Department of the University of Texas at Austin. Past and present members of the RTS Group directly involved in the work reported herein are: Paul Clements, Farnam Jahanian, Tei-Wei Kuo, Doug Stuart, Supoj Sutanthavibul and Farn Wang.

REFERENCES

[1] **F. Jahanian and A. Mok**, "A Graph-Theoretic Approach for Timing Analysis and Its Implementation", *IEEE Transactions on Computers, August 1987.*

[2] **F. Jahanian and A. Mok**, "Safety Analysis of Timing Properties in Real-Time Systems", *IEEE Transactions on Software Engineering, September 1986.*

[3] **F. Jahanian, R. Lee and A. Mok**, "Semantics of Modechart in Real Time Logic", *Proceedings of the 21st Hawaii International Conference on System Science, January 1988.*

[4] **A. Mok and S. Sutanthavibul**, "Modeling and Scheduling of Dataflow Real-Time Systems", *Proceedings of the 1985 Real-Time Systems Symposium, 1985.*

[5] **A. Mok**, "The Design of Real-Time Programming Systems Based on Process Models", *Proceedings of the IEEE Real-Time Systems Symposium, Austin, Texas, December 1984.*

[6] **J. Leung and M. L. Merrill**, "A Note on Preemptive Scheduling of Periodic, Real-time Tasks", *Information Processing Letters, 11, pp. 115-*

118.

[7] **A. Mok**, "Fundamental Design Problems of Distributed Systems for the Hard-Real-Time Environment", *Ph.D Thesis, Department of Electrical Engineering and Computer Science, Massachusetts Institute of Technology, Cambridge, Massachusetts, May, 1983.*

[8] **M. Dertouzos**, "Control Robotics : the Procedural Control of Physical Processes", *Proceedings of the 1974 IFIP Congress, pp. 807-813.*

[9] **C. L. Liu and J. W. Layland**, "Scheduling Algorithms for Multiprogramming in a Hard-Real-Time Environment", *JACM, vol. 20, 1973, pp. 46-61.*

[10] **M. Garey and D. Johnson**, *Computers and Intractibility: a Guide to the Theory of NP-Completeness, W. H. Freeman, San Francisco, California, 1979.*

[11] **A. Mok and S. Sutanthavibul**, "Modeling and Scheduling of Dataflow Real-Time Systems", *to appear in Acta Informatica, an earlier version appeared in the proceedings of the IEEE Real-Time Systems Symposium, 1985.*

[12] **A. Mok, P. Amerasinghe, M. Chen, S. Sutanthavibul and K. Tantisirivat**, "Synthesis of a Real-Time Message Processing System with Data-Driven Timing Constraints", *Proceedings of the IEEE Real-Time Systems Symposium, 1987.*

[13] **A. Mok**, "Annotating Ada for Real-Time Program Synthesis", *Proceedings of the IEEE COMPASS '87 Conference, June 1987.*

CHAPTER 2

Derivation of Sequential,

Real-Time, Process-Control Programs

Keith Marzullo[*]

Fred B. Schneider[**]

Navin Budhiraja[*]

Department of Computer Science
Cornell University
Ithaca, New York 14853

Abstract

The use of weakest-precondition predicate transformers in the derivation of sequential, process-control software is discussed. Only one extension to Dijkstra's calculus for deriving ordinary sequential programs was found to be necessary: function-valued auxiliary variables. These auxiliary variables are needed for reasoning about states of a physical process that exist during program transitions.

---

[*]Supported in part by the Defense Advanced Research Projects Agency (DoD) under NASA Ames grant number NAG 2-593 Contract N00140-87-C-8904 and a grant from Xerox Corporation. Any opinions, findings, and conclusions or recommendations expressed in this publication are those of the author and do not reflect the views of these agencies.

[**]Supported in part by the Office of Naval Research under contract N00014-86-K-0092, the National Science Foundation under Grant No. CCR-9003440, and Digital Equipment Corporation. Any opinions, findings, and conclusions or recommendations expressed in this publication are those of the author and do not reflect the views of these agencies.

1. Introduction

For the past few years, we have been exploring the use of assertional reasoning in the construction of process-control software. Our intent was to employ an existing method, perhaps with a few extensions, and systematically derive process-control programs from specifications. Use of an existing method had both a scientific and a pragmatic motivation. The scientific motivation was based on our expectation that the difficulties we encountered by using an extant method would provide insights into what distinguishes process-control programs from ordinary sequential and concurrent programs. The pragmatic motivation was that extending a well understood method was likely to be easier than developing a new one.

Our investigations have been structured as a series of experiments. Each experiment is based on a simple process-control problem that (we feel) epitomizes some aspect of process-control programming. We started with the simplest process-control problem imaginable—a sequential control-program running on a single, fault-free processor. By reading sensors and writing to actuators, this program controls an on-going physical process. Solving such a problem requires reasoning about control-program execution times, something that has long been considered an integral part of process-control programming. We are well aware, however, that any conclusions from this experiment would have to be regarded as tentative. By considering a sequential control-program, problems arising due to resource contention are avoided; and by assuming a fault-free processor, complications associated with implementing fault-tolerance are being ignored.

Simplifying assumptions not withstanding, our first experiment did lead to some insights about the use of assertional reasoning in writing process-control programs. These insights are the subject of this paper. In section 2, we describe extensions to Dijkstra's weakest-precondition calculus [2] [3] that we found necessary for deriving sequential process-control programs. Section 3 illustrates the use of these extensions and the calculus by giving an example derivation of a control program. Conclusions appear in section 4.

2. Using Weakest Preconditions with Physical Processes

Process-control problems are often specified in terms of restrictions on permissible states of some physical system. By setting actuators to manipulate the process being controlled, a *control program* ensures that none of these proscribed states is ever entered. The actions of the control program are, therefore, closely linked to the state of the physical process being controlled. Consequently, when deriving a control program, it is necessary to reason about both the program state and the state of the physical process being controlled.

Assertional methods for deriving programs are based on manipulating logical formulae, called *assertions*, that characterize sets of program states. One way to employ assertional methods in the design of a process-control program is to augment the program state space so that it includes information about the state of the physical process being controlled. Doing so, however, requires extending the rules used to reason about program execution, as follows.

(1)   While a program statement is executed, changes occur to the state of the physical process being controlled. Rules characterizing the effects of program execution must be modified to reflect these other state changes.

(2)   Statements whose execution involves interaction with sensors and/or actuators must be axiomatized as rules relating states before, during, and after execution.

The remainder of this section discusses these extensions.

2.1. Reality Variables

The state space of physical system is usually defined by a collection of *state components*, each of which is indexed by some independent (physical) parameters. For example, the state of a railroad train at a time T can be characterized by its position $X(T)$, its speed $V(T)$, and its acceleration $A(T)$. Note that the choice of time as the independent parameter is arbitrary. If its velocity is always greater than 0, then a train at position X could equally well be described by time $T(X)$, speed $V(X)$, and acceleration $A(X)$. As physicists learned long ago, quantities that are convenient for the task at hand should be selected as the independent parameters.

The state space of a program can be augmented to include the state of a physical process. For each state component Q_i, we add to the program state space a function-valued program variable q_i, called a *reality variable*.[1] Each reality variable replicates (in the program's state space) information about a physical system during program execution. Initially, the domain of a reality variable q_i will be empty; as the independent parameter P_i for Q_i changes, the domain of q_i is extended to include the values over which P_i has ranged. Reality variables are entirely fictional. They allow us to describe and reason about the state of a physical system by using assertions, but they are not actually maintained in memory. Thus, they are a form of auxiliary variable [1].

In order to define and manipulate expressions involving function-valued program variables, like reality variables, it will be convenient to have some notation. Following [2], given a function f with domain $dom(f)$, the function expression

$$(f;\ x \in D : g(x))$$

is defined to be a function whose domain is $dom(f) \cup D$ and whose value at any point a is $g(a)$ if $a \in D$ and $f(a)$ otherwise. As a notational convenience, we define:

$$(f;\ x \in D : g(x);\ x \in D' : h(x)) = ((f;\ x \in D : g(x));\ x \in D' : h(x))$$

And, in specifying domains, we use the notation *low .. high* to denote the set $\{a \mid low \leq a \leq high\}$.

2.2. Preserving the Fiction: Updating Reality Variables

The state of a physical system is changed by a physical process. Typically, the changes can be characterized by a set of equations relating the current values of various state components to their recent values. We cannot expect a physical process to update the reality variables being used in modeling the state of a physical system. And, since the weakest-precondition calculus is based on the presumption that all changes to the truth of an assertion are the result of program execution, we have no choice but to regard the program itself as performing updates to reality variables. Program statements can compute these updates by using the equations that characterize the way

---

[1]In the sequel, we use upper-case identifiers to denote (physical) state components and the corresponding lower-case identifier to denote the reality variables that model these.

the physical state components change.

Consider some physical state component $Q(P)$ being modeled by a reality variable $q(p)$, and suppose that as long as no actuator changes during some interval from P to $P+\delta$, changes to Q are characterized by the following continuous equation.

(2.1) $Q(P+\Delta) = \mathcal{F}(Q(P), \Delta)$ for $0 \leq \Delta \leq \delta$

Let $\langle S \rangle_\delta$ denote a statement whose execution coincides with a change of δ by parameter P. Then, execution of $\langle S \rangle_\delta$ is equivalent to executing S and, as part of the same atomic action, changing p and q in accordance with (2.1). This state change is modeled by a program fragment:

$$S; \; p, q := p+\delta, (q; \; i \in p \,..\, p+\delta : \mathcal{F}(q(p), i-p))$$

Using the weakest-precondition predicate transformers for multiple-assignment and statement composition, we obtain the following predicate transformer characterization for $\langle S \rangle_\delta$.

$$wp(\langle S \rangle_\delta, R)$$
$$= \quad \text{«}wp \text{ definition of ";"»}$$
$$wp(S, wp(p, q := p+\delta, (q; \; i \in p \,..\, p+\delta : \mathcal{F}(q(p), i-p)), R))$$
$$= \quad \text{«}wp \text{ definition of ":="»}$$
$$wp(S, R^{p, q}_{p+\delta, (q; \; i \in p \,..\, p+\delta : \mathcal{F}(q(p), i-p))})$$

Notice that when the independent parameter δ in $\langle S \rangle_\delta$ models the passage of time, $\langle S \rangle_\delta$ is a statement that executes for δ seconds. The definition of $wp(\langle S \rangle_\delta, R)$ then asserts that after executing $\langle S \rangle_\delta$ the current time has been incremented by δ and all other reality variables have been updated as if δ seconds had elapsed. However, our characterization of $\langle S \rangle_\delta$ also allows the independent parameter δ to be a quantity other than time, making it possible to reason in the coordinate system best suited for the problem at hand. Also notice that, according to our weakest precondition characterization of $\langle S \rangle_\delta$, an ordinary statement S must be regarded as being equivalent to $\langle S \rangle_0$. This is because

$$wp(\langle S \rangle_0, R) = wp(S, R)$$

holds, since $\mathcal{F}(q(p), 0) = q(p)$ according to (2.1).

To illustrate the use of $wp(\langle S \rangle_\delta, R)$ in an actual process-control programming problem, suppose we are interested in controlling the speed of a railroad train. Define reality variable $v(x)$ to be the speed of the train when it is at a given position x. From Newton's Laws of Motion, we know that if the train does not accelerate during an interval of δ seconds, then reality variable v can be characterized by the following equation:

(2.2) $v(x + \Delta) = v(x)$ for $0 \le \Delta \le v(x) * \delta$

Thus, according to our definition for $wp(\langle S \rangle_\delta, R)$, we have the following weakest precondition characterization for a statement $\langle S \rangle_\delta$ that takes duration δ seconds and is executed while a train is not accelerating.

$$
\begin{aligned}
& wp(\langle S \rangle_\delta, R) \\
= \quad & \text{«(2.2) and } wp \text{ definition for } \langle S \rangle_\delta \text{»} \\
& wp(S, R^{x, v}_{x + v(x) * \delta, \, (v; \, l \in x \, .. \, x + v(x) * \delta: \, v(x))})
\end{aligned}
$$

2.3. Interacting with a Physical Process

To have broad applicability, a method for reasoning about process-control programs must not restrict the types of sensors and actuators that it can handle. Rules for reasoning about sensors and actuators can be derived by

(1)   modeling interactions with sensors and actuators by statements that read and update reality variables, and then

(2)   using the rules provided for reasoning about ordinary statements to derive rules for reasoning about these models.

As long as reality variables correctly model the physical process, the resulting rules will be sound and can be used to reason about how a control program interacts with the process it controls.

To illustrate how sensors and actuators are modeled, we return to railroad control. Consider an actuator **go**(t) and a sensor **await**(c). Executing **go**(t) causes the train to accelerate/decelerate with some maximum constant acceleration ACC (say) until target speed t is reached; execution terminates only when the train reaches its target speed. **await**(c), if invoked while the train is not accelerating, delays execution of a program until the train is at location $c.$[2]

Define $Vlen(u, t)$ to be the distance that a train travels while it is accelerating from a speed u to target speed t:

$$Vlen(u, t) = |(u^2 - t^2)/(2*ACC)|$$

Define $Vat(u, t, x)$ to be the speed of a train after having traveled x meters, $0 \le x \le Vlen(u, t)$, from the point at which it started accelerating from speed u to t:

$$Vat(u, t, x) = \begin{cases} \sqrt{u^2 + 2*x*ACC} & \text{if } u < t \\ \sqrt{u^2 - 2*x*ACC} & \text{if } u > t \\ u & \text{if } t = u \end{cases}$$

The effect of executing **go**(t) can be modeled as an update to reality variables x and v. The value of x is increased by $Vlen(v(x), t)$ and the domain of v is extended to include $x .. x + Vlen(v(x), t)$:

$$\textbf{go}(t): \quad x, v := x + Vlen(v(x), t),$$
$$(v; \ l \in x .. x + Vlen(v(x), t): Vat(v(x), t, l-x))$$

This multiple-assignment statement model provides a basis for calculating $wp(\textbf{go}(t), R)$:

$$wp(\textbf{go}(t), R)$$
$$= \quad \text{«model of \textbf{go}}(t)\text{»}$$
$$wp(x, v := x + Vlen(v(x), t),$$
$$(v; \ l \in x .. x + Vlen(v(x), t): Vat(v(x), t, l-x)), R)$$
$$= \quad \text{«}wp \text{ definition of ":="»}$$
$$R^{x, v}_{x+Vlen(v(x), t), (v; \ l \in x .. x + Vlen(v(x), t): Vat(v(x), t, l-x))}$$

Similarly, **await**(c) can be modeled by an alternative command:

---

[2]If **go**(t) is the only actuator that can cause acceleration, then the condition that **await**(c) is never executed while the train is accelerating is equivalent to stipulating that a train is controlled by a single sequential program.

$$\textbf{await}(c)\text{:} \quad \textbf{if } x \le c \wedge 0 < v(x) \to x, v := c, (v;\ l \in x \mathinner{\ldotp\ldotp} c : v(x))\ \textbf{fi}$$

Our model for $\textbf{await}(c)$ updates reality variables x and v if $x \le c$ and $0 < v(x)$ hold; otherwise, it delays forever. Using the weakest precondition for $\textbf{if}$, we can calculate a weakest precondition predicate transformer for $\textbf{await}(c)$:

$$
\begin{aligned}
&wp(\textbf{await}(c), R) \\
=\quad &\text{«model of } \textbf{await}(c)\text{»} \\
&wp(\textbf{if } x \le c \wedge 0 < v(x) \to x, v := c, (v;\ l \in x \mathinner{\ldotp\ldotp} c : v(x))\ \textbf{fi}, R) \\
=\quad &\text{«}wp \text{ definition of } \textbf{if}\text{»} \\
&x \le c \wedge 0 < v(x) \\
&\quad \wedge (x \le c \wedge 0 < v(x) \Rightarrow wp(x, v := c, (v;\ l \in x \mathinner{\ldotp\ldotp} c : v(x)), R)) \\
=\quad &\text{«}wp \text{ definition of "}{:=}\text{" and predicate logic»} \\
&x \le c \wedge 0 < v(x) \wedge R^{x,\, v}_{c,\, (v;\ l \in x \mathinner{\ldotp\ldotp} c : v(x))}
\end{aligned}
$$

3. An Example

Other than the extensions mentioned above, the methodology of [2] and [3] for deriving ordinary sequential programs can be used, unchanged, for deriving sequential process-control programs. In this section, we illustrate that methodology with a simple railroad-control problem.

Railroad tracks are typically partitioned into segments, called *blocks*. Each block i, has an associated starting location b_i and ending location b_{i+1}, where $b_i \le b_{i+1}$, and a range of permissible speeds $mn_i \mathinner{\ldotp\ldotp} mx_i$, where $0 \le mn_i < mx_i$. Desired is a program to control the speed of a point train[3] so that it travels from b_0 to b_n, maintaining safe speeds along the way. Use $\textbf{go}(t)$ and $\textbf{await}(c)$, as defined above, for interactions between a single sequential control program and the train.

First, we formalize the problem. The train has made a safe passage from location a to b provided the following holds.

---

[3]Assuming a point train is not fundamental. It merely simplifies some of the derivation that follows. By using a configuration space transformation [4], the control problem for a length L train can be transformed to a control problem for a point train on a track with additional blocks.

Safe (a, b): $a .. b \subseteq dom(v)$
$$\wedge \; (\forall l: \; a \leq l \leq b: \; b_i \leq l \leq b_{i+1} \Rightarrow mn_i \leq v(l) \leq mx_i)$$

The first conjunct of *Safe* (a, b) asserts that the train has actually traveled from a to b, and the second conjunct asserts that the train's speed satisfied the restrictions associated with each block it occupied. Using *Safe* (a, b), we can specify the above railroad control problem in terms of weakest preconditions:

(3.1) $x = b_0 \wedge v = (; \; b_0 : v_0) \Rightarrow wp(S, Safe(b_0, b_n) \wedge x = b_n)$

This formula constrains S to be a program that terminates with the train at location b_n after having traveled at safe speeds to get there, provided S is started with the train at location b_0 traveling with speed v_0.[4]

3.1. A First Try

Having formalized the specification for a correct control program S, we now proceed with the derivation. The universal quantifier in conjunct $Safe(b_0, b_n)$ of the result assertion is a tip-off that S should be structured as a loop. Thus, we employ a standard hueristic from [2]—replacing a constant by a variable—and derive a loop invariant from the result assertion. Replacing n in the result assertion by a new program variable h (for "here") we get:

    I: $Safe(b_0, b_h) \; \wedge \; x = b_h \; \wedge \; 0 \leq h \leq n$

Since $I \wedge h = n$ implies result assertion $Safe(b_0, b_n) \wedge x = b_n$, we conclude that the loop guard must be $h \neq n$ (or something that implies $h \neq n$) and conjecture that S has the following structure:

    S: S_1 $\{I\}$
        do $h \neq n \rightarrow \{I \wedge h \neq n\} \; S_2 \; \{I\}$ **od** $\{h = n \wedge I\}$
        $\{Safe(b_0, b_n)\}$

Program S will satisfy its specification provided we find statements S_1 and S_2 that satisfy the following specifications.

---

[4]If the conjunct $x = b_n$ is omitted from the result assertion, then it would be permissible for control program S to terminate long after the train had passed point b_n. We have deemed such behavior unacceptable and so our specification prohibits it.

(3.2) $x=b_0 \wedge v=(;\ b_0{:}v_0) \Rightarrow wp(S_1, I)$

(3.3) $I \wedge h \neq n \Rightarrow wp(S_2, I)$

Formula (3.2) is the specification for the loop initialization; (3.3) is the specification for the loop body.

According to specification (3.2), S_1 must establish I. Observe that an easy way to establish I is by setting h to 0. So, we use wp to calculate an assertion that must hold before executing $h := 0$ in order for I to hold afterwards.

$$wp(h := 0, I)$$
$$= \quad \text{«wp definition of ":="»}$$
$$(Safe(b_0, b_h) \wedge x=b_h \wedge 0 \leq h \leq n)_0^h$$
$$= \quad \text{«textual substitution»}$$
$$Safe(b_0, b_0) \wedge x=b_0$$
$$= \quad \text{«definition of $Safe(a, b)$»}$$
$$b_0 \in dom(v) \wedge mn_0 \leq v(b_0) \leq mx_0 \wedge x=b_0$$

Notice that $x=b_0 \wedge v=(;\ b_0{:}v_0)$, the antecedent of specification (3.1) for S, implies $wp(h := 0, I)$ only if $mn_0 \leq v_0 \leq mx_0$. Thus, executing $h := 0$ establishes the loop invariant only under certain conditions—the initial speed of the train must be safe for travel in block b_0. We identify this requirement explicitly.

Assumption AS1. $mn_0 \leq v_0 < mx_0$

In retrospect, this requirement should not be surprising. It is worth noting, however, that this implicit assumption was exposed simply by adhering to a rigorous calculus in deriving the program. Including this assumption in the program we have developed so far, we get:

$$S: \{x=b_0 \wedge v=(;\ b_0{:}v_0) \wedge AS1\}$$
$$h := 0 \ \{I: \ Safe(b_0, b_h) \wedge x=b_h \wedge 0 \leq h \leq n\}$$
$$\textbf{do } h \neq n \rightarrow \{I \wedge h \neq n\} \ S_2 \ \{I\} \textbf{ od } \{h=n \wedge I\}$$
$$\{Safe(b_0, b_n)\}$$

We now refine S_2, the body of the loop. Based on our choice of guard, we know that the loop will terminate when h equals n. Initially, h is 0. Thus, for S_2 to make progress towards termination, h must be increased; and for S_2

to satisfy specification (3.3), S_2 must reestablish I. To investigate the feasibility of increasing h by 1, we calculate $wp(h := h+1, I)$.

$$wp(h := h+1, I)$$
=   «wp definition of ":="»
$$(Safe(b_0, b_h) \land x=b_h \land 0 \leq h \leq n)_{h+1}^{h}$$
=   «textual substitution»
$$Safe(b_0, b_{h+1}) \land x=b_{h+1} \land 0 \leq h+1 \leq n$$
=   «$a \leq b \leq c \Rightarrow (Safe(a, c) = (Safe(a, b) \land Safe(b, c)))$»
$$Safe(b_0, b_h) \land Safe(b_h, b_{h+1}) \land x=b_{h+1} \land 0 \leq h+1 \leq n$$

Since $I \land h \neq n$ holds at the start of S_2, we know that the first and last conjuncts of $wp(h := h+1, I)$ hold before S_2 executes. We must, therefore, arrange for the remaining conjuncts to hold.

$$Safe(b_h, b_{h+1}) \land x=b_{h+1}$$
=   «definition of $Safe(a, b)$»
$$b_h .. b_{h+1} \subseteq dom(v)$$
$$\land \; (\forall l: b_h \leq l \leq b_{h+1}: b_i \leq l \leq b_{i+1}$$
$$\Rightarrow mn_i \leq v(l) \leq mx_i) \land x=b_{h+1}$$
=   «$x=b_{h+1} \Rightarrow b_0 .. b_{h+1} \subseteq dom(v)$»
$$(\forall l: b_h \leq l \leq b_{h+1}: b_i \leq l \leq b_{i+1} \Rightarrow mn_i \leq v(l) \leq mx_i) \land x=b_{h+1}$$
=   «predicate logic»
(3.4) $(\forall l: b_h \leq l < b_{h+1}: b_i \leq l \leq b_{i+1} \Rightarrow mn_i \leq v(l) \leq mx_i)$
$$\land \; max(mn_h, mn_{h+1}) \leq v(b_{h+1}) \leq min(mx_h, mx_{h+1}) \land x=b_{h+1}$$

We consider the final conjunct first. It is easy to establish this conjunct by executing **await**(b_{h+1}), so we compute:

$$wp(\mathbf{await}(b_{h+1}), (3.4))$$
=   «wp calculus»
$$x \leq b_{h+1} \land 0 < v(x)$$
$$\land \; ((\forall l: b_h \leq l < b_{h+1}: b_i \leq l \leq b_{i+1} \Rightarrow mn_i \leq v(l) \leq mx_i)$$
$$\land \; max(mn_h, mn_{h+1}) \leq v(b_{h+1}) \leq min(mx_h, mx_{h+1})$$
$$\land \; x=b_{h+1})_{b_{h+1}, (v; \, l \in x .. b_{h+1}: v(x))}^{x, v}$$
=   «textual substitution and simplification»

(3.5) $x \le b_{h+1} \land 0 < v(x)$
$\land (\forall l: b_h \le l < b_{h+1}: b_i \le l \le b_{i+1} \Rightarrow$
$mn_i \le (v; l \in x .. b_{h+1}: v(x))(l) \le mx_i)$
$\land \max(mn_h, mn_{h+1})$
$\le (v; l \in x .. b_{h+1}: v(x))(b_{h+1})$
$\le \min(mx_h, mx_{h+1})$

Unfortunately, (3.5) is not implied by what is known to hold at the start of S_2, $I \land h \ne n$. We must therefore employ additional statements to transform the state from one satisfying $I \land h \ne n$ to one satisfying (3.5). The final conjunct of (3.5) can be established by executing $go(\tau)$, where τ is any speed that is safe and is attainable by accelerating from $v(b_h)$. That is, τ must satisfy:

(3.6) $\max(mn_h, mn_{h+1}) \le \tau \le \min(mx_h, mx_{h+1})$
$\land Vlen(v(b_h), \tau) \le b_{h+1} - b_h$

Nothing stated thus far implies that it should be possible to accelerate from any safe $v(b_h)$ to a safe $v(b_{h+1})$ in at most a distance of $b_{h+1} - b_h$, and so without making further assumptions about speed constraints, our control problem is unsolvable. We have uncovered another hidden assumption required to control a train:

Assumption AS2. $(\forall i, s: 0 < i < n \land \max(mn_{i-1}, mn_i) \le s \le \min(mx_{i-1}, mx_i):$
$(\exists s': \max(mn_i, mn_{i+1}) \le s' \le \min(mx_i, mx_{i+1}):$
$Vlen(s, s') \le b_{i+1} - b_i)))$

Henceforth, we assume that speed constraints for blocks do satisfy AS2. (It is not difficult to prove that any control problem for which there is a safe path from b_0 to b_n can always be reformulated as one with more restrictive minimum and maximum speeds satisfying AS2.)

A target speed τ satisfying (3.6) can now be computed as follows. First, due to the definition of $Vlen(u, t)$, the set of attainable speeds s—both safe and unsafe—starting from position b_h is characterized by:

$$\sqrt{v(b_h)^2 - 2*ACC*(b_{h+1} - b_h)} \le s \le \sqrt{v(b_h)^2 + 2*ACC*(b_{h+1} - b_h)}$$

Second, the set of safe speeds s for location b_{h+1} is given by:

$$\max(mn_h, mn_{h+1}) \le s \le \min(mx_h, mx_{h+1})$$

The intersection of these sets, therefore, is the set of safe and attainable speeds; the maximum of this intersection is the greatest safe speed—time is money for a railroad.

$$\tau = \min(\sqrt{v(b_h)^2+2*ACC*(b_{h+1}-b_h)},\ mx_h,\ mx_{h+1})$$

Using this value of τ for the target speed ensures that the final conjunct of (3.5) will hold.

The penultimate conjunct of (3.5) now is implied by our choice of τ and $Safe(b_0, b_h)$. Thus, our only remaining obligation is the truth of the second conjunct of (3.5), $0<v(x)$. Recall that $0\le mn_i<mx_i$ holds, by assumption. Thus, for all i, $mx_i\ne0$ and so successive values of τ are each non-zero. Provided $v_0\ne0$, we can strengthen the loop invariant to include $0<v(x)$ as a conjunct. This results in the following program.

S: $\{x=b_0 \wedge v=(;\ b_0{:}v_0) \wedge AS1 \wedge 0<v_0 \wedge AS2\}$
$\quad h := 0$
$\quad \{I:\ Safe(b_0, b_h)\ \wedge\ x=b_h\ \wedge\ 0\le h\le n\ \wedge\ 0<v(x)\}$
$\quad \textbf{do } h\ne n \to \{I \wedge h\ne n\}$
$\qquad\qquad S_2:\ t := \min(sqrt(v(b_h)^2+2*ACC*(b_{h+1}-b_h)),$
$\qquad\qquad\qquad\qquad\qquad mx_h,\ mx_{h+1});$
$\qquad\qquad \textbf{go}(t);$
$\qquad\qquad \textbf{await}(b_{h+1});$
$\qquad\qquad h := h+1$
$\qquad\qquad \{I\}$
$\quad \textbf{od } \{h=n \wedge I\}$
$\quad \{Safe(b_0, b_n)\}$

As the final step of the derivation, we delete references to reality variables from program statements. Recall, reality variables are auxiliary and, therefore, may not affect program execution. The only reference to a reality variable from within statements in the program above is the expression $v(b_h)$. We can maintain this value in a program variable *vel* by strengthening the loop invariant and adding assignments after each **go** statement. Making these changes results in the following control program; it solves the railroad control problem.

S: $\{x=b_0 \wedge v=(; \ b_0:v_0) \wedge AS1 \wedge 0<v_0 \wedge AS2\}$

$\quad h := 0; \quad vel := v_0$

$\quad \{I: \ Safe(b_0, b_h) \ \wedge \ x=b_h \ \wedge \ 0 \leq h \leq n \ \wedge \ 0 < v(x)$

$\qquad \wedge \ vel = v(b_h)\}$

$\quad \mathbf{do} \ h \neq n \rightarrow \{I \wedge h \neq n\}$

$\qquad\qquad S_2: \ t := \min(sqrt(vel^2 + 2*ACC*(b_{h+1}-b_h)),$

$\qquad\qquad\qquad\qquad\qquad mx_h, \ mx_{h+1});$

$\qquad\qquad\quad \mathbf{go}(t);$

$\qquad\qquad\quad vel := t;$

$\qquad\qquad\quad \mathbf{await}(b_{h+1});$

$\qquad\qquad\quad h := h+1$

$\qquad\qquad\quad \{I\}$

$\quad \mathbf{od} \ \{h=n \wedge I\}$

$\quad \{Safe(b_0, b_n)\}$

3.2. An Improved Control Program

Although correct, the control program just derived does not always permit a train to travel as quickly as possible. Modifying the derivation to maximize train speed is not difficult, however. First, we rewrite (3.4) as follows:

$(\forall l: \ b_h < l < b_{h+1}: \ b_i \leq l \leq b_{i+1} \Rightarrow mn_i \leq v(l) \leq mx_i)$

$\quad \wedge \ \max(mn_{h-1}, mn_h) \leq v(b_h) \leq \min(mx_{h-1}, mx_h)$

$\quad \wedge \ \max(mn_h, mn_{h+1}) \leq v(b_{h+1}) \leq \min(mx_h, mx_{h+1}) \ \wedge \ x=b_{h+1}$

Then, rather than allowing the final conjunct to drive the derivation (as it did above), we concentrate on the penultimate conjunct. The loop body that results from this strategy is:

S_2: $\mathbf{go}(t_1);$

$\qquad \mathbf{await}(b_{h+1} - Vlen(t_1, t_2));$

$\qquad \mathbf{go}(t_2);$

$\qquad h := h+1$

where t_1 and t_2 are the largest speeds satisfying:

$Vlen(v(b_h), t_1) + Vlen(t_1, t_2) \leq b_{h+1} - b_h \ \wedge \ mn_h \leq t_1 \leq mx_h$

$\quad \wedge \ \max(mn_h, mn_{h+1}) \leq t_2 \leq \min(mx_h, mx_{h+1})$

Computing values for t_1 and t_2 and using this new S_2 as a loop body, we get the following revised control program.

$S:$ $\{x=b_0 \wedge v=(; \ b_0:v_0) \wedge AS1 \wedge 0<v_0 \wedge AS2\}$
$\quad h := 0; \quad vel := v_0$
$\quad \{I: \ Safe(b_0,b_h) \ \wedge \ x=b_h \ \wedge \ 0\leq h\leq n \ \wedge \ 0<v(x)$
$\qquad \wedge \ vel=v(b_h)\}$
$\quad \textbf{do } h\neq n \rightarrow \{I \wedge h\neq n\}$
$\qquad S_2: \ t_1 := \min(mx_h,$
$\qquad\qquad\qquad sqrt(vel^2+2*ACC*(b_{h+1}-b_h)),$
$\qquad\qquad\qquad sqrt(\dfrac{mx_{h+1}^2}{2}+\dfrac{vel^2}{2}+ACC*(b_{h+1}-b_h))));$
$\qquad t_2 := \min(t_1, ms_{h+1});$
$\qquad \textbf{go}(t_1);$
$\qquad \textbf{await}(b_{h+1}-Vlen(t_1,t_2));$
$\qquad \textbf{go}(t_2);$
$\qquad vel := t_2;$
$\qquad h := h+1$
$\qquad \{I\}$
$\quad \textbf{od } \{h=n \wedge I\}$
$\quad \{Safe(b_0,b_n)\}$

4. Discussion

We were pleased to discover that only minor modifications were needed in order to employ Dijkstra's weakest-precondition calculus in deriving sequential, real-time, process-control programs. Dijkstra's calculus, unfortunately, is based on regarding a program as a relation between sets of states and, therefore, does not scale-up to concurrent and distributed programs, which are best thought of as "invariant maintainers". The extensions derived in section 2 for handling the state of a physical process—the contribution of this paper—do scale up. For example, we have been able to use them along with a logic for proving arbitrary safety properties of concurrent programs, Proof Outline Logic [5].

Second, both of the control programs we developed assumed that assignment statements are instantaneous. In reality, executing assignment statements does take time, and the state of the controlled process can change during that interval. It is not difficult to derive control programs for this more realistic setting. The predicate logic details become a bit messier as do the constants, but nothing about the structure of the derivation or resulting programs changes.

Reality variables are history variables—they encode in the current program state information about past system states. Using history variables for reasoning about programs is usually a bad idea, because it introduces distinctions that should be irrelevant. The current state—not how it was computed—should be of concern when reasoning about what a program will do next. In reasoning about process-control systems, however, one has no choice but to employ history variables of some sort. This is because the past instants for which the state of a physical process is defined is a strict superset of the past instants for which the state of a control program is defined. A program implements a discrete transition system, while a physical process is likely to implement a continuous transition system. History variables allow us to reason about all of the behavior of the physical process, including those states that exist while the program state is in transition, hence undefined.

Acknowledgment. Richard Brown read an early version of this paper and provided helpful comments.

References

[1]   Clint, M. Program proving: Coroutines. *Acta Informatica 2*, 1 (1973), 50-63.

[2]   Gries, D. *The Science of Programming.* Springer-Verlag, New York, 1981.

[3]   Dijkstra, E.W. *A Discipline of Programming.* Prentice Hall, N.J., 1976.

[4]   Lozano-Perez, T. Spatial planning: A configuration space approach. *IEEE Trans. on Computers C-32*, 2, 1983, 108-120.

[5]   Schneider, F.B. and G. R. Andrews. Concepts for concurrent programming. In *Current Trends in Concurrency.* (J.W. de Bakker, W.P. de Roever, and G. Rozenberg, eds.) Lecture Notes in Computer Science, Volume 224, Springer-Verlag, New York, 1986, 669-716.

CHAPTER 3

Mathematical Models of Real-Time Scheduling

Victor Yodaiken and Krithi Ramamritham
Department of Computer and Information Science
University of Massachusetts
Amherst, MA 01003, USA

Abstract

Real-time scheduling problems appear to be inherently difficult, but the weakness of available mathematical techniques for reasoning about the problem presents a further obstacle. In this paper, we begin to develop a mathematical "testbed" for real-time scheduling algorithms. The testbed consists of a specification of a real-time job scheduling system given in terms of the modal primitive recursive (m.p.r.) arithmetic. The m.p.r. arithmetic allows us to develop a formal model which in which the scheduling and communication mechanisms are visible and easily configured to match different algorithms or environments. We are able to describe the system, without relying on a simplified model of concurrency, such as those provided by interleaving or maximal parallelism. Despite this, we are able to take into account both the limited resources available in real-world real-time systems, and the inherent lack of accuracy in timing devices.

This work was supported by ONR under contract NOOO14-85-K-0398.

INTRODUCTION

A common configuration for a real-time system involves a processing device which accepts *jobs* or tasks of some sort from the environment and attempts to complete the computation involved for each job within a given deadline. Since jobs often will not require the full processing power of the system, and since the job stream may generate jobs out of priority order, it is not unusual to consider the problem of queueing and then scheduling jobs in some priority based ordering. In this paper, we consider the specification of a system which multi-tasks real-time jobs. First, we will develop an abstract specification, describing the intended visible behavior of the system. We then turn to a possible multi-processor implementation of the system. The implementation will contain a clock, a scheduler, and some number of processing elements. The function of the scheduler is to map the components of a job on to the processing elements in conformance with some scheduling algorithm. In order to make the system a little more flexible, we suppose that some of the processing elements may, themselves, be job scheduling systems. These *sub-systems* may accept several tasks from the scheduler, and process them in some concurrent fashion, possibly using specialized resources and/or different scheduling algorithms. The clock in our system will generate interrupts to permit the scheduler to keep track of the passage of time. Figure 1 provides a graphical depiction of the system organization.

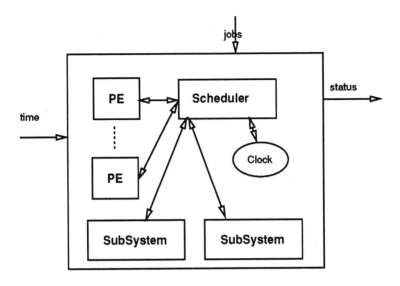

Figure: 1   The scheduling system

The specification is given in the modal primitive recursive (m.p.r.) arithmetic [14], an extension of integer mathematics that is intended to allow for concise description and analysis of finite state machines. The next section of this paper consists of an introduction to the m.p.r. arithmetic, and the third section contains the development of the scheduling system.

REAL-TIME STATE MACHINES

Mathematical techniques for the specification and verification real-time systems would both aid in the deign process and improve confidence in the correctness of a system design or implementation. But, if the mathematical techniques are themselves extremely complex and un-intuitive, then they may, instead, serve as an impediment to design. In this paper, we argue that finite state machines and integer valued functions provide a sufficient basis for formal reasoning about real-time systems, including those composed of concurrent sub-systems. Our approach relies on the *modal primitive recursive* (m.p.r.) functions, a class of integer-valued functions which allow us to describe state machines abstractly: without enumerating state sets or transition functions. Because m.p.r. functions allow for very compact descriptions of large-scale state machines, we can employ an especially simple model of real-time. We provide state machines with two types of transitions: control transitions which we consider to be instantaneous, and time transitions representing the passage of units of physical time. For example, in the system of figure 1, we will have both tick transitions, which represent a single discrete instant of physical time, and start.j transition, which represent commands to start job j. The amount of time which passes during a sequence of state transitions can, then, be determined by counting the tick transitions in the sequence.

Composite and concurrent systems. For composite systems with concurrent sub-systems, we turn to *product form state machines*. Briefly, a product form state machine connects some number of previously defined state machines, called *components* via a connection defined by *feedback functions*. Each component is associated with its own feedback function, and when the product state machine accepts an input, the feedback functions *induce* some sequence of parallel state transitions in each of the components. That is, as the composite system changes state, each component sub-system changes state concurrently. The feedback functions depend not only on the input to the product state machine, but on the *feedback* — the output of the other components. For example, in the system depicted in figure 1, the inputs to the scheduler depend on the system input, its own internal state, and the outputs of the clock, processing element, and subsystem components. A single tick transition might cause the scheduler to follow the path $\langle tick, int\_clk \rangle$ if the clock is generating a clock interrupt. Since each component may also be in product form, we can have multiple levels of connected components. Although product form state machines are not simple objects, we have developed techniques for specifying and reasoning about them quite concisely.

Related Work. M.p.r. arithmetic makes use of temporal logic style operators similar to those used by [12] and real-time operators similar to those used by [7]. We also share a state machine based semantics with many researchers (c.f., [10, 4, 12]), and an event/trace based view of computation with an even larger group that includes [3, 9, 6]. The m.p.r. arithmetic, however, differs sharply from these methods in several key respects.

- M.p.r. arithmetic provides a unified mathematical language for describing both high-level properties and detailed algorithmic design.

- M.p.r. arithmetic is free from programming language derived assumptions about the character of real-time systems and environments. We *do not* assume the existence of assignable storage, processes, inter-process communication channels, program counters or any other system dependent mechanism. These mechanisms *can* be defined within the m.p.r. arithmetic, but are not part of the model.

- M.p.r. arithmetic composition supports full encapsulation. The alphabets of components do not need to have any relationship to each other or to the alphabet of the product system. Thus, the details of lower-level components can be completely hidden, without use of non-determinism (c.f. [11]).

- The m.p.r. model of concurrency supports true parallelism without assuming anything about scheduling. The feedback functions allow us to model arbitrary parallel schemes: including systems containing sub-systems which change state at different rates or even *drift* apart. We do not assume maximal parallelism [8], interleaving [5], unbounded parallelism [13], or priority based scheduling [3]. Any of these schemes can be employed in a m.p.r. specification, either by using one of the components to control the others, or directly through the feedback functions.

- M.p.r. proofs are similar in style to proofs of standard algebra, and do not require any of the machinery of formal logic.

In this section, we provide an informal introduction to m.p.r arithmetic. A formal syntax and semantics can be found in [14].

Implicit specification. During the design or development of a digital system it seems natural to think about state indirectly. For example, one of the correctness conditions of a scheduling device might be written:

$$\neg \mathsf{Selected}(\mathsf{Job}_i) \rightarrow \mathsf{Priority}(\mathsf{Job}_i) \leqslant \mathsf{Priority}(\mathsf{SelectedJob}).$$

This expression implicitly references the current state of the device. Pictorially, the expression might be re-written:

$$\boxed{\textbf{Device Context}} \quad \text{Priority}(\text{Job}_j) \leqslant \text{Priority}(\text{SelectedJob}).$$

The boxed symbol on the left of the expression is a *context*, and represents the current state and possible future behavior of the device. The expression on the right is a *formal expression*, with a concrete meaning that depends on the context. The technique of separating semantics (context) from formal expressions is basic to formal logic. The advantage of this approach is that formal expressions can be made independent of the particular details of the context. For example, the boolean function SelectedJob, can be defined without worrying about how the algorithm is implemented. If SelectedJob had to be written with the state as a parameter, these details would have to be made explicit.

Contexts and m.p.r functions

We say that a sequence of transition symbols $w = \langle a_1, ..., a_n \rangle$ is a *trace* of state machine M iff w contains only symbols in the alphabet of M and w describes a path starting at the initial state of M and never driving M into an undefined state. That is, w is a trace of M iff w represents a possible behavior of M. In m.p.r. arithmetic, a context consists of a pair (M, w) where M is a finite state transducer (automaton with output) and w is a trace of M. Thus, (M, w) represents a system modeled by M in the state reached by following w. If **D** is a state machine representing the behavior of the scheduling device, we can re-write our example specification as follows:

$$\left[\ \boxed{\boxed{\textbf{D}}\atop w} \quad \text{Priority}(j) \leqslant \text{Priority}(\text{SelectedJob}) \ \right]$$

We *never* make the context explicit. We always describe the context in terms of the values of m.p.r. functions or expressions. We say an integer-valued expression is *true* in the context of (M, w) if and only if the value of the expression in the context of (M, w) is not zero. It should come as no surprise, that we say an expression is *false* iff its value is

0. We say a state machine M is *specified* by an expression $f(n)$ if and only if $f(n) > 0$ in the context of (M, w) for every trace w of M. Thus, every integer valued m.p.r. expression specifies some (possibly empty) family of state machines. To prove that a specification $S(m)$ *implements* a higher-level specification $S'(n)$, we just need to show that $S(m) \to S'(n)$ — an explicit state mapping from implementation to specification is not required.

The Basic Functions. We can describe a large range of systems using just two m.p.r. functions, Initial and Enable, and a modal operator *after* which allows us to refer to future values of expressions and functions. To describe composite systems (product form state machines) we also need a function Effect which describes the system feedback, and an operator *in* which allows us to refer to the value of an expression *within* a particular sub-system (component state machine).

The boolean function Initial : $\emptyset \to \{0, 1\}$ is true if and only if the system is in its initial state[1].

$$\left[\boxed{\begin{array}{c} \boxed{\mathbf{M}} \\ w \end{array}} \quad \text{Initial} \right] = \begin{cases} 1 & \textbf{if } w = \langle \rangle; \\ 0 & \textbf{otherwise.} \end{cases}$$

Thus, the value of Initial in context (M, w) is 1 iff w is the empty trace (the trace which leaves M in its initial state). Similarly, the boolean function Enable tests whether or not paths are *enabled* in the current context.

$$\left[\boxed{\begin{array}{c} \boxed{\mathbf{M}} \\ w \end{array}} \quad \text{Enable}(u) \right] = \begin{cases} 1 & \textbf{if } wu \textbf{ is a} \\ & \text{trace of M;} \\ 0 & \textbf{otherwise.} \end{cases}$$

Thus, Enable$(u) = 1$ in context (M, w) iff the sequence wu obtained by concatenating w and u does not drive M into an undefined state. We will often be interested in testing to see if a single state transition is enabled in the current state: that is, we will want to know iff Enable$(\langle a \rangle) = 1$ for some transition symbol a. By convention, we will omit the angle-braces, writing Enable(a) for Enable$(\langle a \rangle)$, whenever no confusion results.

---

[1] For simplicity of notation we will omit the empty parenthesis from functions with 0 arguments, writing *Initial* in place of *Initial( )*.

Future states. When we write $f(n)$, we are referring to the value of $f(n)$ in the current context. We can also refer to the value of an expression in a the context of a future state. The expression $(after\, u)f(n)$ refers to the value of $f(n)$ in the future state reached by following path u from the current state. Pictorially:

$$\left[\; \boxed{\boxed{\mathbf{M}} \atop w} \quad (after\, u)f(n) \right] \;=\; \left[\; \boxed{\boxed{\mathbf{M}} \atop wu} \quad f(n) \right]$$

That is, we evaluate $(after\, u)f(n)$ in the context (M, w), by evaluating $f(n)$ in the context of (M, wu).

Composite systems. We can consider a product form context to contain a product state machine, its trace, and context for each component.

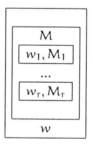

An expression $(in\, c)f(n)$ refers to the value of $f(n)$ *within* the context of the component state machine named c. We evaluate such an expression by replacing the current context with the context of state machine c.

$$\left[\; \boxed{\begin{array}{c} \mathbf{M} \\ \boxed{w_1, \mathbf{M}_1} \\ \cdots \\ \boxed{w_r, \mathbf{M}_r} \\ w \end{array}} \quad (in\, c)f(n) \right] \;=\; \left[\; \boxed{\boxed{\mathbf{M}_c} \atop w_c} \quad f(n) \right]$$

The function $\mathrm{Effect}(u, c)$ defines the *effect* of a path u on component c. If the product form state machine follows u from the current state, the component state machine named c will follow Effect(a, c) in parallel. For example, we might have

$$\text{Effect}(\langle \text{tick}\rangle, \text{dev1}) = \langle \text{tick}, \text{reset}\rangle$$

if $(\text{in dev2})\text{Reset} = 1$, and have

$$\text{Effect}(\langle \text{tick}\rangle, \text{dev1}) = \langle \text{tick}\rangle$$

otherwise. Thus, the output of dev2 controls the operation of dev1. Following our, by now familiar, convention, we will write Effect(a, c) in place of Effect$(\langle a\rangle, c)$ whenever no confusion results.

Expressions. We can use *after* and *in* as operators on arbitrary expressions as well as on functions. For example, $(\text{after } u)(f(n) > g(m))$ refers to the value of the expression $(f(n) > g(m))$ in the future state reached by following u. Similarly, $(\text{in } c)(f(g(m)))$ refers to the value of the entire expression $f(g(m))$ in the context of component c. As with more familiar operators, such as $\sum$ and $\forall$, the we have conventions that limit the scope of *after* and *in*. The expression $(\sum_{i=1}^{n} f)(g(i))$ is not equivalent to the expression $(\sum_{i=1}^{n}(f(g(i)))$, and $(\text{after } u)f(g(m))$ is <u>not</u> equivalent to $(\text{after } u)(f(g(m)))$. To evaluate $(\text{after } u)(f(g(m)))$ in the context of (M, w) we evaluate $(f(g(m)))$ in the context of (M, wu). But to evaluate $(\text{after } u)f(g(m))$, we evaluate $g(m)$ in the context of (M, w) to get some k, and then we evaluate $f(k)$ in the context of (M, wu). Similarly, $(\text{in } c)(f(g(m)))$ refers to the value of $(f(g(m)))$ within component c, while $(\text{in } c)f(g(m))$ refers to the value of $f(k)$ within component c, where k is the value of $g(m)$ in the current context.

Proof rules. We will begin with a very simple, but quite useful proof rule which permits us to get rid of the modal quantifiers in and after in some situations. If f is a function or predicate of ordinary arithmetic, then $(\text{after } u)f(n) = (\text{in } c)f(n) = f(n)$. For example $(\text{after } u)(n+1) = n+1$ — addition does not depend on the context. We will sometimes refer to this as the *context independence* property.

Another important property allows *path division*. That is, given an expression $(\text{after } uv)f(n)$, we can replace it with an equivalent expression $(\text{after } u)(\text{after } v)f(n)$. Let $a : u$ abbreviate $\langle a\rangle u$ and let $u : a$ abbreviate $u\langle a\rangle$. In keeping with our practice of simplifying notation, we write $(\text{after } a)f(n)$ in place of $(\text{after}\langle a\rangle)f(n)$ whenever it is clear that a is a transition symbol, not a path. Note that $(\text{after } a : u)f(n) = (\text{after } a)(\text{after } u)f(n)$, and $(\text{after } u :: a)f(n) = (\text{after } u)(\text{after } a)f(n)$. The path division property can be verified by examining the evaluation of *after*.

There is a distributive law for *after* and *in*. For arbitrary expression E_i, we know that

1. $(\text{after } u)(f(E_1, ..., E_n)) = (\text{after } u)f((\text{after } u)E_1, ..., (\text{after } u)E_n)$
2. $(\text{in } c)(f(E_1, ..., E_n)) = (\text{in } c)f((\text{in } c)E_1, ..., (\text{in } c)E_n)$.

We can often use the distributive law to simplify expressions. For example, consider $(\text{after } u)(E \wedge E')$. Rewriting this expression in function form we get an equivalent expression $(\text{after } u)(\text{and}(E, E'))$. By the distributive law we can derive a third equivalent expression:

$$(\text{after } u)\text{and}((\text{after } u)E, (\text{after } u)E').$$

But, since $\wedge$ is clearly a context independent function, we see that $(\text{after } u)\text{and}(x, y) = \text{and}(x, y)$. Thus, we can simplify our expression again to get $(\text{after } u)E \wedge (\text{after } u)E'$.

Finally, there is a property of expressions that allows us to *invert* expressions of the form $(\text{after } u)(\text{in } c)f(n)$. Note that we evaluate such an expression in a context (M, w) by evaluating $(\text{in } c)f(n)$ in the context of (P, wu). Essentially, we want to advance the state of the whole system by u, and then examine the value of $f(n)$ within component c. We can, equivalently, just advance the state of the component c by the path induced by u for c. That is, $(\text{after } u)(\text{in } c)f(n) = (\text{in } c)(\text{after Effect}(u, c))f(n)$. By convention, we will evaluate $(\text{in } c)(\text{after } E)f(n)$ by evaluating E within the current context. Thus, $(\text{in } c)(\text{after Effect}(u, c))f(n)$ is evaluated by finding the path z induced by u for component c, and then evaluating $(\text{after } z)f(n)$ within the context of component c. We call this rule, the *inversion rule*.

Temporal logic style operators.
Interval style operators. We can derive new operators from *after* which test to see if a property holds in any (every) state visited by a path. We let $(\text{sometimes } u)f(n)$ be true iff $f(n)$ attains a non-zero value at some

point during the computation of u. And we let $(always\, u)f(n)$ be true if every state visited by path u makes $f(n)$ true. Finally, let $(cumu\ u)f(n)$ be the *cumulative* value obtained by adding the value of $f(n)$ in each state reached during u. Let $v \prec u$ be true if and only if $(\exists z)vz = u$. That is, $v \prec u$ is true iff v is a *prefix* of u. Note that $\langle\rangle \prec u$ and $u \prec u$. We can define sometimes, always, and cumu using prefixes quite easily.

Definition 1:

$$(\mathrm{sometimes}\ u)f(n) \stackrel{\mathrm{def}}{=} (\exists v \prec u)(\mathrm{after}\, v)f(n) > 0$$
$$(\mathrm{always}\, u)f(n) \stackrel{\mathrm{def}}{=} (\forall v \prec u)(\mathrm{after}\, v)f(n) > 0$$
$$(\mathrm{cumu}\ u)f(n) \stackrel{\mathrm{def}}{=} \sum_{v \prec u}(\mathrm{after}\, v)f(n)$$

Henceforth. We write $\Box f(n)$ to assert that $f(n) > 0$ in the current and all reachable future states.

Definition 2:

$$\Box f(n)$$
$$\stackrel{\mathrm{def}}{=} (\forall u)(\mathrm{Enable}(u) \rightarrow (\mathrm{after}\, u)f(n) > 0)$$

Thus, $\Box f(n)$ is true iff every enabled path leads to a state where $f(n) > 0$. Since $\langle\rangle$ must be enabled unless the current state is undefined, $\Box f(n)$ implies that $f(n)$ is true both currently and *henceforth*. The symbol $\Box$ is used in a similar way in the branching temporal logics [1, 2].

Until. We want $E\,\mathrm{until}\,E'$ to be true iff for every enabled path u, u does not visit a state where E is false *until* it has visited a state where E' is true.

Definition 3:

$$f(n)\,\mathrm{until}\,g(m) \stackrel{\mathrm{def}}{=} (\forall u)(\mathrm{Enable}(u) \rightarrow (\mathrm{always}\, u)f(n) \bigvee (\mathrm{sometimes}\ u)g(m).$$

To see that this definition captures our intuitive notion of until, suppose that $f(n)$ until $g(m)$ is true, and consider an enabled path u.

If (always u)f(n), then u clearly satisfies our intuitive definition. Suppose that (always u)f(n) is false. Then, by definition (sometimes u)g(m). Now suppose that, contrary to our intuitive definition, f(n) becomes false along u *before* g(m) becomes true. Then there must be some prefix $v \prec u$, so that (sometimes v)g(m) and (always v)f(n) are both false. But, note that $v \prec u \rightarrow$ Enable(u) $\rightarrow$ Enable(v). By the definition of until, we are assuming that (always v)f(n) $\bigvee$(sometimes v)g(m) must be true. Thus, it is impossible for any prefix of u to make f(n) false before making g(n) true.

An *until* theorem. Synchronization of devices is often accomplished by letting one device wait until the second device is ready. The next m.p.r. theorem states that if an expression E is non-zero, and E until (E $\bigwedge$ F), and (sometimes u F), then if u is enabled, (sometimes u (E $\bigwedge$ F)). That is, if device X signals its intention to synchronize until both its own signal and the signal of device Y are sensed, and if the signal from Y will be sensed during the same interval, we can conclude that the synchronization will take place.

M.p.r. theorem 1: Until latching.

$$
\square \left(\begin{array}{l} \text{E until } (\text{E} \bigwedge \text{F}) \\ \bigwedge \text{Enable}(u) \\ \bigwedge (\text{sometimes } u)\text{F} \\ \rightarrow (\text{sometimes } u)(\text{E} \bigwedge \text{F}) \end{array} \right)
$$

The proof of m.p.r. theorem 1 is straightforward. We assume the theorem hypothesis. From (sometimes u)F there must be some $v_0 \prec u$, so that (after v_0)F. We note that, by definition of until, every enabled path u must satisfy (always u)E $\bigvee$(sometimes u)(E $\bigwedge$ F). If the second case is true, we are done. If (always u)E is true, then for every $v \prec$ u, we must have (after v)E. Thus, (after v_0)F $\bigwedge$(after v_0)E. Writing $\bigwedge$ in functional form, we have and((after v_0)E, (after v_0)F). Since and is context independent, we can move it down into the scope of the *after* and conclude (after v_0)and(E, F)), i.e., (after v_0)(E $\bigwedge$ F). **EndProof.**

The final temporal operator that we want to simulate is $\bigcirc$. We write $\bigcirc f(n)$ to assert that $f(n)$ must be non-zero in the next state.

Definition 4:

$$\bigcirc f(n) \overset{\text{def}}{=} (\forall a)(\textit{after } a)(f(n) > 0).$$

We conclude this section with a m.p.r. theorem which allows us to prove E until F *inductively* on paths. That is, we show that if in all future states, E implies that $F \vee \bigcirc (E \vee F)$ is true, then we must have $E \to (E \text{ until } F)$.

M.p.r. theorem 2: Until induction.

$$\square((E \to (F \vee \bigcirc (E \vee F))) \to E \text{ until } F$$

It is possible to define m.p.r. analogs of all the temporal operators, and it is also possible to eliminate the unbounded quantification used here. For details see [14].

Real-time operators and functions. In this paper, we will use the transition symbol tick to mark the passage of one unit of physical time. Note that tick does not represent a tick of a timing device, it represents time passing in the physical world. We do not need to assume that real-time devices can accurately measure the passage of time, we may, for example, specify that a property must hold at least once every t physical time units, and at most once every t' time units. But, before we can begin to describe such properties, we need to be able to count the tick symbols in a path or trace.

Definition 5: The function TLen.

$$\text{TLen}(\langle \rangle) \overset{\text{def}}{=} 0,$$
$$\text{TLen}(u :: a) \overset{\text{def}}{=} \begin{cases} \text{TLen}(u) & \text{if } a \neq \text{tick}; \\ \text{TLen}(u) + 1 & \textbf{otherwise} \end{cases}$$

Definition 6: The function duration.

$$\text{duration}(u) \overset{\text{def}}{=} \text{TLen}(u) * \text{Enable}(u).$$

Thus, $\text{duration}(u) > 0$ implies that u is an enabled path, during which $\text{duration}(u)$ time units pass.

We can define specialized real-time versions of $\square$ and $\diamond$ which depend on the number of ticks which are traversed by a path. Intuitively, $\square_t f(x)$ should be true if and only if $f(x) > 0$ for at least the next t time units. Similarly, $\diamond_t f(x)$ should be true if and only if $f(x) > 0$ *within* at most t time units. These functionals are analogous to the real-time temporal modifiers found in [7].

Definition 7: Timed versions of henceforth and eventually.

$$\square_t f(n) \overset{\text{def}}{=} (\forall u)(\text{Enable}(u) \wedge \text{duration}(u) \leqslant t$$
$$\rightarrow (\text{after } u)f(n))$$
$$\diamond_t f(n) \overset{\text{def}}{=} (\forall u)(\text{ duration}(u) \geqslant t$$
$$\rightarrow (\text{sometimes } u)f(n))$$

We can prove some elementary facts about $\diamond_t$ and $\square_t$ that will be useful in gaining intuition about their behavior.

M.p.r. theorem 3: Elementary results about $\diamond_n$ and $\square_n$.

1. $(\diamond_n E \wedge \square(E \rightarrow F)) \rightarrow \diamond_n F$
2. $(\square_{n+1} E \wedge \text{Enable}(\text{tick}) \rightarrow (\text{after tick})\square_n E)$
3. $\square \diamond_n E \wedge \text{duration}(u) \geqslant k * n$
$\rightarrow (\text{cumu } u)E \geqslant k$

Proof. For 3.1 we simply note that $\text{duration}(u) \geqslant n$ implies that for some $v \prec u$ we have $(\text{after } v)E$. By the premise, we have $(\text{after } v)(E \rightarrow F)$, and thus, we have shown $(\text{after } v)F$. For the second part of the theorem we note that $\text{duration}(u) \leqslant n+1 \rightarrow (\text{always } u)E$. Suppose that $(\text{after tick})\text{duration})(v) \geqslant n$. Then $\text{Enable}(\text{tick})$ implies that $\text{duration}(\text{tick} \cdot v) \geqslant n+1$. Thus $(\text{always tick} : v)E$, and $(\text{after tick})(\text{always } v)E$. To prove m.p.r. theorem 3.3 divide u into $(k+1)$ segments, each of which contains at least n ticks. **EndProod.**

Less trivially, consider a system where property E becomes true and stays true until both E and F are true. For example, a "handshake" protocol requires one device to signal its request and maintain the request until a second device signals its response. Formally, we write such a requirement as $\Box\Diamond_m(E \text{ until } (E \wedge F))$. That is, every m time units E will become true and stay true until $(E \wedge F)$ becomes true. Now suppose that F becomes true every n time units: $\Box\Diamond_n F$. It should follow that within $n + m$ time units both E and F will be true.

M.p.r. theorem 4: Duration upper bound.

$$\Box(\Diamond_m(E \text{ until } (E \wedge F)) \wedge \Diamond_n F) \rightarrow \Diamond_{n+m}(E \wedge F))$$

For a related theorem consider the case where condition E interferes with the handling of condition F. For example, if E is a request which has higher priority than F. In this case, we may want to specify that E must periodically stay false long enough for $(F \wedge \neg E)$ to become true. We write $\Diamond_t \Box_n \neg E$ to assert that within t time units the system will enter an interval of duration n, during which E will stay false. Suppose that $\Box\Diamond_m F$ is true, and that $\Diamond_t \Box_n \neg E$ is also true, for $n > m$. Thus, within t time units, E will be false for at least n time units. Within those n time units, F must become true. So these two conditions ensure that $\Diamond_{t+m}(\neg E \wedge F)$.

M.p.r. theorem 5: Duration lower bound.

$$(n > m \wedge \Diamond_t \Box_n \neg E \wedge \ \Box\Diamond_m F)$$
$$\rightarrow \Diamond_{t+m}(\neg E \wedge F))$$

THE SCHEDULING SYSTEM

Suppose that we have a set $\mathcal{J}$ of *jobs*, a range $\{1, ..., \text{MaxDead}\}$ of deadlines, and a range $\{1, ..., \text{MaxId}\}$ of job *identifiers*. We want to design a system which accepts requests $(job, deadline, id)$ to compute the named job within the given deadline. In this paper, we will develop a mathematical model of a *real-time job scheduling system* (RTJSS) which will accept requests of this form and try to compute each job in a timely fashion. We begin with a high-level abstract specification of the system requirements.

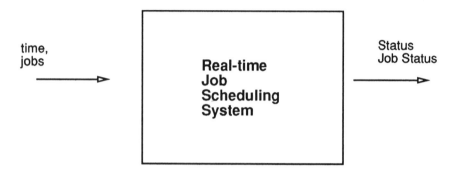

time,
jobs

Real-time Job Scheduling System

Status
Job Status

Figure: 2   The real-time job scheduling system

The system of figure 2 accept ticks, to indicate the passage of physical time, commands of the form start(j, d, i) to initiate an effort to complete job j within deadline d, and commands of the form ack.i to acknowledge the terminal status of a job. We let deadlines be given in relative form, i.e., a deadline of n means finish up within n time units. The time units for deadlines will be less fine than the time units for ticks. A tick represents the finest interval of discrete time that can change system state. For example, in many systems ticks might well represent nano-seconds. A deadline, on the other hand, will be given in some grosser unit, say milli-seconds. Let U denote the multiplicity of deadline time units in tick time units. That is, U ticks will pass during a single deadline time unit. When the environment provides the system with a job (j, d.i), they system will generate a status output for id i indicating that status of job id i is either Done or Fail. Ideally, the time required for this output should be d, but communication and processing delays are inevitable, so we allow for a fudge factor delay. The system expects that the environment will acknowledge the terminal status of job id i at some point. Until the environment generates the acknowledgment, the system will refuse to accept new jobs using the same id. Note, we do not assume anything about when, or the environment will generate requests or acknowledgments: we are modeling the scheduling system, not its clients. We formalize the system requirements below, in figure 3

Figure: 3   A RTJSS

$Rtjss(\mathcal{J}, MaxId, MaxDead, U, delay) \overset{\text{def}}{=}$

{

  Alphabet = { tick,

                start.(j, d, i): $0 \leqslant i < MaxId$,

                             $j \in \mathcal{J}, 0 \leqslant d < MaxDead$,

                             ack.$i : 0 \leqslant i < MaxId$

        }

$\bigwedge$ Outputs $= \{SysStatus, Status\}$

$\bigwedge$ SysStatus $\in \{Ready, Fail, Busy\}$

$\bigwedge$ Status$(i) \in \{Idle, Active, Fail, Done\}$

$\bigwedge$ Initial $\rightarrow (\forall i) Status(i) = Idle$

$\bigwedge (after\ a) Status(i) = \begin{cases} Active & \textbf{if } a = start.(j, d, i); \\ Idle & \textbf{else if } a = ack.i \\ & \textbf{or if } Status(i) = Idle \\ Fail & \textbf{else if } Status(i) = Fail \\ Done & \textbf{else if } Status(i) = Done \end{cases}$

$\bigwedge (after\ start.(j, d, i)) \Diamond_{U*(delay+d)} Status(i) \in \{Done, Fail\}$

$\bigwedge SysStatus = \begin{cases} Fail & \textbf{if } (\exists i) Status(i) = Fail; \\ Ready & \textbf{else if } (\exists i)(Status(i) = Idle); \\ Busy & \textbf{otherwise.} \end{cases}$

$\bigwedge$ Enable(tick) $= 1$

$\bigwedge$ Enable(start$(i, p.l)$) $\leftrightarrow$

                        (SysStatus $= Ready \bigwedge$ Status$(i) = Idle$)

}

The real-time job scheduling system (RTJSS) has an alphabet consisting of tick, transitions start.(j, d, i), and transitions ack.i. It has two output functions, SysStatus , which has no arguments, and Status:

$\{0, ... MaxId-1\} \rightarrow \{Idle, Active, Fail, Busy\}$. In the initial state, $Status(i) = Idle$ for each id i — the system is not runing any jobs. After a $start.(j, d, i)$ transition, the $Status(i) = Active$. At some later time (within $U*(delay+d)$ time units. $Status(i)$ will either take the value $Done$ or $Fail$. If $Status(i) = Idle$, then any transition that is not a $start.(j, d, i)$ transition, will leave $Status(i)$ unchanged. If a is an $ack.i$ transition, then after a, $Status(i) = Idle$. If $Status(i) \in \{Fail, Done\}$ and $a \neq ack.i$, then after a the status will remain unchanged. The value of $SysStatus$ is a summary of the values of $Status(i)$ on all the job id's. Note that we let the system accept as many jobs as it has idle job identifiers. Also note that once the system fails, it remains in a failed state indefinitely.

Job scheduling

We'll suppose that each job j can be mapped to a set $tasks(j) = \{j_1, ..., j_n\}$ where each j_i is a task computing some part of j. The elements of $task(j)$ can be computed in any order, or in parallel. Thus, when we are given a request (j, d, i) we need to compute every element of $tasks(j)$ before the deadline given by d is reached. Clearly, we gain some benefit from having multiple processing elements (p.e.'s) to allow for parallel computation of the individual tasks. Some of the p.e.'s will be simple processing devices. But, sometimes we will need processing elements that are more complex: for example, processing elements that multi-task or contain specialized resources or processing elements of their own. These, more complex p.e.'s will be real-time job scheduling systems in their own right. Thus, we might have a hierarchy of systems with a RTJSS at the top containing p.e.'s, a clock, and subsidiary RTJSS's. Note that a system containing subsidiary RTJSSs can treat them as if they were additional p.e.'s. That is, if a subsidiary RTJSS can accept up to k concurrent jobs, then it can be treated, in some respects, as a collection of k p.e.'s.

Given a request (j, d, i) we can generate a triple $(tasks(j), d, i)$ which is the "compiled" version of the request. We use the notation $(x_0, ..., x_n)_i = x_i$ to index elements of a tuple. We can call the first element of such a triple $(T, d, i)_0 = T$ the *pending tasks* for request i. Suppose that we have a scheduling function which will pick the next task to run from a set of triples (T, d, i) and a list of available processing elements. Let X be a set of triples and let P be a list of idle processing elements. We want NextTask(X, P) to select the most "urgent" task belonging to any job in X. We let NextTask(X, P) = (s, d, i, p) if and only if there is some p ∈ P and **some** (T, d, i) ∈ X so that s ∈ T and, by some criterion, s should be selected **next.** The function NextTask can implement an arbitrary scheduling **algorithm** and may use information about which p.e.'s are best suited to run which tasks. In this paper, we do not care how NextTask works, we want to set up a mathematical testbed for examining the properties of the algorithm.

Let's consider the simpler components, the processing elements and the clock. The processing elements accept jobs, run them in real time, and then assert a signal indicating that they are done. When an ack input is given to a processing element, it enters an idle state and waits for a new task. We give each processing element a map timetorun:TaskSet → $\mathcal{N}$ which provides the upper bound of time required for processing a task (instruction).

Figure: 4 The Processing Element (p.e.).

$ProcessingElement(timetorun, TaskSet) \stackrel{\text{def}}{=}$
{
    $Alphabet = \{tick, ack, run.j : j \in TaskSet\}$
    $\wedge \, Outputs = \{Status\}$
    $\wedge \, Status \in \{Idle, Busy, Done\}$
    $\wedge \, Initial \rightarrow Status = Idle$
    $\wedge (after\ a)CurrentTask = \begin{cases} j & \textbf{if } a = run.j \\ CurrentTask & \textbf{otherwise.} \end{cases}$
    $\wedge (after\ run.j)Status = Busy\ \textbf{until}\ Status = Done$
    $\wedge \, Status \in \{Idle, Done\} \rightarrow (after\ tick)Status = Status$
    $\wedge (after\ ack)Status = Idle$
    $\wedge \, Status = Busy \rightarrow \Diamond_{timetorun(CurrentTask)}Status = Done$
    $\wedge \, Enable(tick) = 1$
    $\wedge \, Enable(run.j) = (Status = Idle)$
    $\wedge \, Enable(ack) = (Status = Done)$
}

The TimerElement just generates an interrupt at least once every $U + drift$ time units, and at most once every $U - drift$ time units. The first constraint is expressed as $\Diamond_{U+d}$Interrupt, meaning that the boolean function Interrupt will be true at least once every $U + d$ time units. The second constraint is expressed by asserting that after a reset, the value of Interrupt will be false for at least $U - d$ time units. After generating an interrupt, the timer waits for a reset.

Figure: 5   The Timer Element.

$$\text{TimerElement}(U, drift) \stackrel{\text{def}}{=}$$
$$\{$$

    $\text{Alphabet} = \{\text{tick}, \text{reset}\}$

    $\wedge \text{Outputs} = \{\text{Status}\}$

    $\wedge \text{Status} \in \{\text{Idle}, \text{Interrupt}\}$

    $\wedge \text{Initial} \rightarrow \text{Status} = \text{Idle}$

    $\wedge (\textbf{after reset})\Box_{U-drift}\text{Status} = \text{Idle}$

    $\wedge \Diamond_{U+drift}\text{Status} = \text{Interrupt}$

    $\wedge \text{Status} = \text{Interrupt} \rightarrow (\textbf{after tick})\text{Status} = \text{Interrupt}$

    $\wedge \text{Enable}(\text{tick}) = \text{Enable}(\text{reset}) = 1$

$$\}$$

The scheduler

Now, we are ready to specify the scheduler. The scheduler is the most complex part of the system, but it does little more than manage a couple of data structures. For each job id i, we have dynamic functions Status(i), Job(i), Deadline(i), Pending(i), and Running(i). When a start.(j, d, i) transition occurs, we set Job(i) = j, Deadline(i) = d, and Status(i) = Active. We also set Pending(i) = Tasks(j), and set Running(i) = $\emptyset$. Thus, Pending(i) holds the set of tasks which must be computed for Job(i). As we dispatch tasks, we will move elements of Pending(i) into Running(i). When a task completes, we will remove it from Running(i). The job is completed when Running(i) $\bigcup$ Pending(i) = $\emptyset$ and Status(i) = Active. We keep track of which processing elements are busy, with the dynamic function ProcStatus. In the initial state ProcStatus(p) = Idle. Whenever we dispatch a task to processing element p, we set ProcStatus(p) = Busy. Whenever processor p completes its task, it generates an interrupt, and we set ProcStatus(p) = Idle again. The set of remaining to be dispatched for job id i is given by Pending(i). Thus, the set $\{(\text{Pending}(i), \text{Deadline}(i), i) : \text{Status}(i) = \text{Active}\}$ is the set of jobs to be dispatched. The set $\{p : \text{ProcStatus}(p) = \text{Idle}\}$ is the set of available processors. Thus, we apply NextTask to these two sets in order to determine which task should be dispatched next.

Figure: 6   Scheduler, part I

$$\text{Sched}(\mathcal{J}, \text{MaxIds}, \text{MaxTime}) \stackrel{\text{def}}{=}$$

$\{$

  Alphabet = { tick,

                dispatch,

                $\text{start}.(i, j, d) : 0 \leqslant i < \text{MaxId}, j \in \mathcal{J}, 0 \leqslant l \leqslant \text{MaxDead}$,

                $\text{int\_done}.i : 0 \leqslant i < \text{MaxId}$,

                int_clk

                }

$\bigwedge$ Outputs = { SysStatus, Status, Time,

                    SelectId, SelectTask, Deadline, Time}

$\bigwedge$ SysStatus = $\begin{cases} \text{Fail} & \textbf{if } (\exists i)\text{Status}(i) = \text{Fail}; \\ \text{Ready} & \textbf{else if } (\exists i)(\text{Status}(i) = \text{Idle}); \\ \text{Busy} & \textbf{otherwise}. \end{cases}$

$\bigwedge$ Initial $\rightarrow$ $(\forall i)\text{Status}(i) = \text{Idle}$

            $\bigwedge$ NextId = 0

            $\bigwedge$ Time = 0

            $\bigwedge$ Dispatching = 0

In the first part of the scheduler specification. part I, we define the alphabet, list the output functions, describe SysStatus, and set the initial conditions. The alphabet contains the usual suspects, start, tick, and ack, plus new symbols representing interrupts and dispatching. The transition symbol dispatch represents the act of dispatching a task to a processing element. The symbol int_done.p, represents an interrupt that is generated by a p.e., to inform the scheduler that the p.e. has completed its task. The symbol int_clk represents a clock interrupt.

In the next part, part II, we set up the basic data structures needed to keep track of jobs and p.e.'s. That is, we define dynamic functions that track the current time, the deadlines for each active job, and the status of each p.e.. We also make sure that we can associate a busy p.e. with both its current task and the id of its current task.

Figure: 7   Scheduler, part II

$$\bigwedge(\text{after } a)\text{Time} = \begin{cases} \text{Time } +1 & \text{if } a = \text{int\_clk;} \\ \quad\quad \text{mod MaxTime} & \\ \text{Time} & \text{otherwise.} \end{cases}$$

$$\bigwedge(\text{after } a)\text{Deadline}(i) = \begin{cases} d & \text{if } a = \text{start.}(j, d, i); \\ \text{Deadline}(i) \dot{-} 1 & \text{if } a = \text{int\_clk;} \\ \text{Deadline}(i) & \text{otherwise.} \end{cases}$$

$$\bigwedge(\text{after } a)\text{ProcStatus}(p) = \begin{cases} \text{Idle} & \text{if } a = \text{int\_done.p;} \\ \text{Assigned} & \text{if } a = \text{dispatch} \\ & \text{and } p = \text{SelectProc;} \\ \text{ProcStatus}(p) & \text{otherwise.} \end{cases}$$

$$\bigwedge(\text{after } a)\text{AssignedTask}(p) = \begin{cases} \text{SelectTask} & \text{if } a = \text{dispatch} \\ & \text{and } p = \text{SelectProc;} \\ \text{Assigned Task}(p) & \\ & \text{otherwise.} \end{cases}$$

$$\bigwedge(\text{after } a)\text{AssignedId}(p) = \begin{cases} \text{SelectId} & \text{if } a = \text{dispatch} \\ & \text{and } p = \text{SelectProc;} \\ \text{AssignedId}(p) & \text{otherwise.} \end{cases}$$

The final part of the scheduler, part III, defines the scheduling operating itself. We collect the sets of active jobs and idle processers needed by NextTask, and specify the dynamic behavior of Pending and Running. Note that the scheduler may detect that a job has failed while tasks belonging to that job are still active on p.e.'s. These tasks will complete, but no other tasks belonging to the failed job will be dispatched.

$$\bigwedge \text{JobsToRun} = \{(\text{Pending}(i), \text{Deadline}(i), i) : \text{Status}(i) = \text{Running}\}$$
$$\bigwedge \text{AvailableProc} = \{p : \text{ProcStatus}(p) = \text{Idle}\}$$
$$\bigwedge \text{SelectTask} = \text{NextTask}(\text{JobsToRun}, \text{AvailableProcs})_0$$
$$\bigwedge \text{SelectDeadline} = \text{NextTask}(\text{JobsToRun}, \text{AvailableProcs})_1$$
$$\bigwedge \text{SelectId} = \text{NextTask}(\text{JobsToRun}, \text{AvailableProcs})_2$$
$$\bigwedge \text{SelectProc} = \text{NextTask}(\text{JobsToRun}, \text{AvailableProcs})_3$$

$$\bigwedge (\text{after } a)\text{Pending}(i) = \begin{cases} \text{tasks}(j) \\ \textbf{if } a = \text{start}(j, d, i); \\[1em] \text{Pending}(i) \setminus \text{SelectTask} \\ \textbf{if } a = \text{dispatch} \\ \textbf{and } i = \text{SelectId} \\[1em] \text{Pending}(i) \\ \textbf{otherwise.} \end{cases}$$

$$\bigwedge (\text{after } a)\text{Running}(i) = \begin{cases} \emptyset \\ \textbf{if } a = \text{start}(j, d, i); \\[1em] \text{Running}(i) \bigcup \text{SelectTask} \\ \textbf{if } a = \text{dispatch} \\ \textbf{and } i = \text{SelectId} \\[1em] \text{Running}(i) \setminus \text{AssignedTask}(p) \\ \textbf{if } a = \text{int\_done}.p \\ \textbf{and } i = \text{AssignedId}(p) \\[1em] \text{Running}(i)\textbf{otherwise.} \end{cases}$$

$$\bigwedge (\text{after dispatch})\neg\text{Dispatching}$$
}

$$\bigwedge \text{Dispatching} \rightarrow \text{JobsToRun} \neq \emptyset$$
$$\bigwedge \text{AvailableProcs} \neq \emptyset$$

$$\bigwedge (\text{after } a)\text{Status}(i) = \begin{cases} \text{Active} & \textbf{if } a = \text{start}.(j, d, i); \\ \text{Idle} & \textbf{else if } a = \text{ack}.i \\ & \textbf{or if } \text{Status}(i) = \text{Idle} \\ \text{Fail} & \textbf{else if } \text{Status}(i) = \text{Fail} \\ & \textbf{or if } \text{Deadline}(i) = 0 \\ & \qquad \bigwedge \text{Status}(i) = \text{Active} \\ \text{Done} & \textbf{else if } \text{Status}(i) = \text{Done} \\ & \textbf{or if } \text{Pending}(i) = \emptyset \\ & \qquad \bigwedge \text{Running}(i) = \emptyset \\ & \textbf{and } \text{Status}(i) = \text{Active} \end{cases}$$

$$\bigwedge \text{Enable}(\text{tick}) = \text{Enable}(\text{clk\_int}) = \text{Enable}(\text{int\_done.p}) = 1$$
$$\bigwedge \text{Enable}(\text{start}(i, \text{p.l}) \leftrightarrow (\text{SysStatus} = \text{Ready}) \bigwedge (\text{Status}(i) = \text{Idle})$$
$$\bigwedge \text{Enable}(\text{dispatch}) \leftrightarrow \text{Dispatching}$$
}

Figure: 8   Scheduler, part III

The implementation

We conclude this section by composing the scheduler, clock, and p.e. specifications to specify a system which implements a RTJSS. The system will contain MaxProc p.e.'s, MaxSub RTJSS subsystems, a clock, and a scheduler. We want to define an implementation, using a boolean function Rtjss so that

$$\square \text{Imp}(\; \mathcal{J}, \text{MaxId}, \text{MaxDead}, \text{MaxSub},$$
$$\text{MaxId}_s (0 \leqslant s < \text{MaxSub}), \text{dl}, \text{del}, U, \text{tr}_p, \text{ts}_p)$$
$$\rightarrow \square \text{Rtjss}(\mathcal{J}, \text{MaxId}', \text{MaxDead}, U, \text{del}')$$

for some MAxId' and del' depending on the arguments to Imp. That is, we want any system which satisfies Imp to also satisfy Rtjss. Note that Imp requires a long list of parameters. This is because Imp must supply all the parameters to all the components we have defined in the previous sections. The specification Imp is actually a *refinement* of Rtjss: supplying more detail about how the system will be implemented.

The p.e.'s will be named proc.p for $0 \leqslant p < \mathsf{MaxProc}$. The subsystems will be named subsys.s for $0 \leqslant s < \mathsf{MaxSub}$. In order to allow the scheduler to treat subsystems as collections of p.e.', we map each job id i on each subsystem s to a *virtual processing element* identifier $\mathsf{VirtProc}(i, s)$. Let MaxId_s be the number of identifiers allowed in subsystem s. Let $\mathsf{VirtProc}(s, i) = (\sum_{s' < s} \mathsf{MaxId}_{s'}) + \mathsf{MaxProcs} + i$. Thus, there are $\mathsf{VirtMaxId} = \sum_s \mathsf{MaxId}_s$ virtual processors, in addition to the $\mathsf{MaxProc}$ "real" processing elements.

In part I, we list the (large number) or parameters, list the components, associate each component with a specification, define the output functions, and define some control functions. The output functions are simple, they just reflect the values of the outputs in the scheduler. The other functions we define are used for interrupt control. A p.e. which has output Done should generate an interrupt for the scheduler. Similarly, an interrupt should be generated if a subsystem has output $\mathsf{Status}(i) = \mathsf{Done}$ for some i. We use the simplest possible algorithm for deciding interrupt priority here. We make p.e.'s have higher priority than subsystems (by selecting a p.e. to schedule if possible, even if there

Figure: 9 The implementation, part I.

Imp($\mathcal{J}$, MaxId, MaxDead, MaxSub, MaxProcs
      MaxId$_s$ $(0 \leqslant s <$ MaxSub$)$, MaxTime
      delay, U
      timetorun$_p$, TaskSet$_p$: $0 \leqslant p <$ MaxProcs$)$)
$\stackrel{\text{def}}{=}$ {

  Alphabet = { tick,
               start.$(i, j, d) : 0 \leqslant i <$ MaxId, $j \in \mathcal{J}, 0 \leqslant l \leqslant$ MaxDead,
               ack.i $: 0 \leqslant i <$ MaxId
          }
$\wedge$ Outputs = {SysStatus, Status}
$\wedge$ Components = {sched, clk, proc.p,
                 subsys.s $: 0 \leqslant p <$ MaxIds, $0 \leqslant s <$ MaxSub}
$\wedge$(in sched)$\square$Sched($\mathcal{J}$, VirtMaxId + MaxId, MaxTime)
$\wedge$(in clk)$\square$TimerElement(U, drift)
$\wedge$($\forall$p)(in proc.p)$\square$ProcessingElement(timetorun$_p$, Taskset$_p$)
$\wedge$($\forall$p)(in subsys.s)$\square$Rtjss($\mathcal{J}$, MaxId$_s$, MaxDead, U, delay)
$\wedge$ SysStatus = (in sched)SysStatus
$\wedge$ Status(i) = (in sched)Status(i)
$\wedge$ BestProc = (min p)(in proc.p)Done
$\wedge$ InterruptProc = (in proc.BestProc)Done
$\wedge$ BestSub = (min s)(in subsys.s)($\exists$i)Status(i) = Done
$\wedge$ BestTask = (min i)(in subsys.BestSub)Status(i) = Done
$\wedge$ InterruptSub = (in subsys.BestSub)Status(BestTask) = Done
$\wedge$ VirtProc(s, i) = $(\sum_{s' < s}$ MaxIds$_s)$ + MaxIds + i

are subsystems that can be scheduled). We let p have higher priority than p' iff $p < p'$. The BestProc is the p.e. that is Done (needs an ack) with the lowest identifying number. The function InterruptProc is true iff there is a p.e. which is generating an interrupt. The BestSub is the subsystem with the lowest identifying number which is generating an interrupt, and BestTask is the task which has the highest interrupt priority (smallest identifier) within the BestSub.

In part II, we define the interaction of the components. A start transition should only change the state of the scheduler. On the other hand, tick transitions may cause any number of components to change state. To simplify the definition of Effect(tick, c) we define a auxilary function act. The value of Effect(tick, c) will be tick : act(c). Every tick must cause every component to traverse a tick in lock-step — after all, physical time passes uniformly. The complex decisions about what interrupts are generated, are made in the act functions.

Figure: 10   The implementation, part II

$$\bigwedge \text{Effect}(\text{start}.(j, d, i), c) = \begin{cases} \langle \text{start}.(j, d, i) \rangle \\ \textbf{if } c = \text{sched}; \\ \langle \rangle \textbf{ otherwise}. \end{cases}$$

$$\bigwedge \text{Effect}(\text{tick}, c) = \text{tick} : \text{act}(c)$$

$$\bigwedge \text{act}(\text{sched}) = \begin{cases} \langle \text{int\_clk} \rangle \\ \textbf{if } (\text{in clk})\text{Interrupt}; \\ \langle \text{int\_done}.\text{BestProc} \rangle \\ \textbf{else if } \text{InterruptProc} \\ \langle \text{int\_done}. \\ \text{VirtProc}(\text{BestSub}, \text{BestTask}) \rangle \\ \textbf{else if } \text{InterruptSub} \\ \langle \text{dispatch} \rangle \\ \textbf{else if } (\text{in sched})\text{Dispatching}; \\ \langle \rangle \textbf{ otherwise}. \end{cases}$$

$$\bigwedge \text{act}(\text{clk}) = \begin{cases} \langle \text{reset} \rangle \\ \textbf{if } (\text{in clk})\text{Interrupt} \\ \langle \rangle \textbf{ otherwise}. \end{cases}$$

$$\bigwedge \text{act}(\text{proc}.p) = \begin{cases} \langle \text{run}.j \rangle \\ \textbf{if } (\text{in sched})\text{Dispatch} \\ \textbf{and } (\text{in sched})\text{SelectProc} = p \\ \textbf{and } (\text{in sched})\text{SelectTask} = j \\ \\ \langle \text{ack} \rangle \\ \textbf{else if } \text{act}(\text{sched}) = \langle \text{int\_done}.p \rangle; \\ \langle \rangle \textbf{ otherwise}. \end{cases}$$

}

$$\wedge\,act(subsys.s) = \begin{cases} \langle start.(j,d,i)\rangle \\ \quad \textbf{if } (\text{in sched})Dispatch \\ \quad \textbf{and} \quad (\text{in sched})SelectProc \\ \qquad = VirtProc(s,i) \\ \quad \textbf{and} \ (\text{in sched})SelectTask = j \\ \quad \textbf{and} \ (\text{in sched}) \\ \quad SelectDeadline = d \\ \quad \langle ack.i\rangle \ \textbf{else if} \ \ ack(sched) \\ \qquad\qquad = \langle int\_done.VirtProc(s,i)\rangle; \\ \langle\rangle \ \textbf{otherwise.} \end{cases}$$

$\wedge\,Enable(tick) = 1$

$\wedge\,Enable \ (start(i,p.l))$
$\qquad \leftrightarrow (SysStatus = Ready \wedge Status(i) = Idle)$

}

CONCLUSION AND FUTURE WORK

We now have a rough model of a system in which scheduling algorithms may be tested. Given a scheduling algorithm NextTask, we can ask how well will it perform under certain job streams, and given varying constraints on clock drift, processing element speed, and scheduler overhead. For example, we might ask if a job stream in which system loading met certain restrictions could cause the system to fail. That is, if $Initial \wedge Enable(u)$ implies that there is a certain distribution of jobs over u, then can a particular scheduling algorithm ensure $(always\ u)Status \neq Fail$. We can also begin to refine our specifications to meet the constraints of an actual scheduling system, e.g., by incorporating timing information for a particular processor into timetorun.

References

[1] M. Ben-Ari, A. Pnueli, and Z. Manna. The temporal logic of branching time. *Acta Informatica*, 20, 1983.

[2] E. A. Emerson and J. Y. Halpern. Sometimes and 'not never' revisited: on branching versus linear time temporal logic. *Journal of the ACM*, 33(1), January 1983.

[3] Richard Gerber and Insup Lee. Communicating shared resources: A model for distributed real-time systems. Technical Report MS-CIS-89-26, University of Pennsylvania, 1989.

[4] D. Harel. Statecharts: A visual formalism for complex systems. Technical report, Weizmann Institute, 1984.

[5] C. A. R. Hoare. *Communicating Sequential Processes*. Prentice-Hall, 1985.

[6] F. Jahanian and A.K. Mok. Safety analysis of timing properties in real-time systems. *IEEE Transactions on Software Engineering*, SE-12(9), September 1986.

[7] R. Kooymans, J. Vytopil, and W.P. DeRoever. Real time programming and asynchronous message passing. In *Proceedings of the 2cd ACM Symp. on Principles of Distributed Programming*, 1983.

[8] R. Koymans, R.K. Shyamasundar, W.P. de Roever, R. Gerth, and S. Arun-Kumar. Compositional semantics for real-time distributed computing. Technical Report 86.4, Eindhoven University of Technology, June 1986.

[9] N.G. Leveson and J.L. Stozy. Safety analysis using petri nets. *IEEE Transactions on Software Engineering*, March 1987.

[10] A. Lynch, N. and M. Merrrit. Introduction to the theory of nested transactions. Technical Report TR-367, Laboratory for Computer Science, MIT, 1986.

[11] R. Milner. *A Calculus of Communicating Systems*, volume 92 of *Lecture Notes in Computer Science*. Springer Verlag, 1979.

[12] J.S. Ostroff and W.M. Wonham. Modelling, specifying, and verifying real-time embedded computer systems. In *Symposium on Real-Time Systems*, Dec 1987.

[13] K. Voss, H.J. Genrich, and G Rozenberg, editors. *Concurrency and Nets: Advances in Petri Nets.* Springer-Verlag, 1987.

[14] Victor Yodaiken. *A Modal Arithmetic for Reasoning About Multi-Level Systems of Finite State Machines.* PhD thesis, University of Massachusetts (Amherst), 1990.

CHAPTER 4

Communicating Shared Resources: A Paradigm for Integrating Real-Time Specification and Implementation

Insup Lee, Susan Davidson, and Richard Gerber
Department of Computer and Information Science
University of Pennsylvania
Philadelphia, PA 19104-6389

Abstract

buted real-time systems can be
Communicating Shared Resources,
ation model of CSR is resource-
es execute synchronously, while
resource are interleaved accord-
es the gap between an abstract
itation environments, but is too
ess algebra. We therefore give
provides the ability to perform
anipulation. We illustrate how
ated into the CCSR formalism
consumer example, and how a
e shown correct using syntactic

op a formal framework for reason-
real-time systems. Such a frame-
tion language, an abstract model

of computation, a notion of equivalence of terms in the model, and tools for automating proofs of equivalence.

Since the timing behavior of a real-time system depends not only on delays due to process synchronization, but also on the availability of shared resources, the computation model must include a notion of resources and how they can be shared as well as a notion of processes and synchronization. These notions are partially addressed in real-time models and scheduling theory, but not adequately combined. While most real-time models capture delays due to process synchronization, they abstract out resource-specific details by assuming idealistic operating environments. On the other hand, while scheduling theory captures the notion of resources, it ignores the effect of process synchronization except for simple precedence relations between processes. Therefore, a contribution of the model we develop is two integrate these two notions.

To help bridge the gap between abstract computation models and implementation environments, we have developed a real-time language called *Communicating Shared Resources*, or CSR. CSR's underlying computational model is *resource-based*, where a resource may be a processor, an Ethernet link, or any other constituent device in a real-time system. At any point in time, each resource has the capacity to execute an action consisting of only a single event or particle. However, a resource may host a set of many processes, and at every instant, any number of these processes may compete for its availability. That is, on a single resource, the actions of multiple processes must be interleaved; "true" parallelism may take place only *between* resources. To arbitrate between competing events, CSR employs a priority-ordering.

CSR syntactically resembles variants of real-time CSP found in [1] and [2]. However, it also has the capacity to specify many constructs commonly found in real-time systems, such as timeouts, deadlines, periodic processes, temporal scopes [3] and exception-handling. CSR also incorporates several of the features of a configuration language, in that processes must be explicitly assigned to the resources on which they reside. We have formalized our constructs using a priority-based denotational semantics, that gives precise meaning to CSR's real-time characteristics, its interleaved resource sharing, and the "pure" concurrency that occurs between resources.

CSR supports a natural, high-level description of real-time systems, and its semantics captures the temporal properties of prioritized resource interaction. However, the CSR language is far too complex to be treated as a process algebra, and thus does not easily lend itself to an equational characterization. To remedy this, we have developed the Calculus for Communicating Shared Resources, or CCSR. Strongly influenced by SCCS [4, 5], CCSR is a priority-sensitive process algebra that uses a synchronous form of concurrency, and possesses a term equivalence based on strong bisimilarity. Thus CCSR provides the ability to perform equivalence proofs by syntactic manipulation. Also, since its prioritized, strong equivalence is a congruence, it allows us to reason about a term's behavior when it is embedded in a real-time "context." CSR and CCSR share the same basic computational model, in that they are both resource-based and rely on a priority arbitration scheme to resolve resource contention.

Section 2 describes the computation model of processes and resources that underlies both CSR and CCSR. Section 3 gives an overview of CSR and shows its use in a real-time periodic producer-consumer example. Section 4 presents an overview of CCSR, and demonstrates how the example of Section 3 can be translated to the CCSR formalism. We conclude the paper in Section 5 by pointing to areas of future research.

THE COMPUTATION MODEL

Events. Our basic unit of computation is the *event*, which we use to model both local resource execution as well as inter-resource synchronization. An event is executed by at most one resource and consumes exactly one time unit. This does not imply that all actions require exactly the same amount of time, rather that the event is a common infinitesimal unit, a building-block with which more complex functions are constructed. We let Σ be the universal set of events.

Actions. In a system composed of multiple resources executing in parallel, the system as a whole may execute a set of events simultaneously. We call such a set of simultaneous events an *action*, which is represented by a set in $\mathcal{P}(\Sigma)$. In general, we let the letters a, b and c range over the event set Σ, and the letters A, B and C range over the action set $\mathcal{P}(\Sigma)$.

We let the Greek letters Δ and Γ range over $\mathcal{P}(\mathcal{P}(\Sigma))$, or subsets of the action domain.

Resources. We let $\mathcal{R}$ represent the set of resources available to a system, and let i, j, and k range over $\mathcal{R}$. Since an event is executed by at most one resource, Σ is partitioned into mutually disjoint subsets, each of which can be considered the set of events available to a single resource. For all i in $\mathcal{R}$ we denote Σ_i as the collection of events exclusively "owned" by resource i:

$$\forall i \in \mathcal{R}, \forall j \in \mathcal{R} . i \neq j, \ \Sigma_i \cap \Sigma_j = \emptyset$$

Furthermore, individual resources are considered to be inherently sequential in nature. That is, a single resource is capable of synchronously executing actions that consist, *at most*, of a single event. We formalize this by defining $\mathcal{D}$, the domain of actions executable by any set of resources, as:

$$\mathcal{D} \ = \ \{A \in p(\Sigma) \,|\, \forall i \in \mathcal{R}, \ |A \cap \Sigma_i| \leq 1\}$$

where $p(\Sigma)$ denotes the set of finite subsets of Σ. For a given action A, we use the notation $\mathcal{R}(A)$ to represent the resource set that executes events in A: $\mathcal{R}(A) = \{i \in \mathcal{R} \,|\, \Sigma_i \cap A \neq \emptyset\}$.

Priority. At any point in time, many events may be competing for the ability to execute on a single resource. We arbitrate such competition through the use of a priority ordering over Σ. There is a finite range of priorities at which events may execute. Letting mp be the maximum possible priority, we denote $PRI = [0, \ldots, mp] \subseteq \mathbf{N}$ as the set of priorities available to events in the system. Thus we can linearly order the events in Σ by a priority mapping $\pi \in \Sigma \to PRI$.

It is often necessary to consider the relative priority of *actions*. Since an action consists of multiple events from different resources, we first consider the priority of an action with respect to a *single* resource: We extend π to singleton (and empty) sets in $\mathcal{P}(\Sigma)$ with the function $\Pi \in \mathcal{P}(\Sigma) \to PRI$ where for each A in $\mathcal{P}(\Sigma)$,

$$\Pi(A) = \begin{cases} \pi(a) & \text{if } A = \{a\} \\ 0 & \text{otherwise} \end{cases}$$

We can now define the partial ordering "$\leq_p$" that reflects our notion of priority over the domain $\mathcal{D}$. For all $A, B \in \mathcal{D}$,

$$A \leq_p B \quad \text{iff} \quad \forall i \in \mathcal{R}, \ \Pi(A \cap \Sigma_i) \leq \Pi(B \cap \Sigma_i)$$

OVERVIEW OF CSR

The CSR language provides the foundation for our real-time specification method, and all of our higher-level constructs are derived from it. In some ways, it syntactically resembles the variants of real-time CSP found in [1] and [6]. However, it significantly differs by including features that take full advantage of our priority semantics. Furthermore, it has the capacity to specify many constructs commonly found in real-time systems, such as timeouts, periodic processes, and exception-handling.

The Role of Events in CSR

Events in CSR can be used to model local computation, "input" communication and "output" communication. If an event models local computation, it can be denoted by any lower-case identifier such as "a", "b", "do_it", or the like. Or, if an event models input communication, it is represented by an identifier followed by a question mark, such as "in_p?", "a?", etc. If an event models output communication, it is represented by an identifier followed by an exclamation point, such as "$out!$" or "$a!$". To avoid confusion, we place the following restriction on Σ: If an identifier "id" is used as a local computation event, there are no events "id?" or "$id!$" in Σ, and *vice versa*.

In CSR, all communication between resources is strictly one-to-one, and is performed by synchronizing events. This means that there is a single resource R_1 that may utilize "$a!$" to denote a "write" action, and a single resource R_2 that may use "$a?$" to denote a "read." When both resources simultaneously agree to communicate, the two events perform a "semantic match" and the events are resolved and thus can be executed On the other hand, events that model local computation are already considered resolved, as they need no communicating partners to ensure their execution.

The Syntax and Informal Semantics of CSR

In CSR, the system consists of a set of resources, each of which is a set of processes. A process is assigned to exactly one resource, and can engage in execution or synchronizing events. The following is a complete grammar for the CSR language:

$$\langle system \rangle ::= \langle resource \rangle \mid \langle system \rangle \parallel \langle system \rangle$$
$$\langle resource \rangle ::= \{\langle process \rangle\}$$
$$\langle process \rangle ::= \langle proc\_id \rangle :: \langle stmt \rangle \mid \langle process \rangle \ \& \ \langle process \rangle$$
$$\langle stmt \rangle ::= \mathbf{wait}\ t \mid \mathbf{skip} \mid a? \mid a! \mid \mathbf{exec}(a, m, n) \mid$$
$$\langle stmt \rangle \ ; \ \langle stmt \rangle \mid \langle guard\_s \rangle \mid \langle within\_s \rangle \mid$$
$$\langle interrupt\_s \rangle \mid \langle loop\_s \rangle \mid \langle every\_s \rangle$$
$$\langle guard\_s \rangle ::= [\langle gd \rangle \rightarrow \langle stmt \rangle \square \quad \dots \square \langle gd \rangle \rightarrow \langle stmt \rangle$$
$$\triangle \ \mathbf{wait}\ t \rightarrow \langle stmt \rangle] \mid$$
$$[\langle gd \rangle \rightarrow \langle stmt \rangle \square \quad \dots \square \langle gd \rangle \rightarrow \langle stmt \rangle]$$
$$\langle gd \rangle ::= a \mid a? \mid a!$$
$$\langle within\_s \rangle ::= \mathbf{within}\ t\ \mathbf{do}\ \langle stmt \rangle\ \mathbf{when}\ t \rightarrow \langle stmt \rangle\ \mathbf{od}$$
$$\langle interrupt\_s \rangle ::= \mathbf{interrupt}\ a\ \mathbf{do}\ \langle stmt \rangle\ \mathbf{when}\ a? \rightarrow \langle stmt \rangle\ \mathbf{od}$$
$$\langle loop\_s \rangle ::= \mathbf{loop}\ \mathbf{do}\ \langle stmt \rangle\ \mathbf{od}$$
$$\langle every\_s \rangle ::= \mathbf{every}\ t\ \mathbf{do}\ \langle stmt \rangle\ \mathbf{od}$$

The **wait** statement specifies a pure delay for t time units, while **skip** is syntactic sugar for the construct **wait** 1. The read statement, $a?$, waits indefinitely for a communicating process to execute the corresponding write statement, $a!$. The $\mathbf{exec}(a, m, n)$ construct denotes local computation – the event a may be executed for a minimum of m, and a maximum of n time units. Sequential composition is similar to that in the traditional, untimed CSP.

The guarded statement is a prioritized variant of that presented in [6]. In the version without a timeout, all of the communication guards delay indefinitely, waiting to be matched with their communicating partners. As soon as the first match is made, the guard with the highest priority takes precedence, and the statement associated with it is executed. Note that local events are allowed as guards, in which case no delay is necessary; the priority arbitration occurs immediately. Furthermore, if a timeout guard, **wait** t, is included in the statement, communication is only attempted for up to t time units, after which the timeout statement is executed.

The **interrupt** operator functions in the following manner: To be interrupted, the main body must currently be executing an event that has lower priority than the interrupting event. If this is the case, control transfers immediately to the interrupt handler. The **within** statement specifies that its body must execute within a specified time limit. If it fails to do so, an exception statement is executed. Note that this facility provides for the specification of nested temporal scopes [3], as **within** statements may themselves be nested. The **loop** statement specifies general, unguarded recursion, while the **every** construct denotes a statement that executes periodically.

There are two types of concurrent operators: Interleaving is denoted by the "&" symbol, while true parallelism is represented by the "∥" symbol. True parallelism can take place only between different resources, while interleaved processes execute on the same resource. In fact, all expansions of the ⟨resource⟩ nonterminal are *required* to be executed on a single resource (or processor). This is guaranteed by the restrictions inherent in the grammar.

To a certain extent CSR provides not only a real-time programming paradigm, but also a configuration language. Unlike other CSP-influenced languages, the structure of our language *mandates* that process-to-resource mapping be performed. After all processes have been assigned to a resource, the resource is closed using the *close* operator, or "{ . }." And after a resource is closed, no other processes may be assigned to it. Only a closed resource can be combined in parallel with other closed resources in the system.

There are several significant restrictions made on the events used both within and between resources. First, if an event *a* represents a synchronizing action, a single resource may not use *a* for both reading and writing. That is, we insist that communication is one-to-one *between* resources. A resource is incapable of communicating with itself since actions on a resource are purely interleaved; thus it is impossible for the read and write actions to occur simultaneously. If interleaved processes need to communicate with each other, they must utilize intermediate resources such as memory, communication media and the like.

Next, two *different* resources may not model a common function using the same event. For example, given an event *a*, two different resources cannot execute the "*a*!" statement. This would also violate our restriction that all communication must be one-to-one. If many-to-one communication protocols are desired, they must explicitly be modeled through guarded statements.

One final restriction is that no two resources may share a single local event. A local event is considered a unique unit from a particular resource, thus sharing it would violate the very resource constraints that we are attempting to model.

It should be noted that our grammar excludes some constructs permitted by other concurrent languages. For example, we do not implicitly allow a simple fork-join program, such as

$$Q = P_1; (P_2 \parallel P_3); P_4$$

Example

We now show how CSR can be used to specify a periodic producer-consumer example. In this example, there are four processes: producers P1 and P2, and consumers C1 and C2. While the producers execute on their own resources, C1 and C2 share a resource. C1 (C2) consumes input produced by P1 (P2) using the synchronizing event i1 (i2).

```
{ P1:: every 6 do
        p1;
        [i1! → exec(p3,3,3) □ wait 2 → skip ]
        od } ||
{ P2:: every 6 do
        p2;
        [ i2! → exec(p4,1,1) □ wait 4 → skip ]
        od} ||
{C1:: loop do i1?; exec(c1,2,2) od &
  C2:: loop do i2?; exec(c2,2,2) od }
```

Since P1 and P2 execute on dedicated resources, there is no contention among events; we therefore assume that $\pi(p1) = \pi(p2) = \pi(p3) = \pi(p4) = 1$ and that $\pi(11!) = \pi(i2!) = 0$, which is also the priority of waiting. For events on the shared resource, we assume the following priorities: $\pi(c1) = \pi(c2) = 3$, $\pi(i1?) = 2$, $\pi(i2?) = 1$. This priority assignment makes $\Pi(\{i1?, i1!\}) <_p \Pi(\{i2!, i2?\})$, thus if $i1?$ and $i2?$ are simultaneously ready, $i1?$ is preferred over $i2?$. Furthermore, if $c1$ (or $c2$) is executing, it cannot be interrupted by any other events.

Informally, the system behaves as in the following diagram, where time is assumed to increase horizontally to the right:

	0	1	2	3	4	5	6	7	...
P1:	p1	i1!	p3	p3	p3		p1	i1!	...
P2:	p2				i2!	p4	p2		...
C1&C2:		i1?	c1	c1	i2?	c2	c2	i1?	...

At time 0, P1 and P2 can both execute their first action, p1 and p2, respectively. P1 and P2 are both ready to synchronize on i1 and i2 respectively, but since $\pi(i1) > \pi(i2)$, C1 and P1 succeed. P1 executes p3 for 3 time units, and then idles another time unit waiting to re-execute the body of **every** 6 **do**. Meanwhile, C1 executes c1 for 2 time units; C2 then synchronizes with P2 on i2 at time 4, executes c2 for 2 time units and becomes ready to re-synchronize with P1 and P2 at time 7. P2, meanwhile, executes p4 for 1 time unit and immediately starts the body of **every** 6 **do** again. P1 and P2 are then both in the same position at time 6 as they were at time 0, and the scenario repeats itself.

What we would like to be able to say about the system is that P1 and P2 never execute their **wait** statements, i.e. they never skip the execution of p3 and p4. While this can be argued informally, we would like to develop a proof system in which we can prove it formally with syntactic manipulation. As a first step, we have developed CCSR.

A CALCULUS FOR COMMUNICATING SHARED RESOURCES

The CSR formalism adequately captures the temporal properties of prioritized resource interaction through a semantics based on linear histories. However, this semantics does not easily lend itself to an equational characterization of the CSR language. For this reason, we developed the Calculus for Communicating Shared Resources, or CCSR. Strongly influenced by SCCS [4, 5], CCSR is a process algebra that uses a synchronous form of concurrency, and possesses a term equivalence based on strong bisimilarity [7]. CSR is syntactically a "richer" formalism than CCSR, in that it contains many real-time language constructs such as timed interrupt-handlers, temporal scopes [3], and periodic processes; however, we believe that CSR constructs can be translated into CCSR. Furthermore, CCSR provides the ability to perform equivalence proofs by syntactic manipulation.

Before describing CCSR, we introduce some notation for termination and synchronization.

Termination. There is one event that has special meaning: the termination event, or "$\sqrt{}$", which can be executed by every resource. We often use the following notation: for any set $A \subseteq \Sigma$, $A^{\sqrt{}}$ means $A \cup \{\sqrt{}\}$ and $A^{\cancel{\sqrt{}}}$ means $A - \sqrt{}$. Also, $\sqrt{}$ is a fixed point of all event renaming functions $\phi \in \Sigma \rightarrow \Sigma$; i.e., for all such ϕ, $\phi(\sqrt{}) = \sqrt{}$.

Synchronization. The lowest form of communication is accomplished through the simultaneous execution of synchronizing events. Our model treats such synchronizing events as being statically "bound" together by the various connections between system resources. To formally treat this property we make use of *connection sets*. A connection set is a set of events that exhibits the "all or none" property of event synchronization: At time t, if any of the events in a given connection set wish to execute, they all must execute. A familiar example of this concept can be drawn from CSP [8, 9], where the alphabet of events is $\{c_1!, c_1?, c_2!, c_2?, c_3!, c_3?, \ldots\}$, where "$c_i$" is a channel, "$c_i!$" is interpreted as a write action, and "$c_i?$" is interpreted as a read action. When a read and a write occur simultaneously on the same channel, the communication is considered successful. The connection sets in such languages are simply $\{c_1!, c_1?\}$, $\{c_2!, c_2?\}$, etc. For the rest of this section, we assume that connections sets contain either one or two elements; one element sets model local execution, and two element sets model one-to-one communication.

Given an action A, we say that A is *fully synchronized* iff, for every input event $a?$ in A, the corresponding output event, $a!$, is also in A (and vice versa). Note that an action containing only local execution events is trivially fully synchronized. We define the predicate $synch(A)$ to be true iff A is fully synchronized. Also, we say that A is synchronized with respect to a resource set $I \subseteq \mathcal{R}$ iff for every input-output pair $\{a!, a?\}$ in $\bigcup_{j \in I} \Sigma_j$, if the input event $a?$ is in A, the corresponding output event, $a!$, is also in A (and vice versa). We define the predicate $sync_{(I)}(A)$ to be true iff A is fully synchronized with respect to the resource set I.

It is often convenient to be able to decompose an action $A \in \mathcal{P}(\Sigma)$ into two parts: that which is fully synchronized, and that which is not. To do this, we make use of the following two definitions:

$$res(A) = \bigcup\{B \subseteq A \mid sync(B)\}$$
$$unres(A) = A - res(A)$$

Priority-Canonical Events. Priority and resource mapping naturally partition Σ into equivalence classes. That is, for events $a, b \in \Sigma$, a is in the class $[b]$ if and only if for some $i \in \mathcal{R}$, $a, b \in \Sigma_i$ and $\pi(a) = \pi(b)$. In CCSR, we use the symbol "τ_i^n" to represent a "canonical" event from each class, where τ_i^n is mapped to resource i and has priority n. Further, for every $i \in \mathcal{R}$, there is a τ_i^0 in Σ_i: every resource has the capacity to execute at the lowest priority level.

There is a unique renaming function, ϕ_π, such that if $a \in [\tau_i^n]$, then $\phi_\pi(a) = \tau_i^n$. It follows that the τ_i^n are fixed-points of priority renaming; that is, $\phi_\pi(\tau_i^n) = \tau_i^n$. All such "canonical" events are local with respect to their own resources; that is, they belong to their own connection sets: For each $a \in \Sigma$ there is a connection set $j \in \mathcal{C}$ such that $\{\phi_\pi(a)\} = C_j$.

The CCSR Language

The syntax of CCSR resembles, in some respects, that of SCCS [4, 5]. Let $\mathcal{E}$ represent the domain of terms, and let E, F, G and H range over $\mathcal{E}$. Additionally we assume an infinite set of free term variables, FV, with X ranging over FV and $free(E)$ representing the set of free variables in the term E. Let $\mathcal{P}$ represent the domain of closed terms, which we call *agents* or alternatively, *processes*, and let P, Q, R and S range over $\mathcal{P}$. The following grammar defines the terms of CCSR:

$$E := NIL \mid A : E \mid E + E \mid E_I\|_J E \mid E \triangle_t^B (E, E, E) \mid [E]_I \mid E\backslash A \mid fix(X.E) \mid X$$

While we give a semantics for these terms in subsequent sections, we briefly present some motivation for them here. The term NIL corresponds to **0** in SCCS – it can execute no action whatsoever. The Action operator, "$A : E$", has the following behavior. At the first time unit, the action A is executed, proceeded by the term E. The Choice operator represents selection – either of the terms can be chosen to execute, subject to the constraints of the environment. For example, the term $(A : E) + (B : F)$ may execute A and proceed to E, or it may execute B and proceed to F.

The Parallel operator $E_I \|_J F$ has two functions. It defines the resources that can be used by the two terms, and also forces synchronization between them. Here, $I \subseteq \mathcal{R}$ is a set of the resources allotted to E, and $J \subseteq \mathcal{R}$ is a set of the resource allotted to F. In the case where $I \cap J \neq \emptyset$, E and F may be able to share certain resources. But as we have stated, such resource-sharing must be interleaved.

The Scope construct $E \triangle_t^B (F, G, H)$ binds the term E by a temporal scope [3], and it incorporates both the features of timeouts and interrupts. We call t the *time bound* and B the *termination control*, where $t \in \mathbf{N}^+ \cup \{\infty\}$ (i.e., t is either a positive integer or infinity), and $B = \{\sqrt{}\}$ or $B = \emptyset$.

While E is executing we say that the scope is *active*. The scope can be exited in a number of ways, depending on the values of E, H, t and B. If E successfully terminates within time t by executing "$\sqrt{}$", then F is initiated. Here, if $B = \{\sqrt{}\}$, the transition from E to F will retain its ability to signal termination, while if $B = \emptyset$, the entire construct will terminate only when F does.

There are two other ways in which the scope may be exited. If E fails to terminate within t units, the "exception-handler" G is executed. Lastly, at any time throughout the execution of E, it may be interrupted by H, and the scope is then departed.

As an example of the Scope operator, consider the following specification: "Execute P for a maximum of 100 time units. If P successfully terminates within that time, then terminate the system. However, if P fails to finish within 100 time units, at time 101 start executing R. At any time during the execution of P, allow interruption by an action $\{a?\}$ which will halt P, and initiate the interrupt-handler S." This system may be realized by the following term: $P \triangle_{100}^{\{\sqrt{}\}} (NIL, R, \{a?\} : S)$.

Now consider this specification: "Execute P for a maximum of 100 time units. If P successfully terminates within that time, "cancel" the termination and proceed to Q. If P fails to finish within 100 time units, at time 101 start executing R." This specification yields the following term: $P \, \Delta_{100}^{\emptyset} \, (Q, R, NIL)$.

We note that sequential composition may be realized by using the Scope operator. To sequentially compose E and F, we may use this term: $E \, \Delta_{\infty}^{\emptyset} \, (F, NIL, NIL)$.

The Close operator, $[E]_I$, denotes that the term E occupies *exactly* the resources represented in the index I. In addition, Close produces a term that totally utilizes the resources in I; that is, it prohibits further sharing of those resources.

The Hiding operator $E \backslash A$ masks events of action A in E up to their resource usage and priority, in that while the events themselves are hidden, their priorities are still observable. The term $fix(X.E)$ denotes recursion, allowing the specification of infinite behaviors.

An Operational Semantics

In this section we present an operational semantics for closed terms, in the style of [10]. We do this in two steps. First, we define a labeled transition system $\langle \mathcal{E}, \rightarrow, \mathcal{D} \rangle$, which is a relation $\rightarrow \subseteq \mathcal{E} \times \mathcal{D} \times \mathcal{E}$. We denote each member (E, A, F) of "$\rightarrow$" as "$E \xrightarrow{\;A\;} F$". We call this transition system *unconstrained*, in that no priority arbitration is made between actions. Thus, if $E \xrightarrow{\;A\;} F$ is in "$\rightarrow$", it means that in a system without preemption constraints, a term E may execute A and proceed to F. After presenting "$\rightarrow$", we use it to define a prioritized transition system $\langle \mathcal{E}, \rightarrow_\pi, \mathcal{D} \rangle$, which is sensitive to preemption. This two-phased approach greatly simplifies the definition of "$\rightarrow_\pi$"; similar tactics have been used by [11] in their treatment of CCS priority, and by [1] in their semantics for maximum parallelism.

Throughout, we use the following notation. For a given set of resources $I \subseteq \mathcal{R}$, we let Σ_I represent the set $\bigcup_{i \in I} \Sigma_i$. Also, $A * B = A^{\sqrt{}} \cup B^{\sqrt{}} \cup (A \cap B)$; that is, the termination event "$\sqrt{}$" is an element of $A * B$ if and only if it is in both A and B.

Tables 1 and 2 present the unconstrained transition system, "$\rightarrow$". The rules for Action, Choice and Recursion are quite straightforward. The other rules, however, require some additional explanation.

Parallel. The four side conditions define both the resource mapping and synchronization constraints imposed on terms that operate in a con-

Action : $A : E \xrightarrow{\ A\ } E$

ChoiceL : $\dfrac{E \xrightarrow{\ A\ } E'}{E + F \xrightarrow{\ A\ } E'}$ **ChoiceR :** $\dfrac{F \xrightarrow{\ A\ } F'}{E + F \xrightarrow{\ A\ } F'}$

Parallel : $\dfrac{P_1 \xrightarrow{\ A_1\ } P_1', \ P_2 \xrightarrow{\ A_2\ } P_2'}{P_1 {}_I\|_J P_2 \xrightarrow{\ A_1 * A_2\ } P_1' {}_I\|_J P_2'} \left(\begin{array}{l} A_1 \subseteq \Sigma_I^{\checkmark}, \ A_2 \subseteq \Sigma_J^{\checkmark}, \\ \mathcal{R}(A) \cap \mathcal{R}(B) = \emptyset, \\ sync_{(I \cup J)}(A_1 * A_2) \end{array} \right)$

ScopeC : $\dfrac{E \xrightarrow{\ A\ } E'}{E \, \Delta_t^B \, (F, G, H) \xrightarrow{\ A\ } E' \, \Delta_{t-1}^B \, (E, F, G)} \quad (t > 1, \ \checkmark \notin A)$

ScopeE : $\dfrac{E \xrightarrow{\ A\ } E'}{E \, \Delta_t^B \, (F, G, H) \xrightarrow{\ A*B\ } F} \quad (t \geq 1, \ \checkmark \in A)$

ScopeT : $\dfrac{E \xrightarrow{\ A\ } E'}{E \, \Delta_t^B \, (F, G, H) \xrightarrow{\ A\ } G} \quad (t = 1, \ \checkmark \notin A)$

ScopeI : $\dfrac{H \xrightarrow{\ A\ } H'}{E \, \Delta_t^B \, (F, G, H) \xrightarrow{\ A\ } H'} \quad (t \geq 1)$

Table 1: Unconstrained Transition System

$$\textbf{Close:} \quad \frac{E \xrightarrow{A} E'}{[E]_I \xrightarrow{A \cup (T_I^0 - T_{\mathcal{R}(A)}^0)} [E']_I} \quad (A \subseteq \Sigma_I^{\checkmark})$$

$$\textbf{Hiding:} \quad \frac{E \xrightarrow{B} E'}{E \backslash A \xrightarrow{\phi_{hide(A)}(B)} E' \backslash A} \quad (sync(A), \; sync(A \cap B))$$

$$\textbf{Recursion:} \quad \frac{E[fix(X.E)/X] \xrightarrow{A} E'}{fix(X.E) \xrightarrow{A} E'}$$

Table 2: Unconstrained Transition System, cont.

current fashion. The first two conditions define the resources on which the terms E_1 and E_2 may execute. That is, A_1 must be hosted on the resources denoted by I, while A_2 must be hosted on the resources denoted by J. Moreover, the third condition stipulates that single resources may not execute more than one event at a time.

The final side condition, "$sync_{(I \cup J)}(A_1 * A_2)$", defines our notion of inter-resource synchronization. Assume that E_1 can execute an action $A_1 \subseteq \Sigma_I^{\checkmark}$, and that E_2 can execute an action $A_2 \subseteq \Sigma_J^{\checkmark}$. Then A_1 and A_2 may execute simultaneously if and only if they are connected in the following sense: If any event in $a \in A_1$ shares a connection set with some event $b \in \Sigma_J$, then b *must* appear in A_2, and *vice versa*. This synchronization constraint is a generalized version of that found in CSP.

Scope. There are four rules for the Scope operator, corresponding to the four actions that may be taken while a term E is bound by a temporal scope. Assume that $E \xrightarrow{A} E'$ with $\checkmark \notin A$, and that $t > 1$. In such a situation, the ScopeC law is used to keep the temporal scope active; i.e., E' is bound by the scope with its time limit decremented to $t - 1$. On the other hand if $\checkmark \in A$ and $t \geq 1$, ScopeE is used. In this case the scope is departed by executing $A * B$, at which time F is initiated. By the definition of "$*$", if $B = \emptyset$, then $A * B = A - \{\checkmark\}$. That is, while

E itself may terminate by executing A, the entire term will terminate when (or if) F does. But if $B = \{\sqrt{}\}$, then $A * B = A$. This means that the entire term may terminate by executing A.

Now assume that $E \xrightarrow{\quad A \quad} E'$ such that $\sqrt{} \notin A$, and that $t = 1$. Thus implies that the ScopeT rule must be used ("T" is for timeout). Here, the scope has "timed out", and thus, first A is executed, followed by the exception-handler G. Finally, the ScopeI rule shows that the term H may interrupt at any time while the temporal scope is active.

Close. The Close operator assigns terms to occupy *exactly* the resource set denoted by the index I. First, the action A may not utilize *more* than the resources in I; otherwise it is not admitted by the transition system. On the other hand, if the events in A utilize less than the set I, the action is augmented with the "idle" events from each of the unused resources. For example, assume E executes an action A, and that there is some $i \in I$ such that $i \notin \mathcal{R}(A)$. In $[E]_I$, this gap is filled by including τ_0^i in A. Here we use the notation T_J^0 to represent *all* of the 0-priority idle events from the resource set J:

$$T_J^0 = \{\tau_j^0 \mid j \in J\}$$

Hiding. Assume that E executes an action B, and that $sync(A)$ and $sync(A \cap B)$ both hold. Then using the Hiding rule, $E \backslash A$ executes an action that reduces the events in $A \cap B$ to their "canonical" priority representation, as described in Section . If $A \subseteq \Sigma$, we construct the function $\phi_{hide(A)}$ as follows. For all a in Σ,

$$\phi_{hide(A)}(a) = \begin{cases} \phi_\pi(a) & \text{if } a \in A \\ a & \text{otherwise} \end{cases}$$

Thus, $\phi_{hide(A)}(B) = (B - A) \cup \phi_\pi(B \cap A)$; i.e., all of the events in $B \cap A$ are mapped to their corresponding "canonical" events.

The reason for this nonstandard hiding construction should be clear when viewed from the perspective of resource usage. As an example, let $a, b \in \Sigma_i$, with $\{a\}$ and $\{b\}$ as connection sets; i.e., both events are completely local to resource i. Now let $E = \{a\} : NIL$ and $F = \{b\} : NIL$. In a more "standard" definition of hiding, $E \backslash \{a\} \xrightarrow{\quad \emptyset \quad} NIL \backslash \{a\}$. In other words, all "$a$" is completely abstracted from the system behavior. But in this definition, we find that $(E \backslash \{a\})_{\{i\}} \|_{\{i\}} F \xrightarrow{\quad \{b\} \quad}$

$(NIL\backslash\{a\})_{\{i\}}\|_{\{i\}} NIL$. This would violate the resource-based execution model, in that two events from resource i would execute simultaneously.

Proposition 1 *All terms in $\mathcal{E}$ are well-defined, in that if $E \in \mathcal{E}$ and $E \xrightarrow{A} E'$, then $A \in \mathcal{D}$.*
The proof follows directly from the definition of the operators. □

We define a prioritized transition system based on a preemption measure, $\prec$, as follows.

Definition 1 *For all $A \in \mathcal{D}$, $B \in \mathcal{D}$, $A \preceq B$ if and only if*

$$\mathcal{R}(A) = \mathcal{R}(B) \land unres(A) = unres(B) \land res(A) \leq_p res(B)$$

The relation "$\preceq$" defines a partial order over $\mathcal{D}$ and thus, we say $A \prec B$ if $A \preceq B$ and $B \npreceq A$, i.e., $\mathcal{R}(A) = \mathcal{R}(B) \land unres(A) = unres(B) \land res(A) <_p res(B)$. □

The prioritized transition system, $\langle \mathcal{E}, \rightarrow_\pi, \mathcal{D} \rangle$, is given by:

Definition 2 *The labeled transition system $\langle \mathcal{E}, \rightarrow_\pi, \mathcal{D} \rangle$ is a relation $\rightarrow_\pi \in \mathcal{E} \times \mathcal{D} \times \mathcal{E}$ and is defined as follows: $(P, A, P') \in \rightarrow_\pi$ (or $P \xrightarrow{A}_\pi P'$) if:*

1. $P \xrightarrow{A} P'$, and

2. *For all $A' \in \mathcal{D}$, $P'' \in \mathcal{E}$ such that $P \xrightarrow{A'} P''$, $A \nprec A'$.* □

Bisimulation and Priority Equivalence

In our semantics, equivalence between agents is based on the concept of *strong bisimulation* [7], which is formally defined as follows:

Definition 3 *For a given transition system $\langle \mathcal{E}, \rightsquigarrow, \mathcal{D} \rangle$, the symmetric relation $r \subseteq (\mathcal{E}, \mathcal{E})$ is a strong bisimulation if, for $(P, Q) \in r$ and $A \in \mathcal{D}$,*

1. *if $P \xrightarrow{A}{\rightsquigarrow} P'$ then, for some Q', $Q \xrightarrow{A}{\rightsquigarrow} Q'$ and $(P', Q') \in r$, and*

2. *if $Q \xrightarrow{A}{\rightsquigarrow} Q'$ then, for some P', $P \xrightarrow{A}{\rightsquigarrow} P'$ and $(P', Q') \in r$.,* □

We let "$\sim_\pi$" denote the largest strong bisimulation over the transition system $\langle \mathcal{E}, \rightarrow_\pi, \mathcal{D} \rangle$, and we call it *prioritized strong equivalence*. Relying on the well-known theory in [4, 5], "$\sim_\pi$" exists. We have shown that "$\sim_\pi$" forms a congruence over the CCSR operators. This property is nice since it allows us to develop a compositional proof system. Indeed, we found a set of equational laws with respect to $\sim_\pi$, which forms a proof system for CCSR terms (see Tables 3 and 4).

An Example

To show the relationship between CSR and CCSR, we will translate the producer-consumer example of the previous section into CCSR. First, we introduce some notation that facilitates a concise specification. For a term P and a nonnegative integer t, let "$\delta_t P$" be the term that *may* delay the execution of P for t time units, and if P is not executed by then it will idle forever. That is:

$$\delta_t P = \begin{cases} \emptyset^\infty & \text{if } t = 0 \\ P + (\emptyset : \delta_{t-1}P) & \text{otherwise} \end{cases}$$

Furthermore, let A^i be shorthand for the Action operator with A repeated i times. For example, $A^2 : P$ is shorthand for $A : A : P$.

To translate P1, we use the δ_2 operator to indicate how long P1 can delay before i1! is accepted. We also pad P1's execution with $\emptyset$ to ensure that its normal execution will not finish before 6 times units after the beginning of each period. This ensures that P1 times-out at the end of each period, and that P1 repeats, i.e. starts a new period. P2 is similarly defined.

$$P1 = (\{p1\} : \delta_2\{i1!\} : (\{p3\})^3 : \emptyset^\infty) \, \Delta_6^\emptyset \, (NIL, P1, NIL)$$
$$P2 = (\{p2\} : \delta_4\{i2!\} : \{p4\} : \emptyset^\infty) \, \Delta_6^\emptyset \, (NIL, P2, NIL)$$

The consumer processes are straightforward: Consumer C1 waits for input from P1 forever, executes c1 for two time units, and repeats. C2 is similarly defined.

$$C1 = \delta_\infty\{i1?\} : (\{c1\})^2 : C1$$
$$C2 = \delta_\infty\{i2?\} : (\{c2\})^2 : C2$$

Choice(1) $E + NIL = E$

Choice(2) $E + E = E$

Choice(3) $E + F = F + E$

Choice(4) $(E + F) + G = E + (F + G)$

Choice(5) $(A : E) + (B : F) = B : F$ if $A \prec B$

Par(1) $E_I \|_J NIL = NIL$

Par(2) $E_I \|_J F = F_J \|_I E$

Par(3) $(E_I \|_J F)_{(I \cup J)} \|_K G = E_I \|_{(J \cup K)} (F_J \|_K G)$ if $I \cap J \cap K = \emptyset$

Par(4) $E_I \|_J (F + G) = (E_I \|_J F) + (E_I \|_J G)$

Par(5) $(A : E)_I \|_J (B : F) =$

$$\begin{cases} (A * B) : (E_I \|_J F) & \text{if } A \subseteq \Sigma_I^{\checkmark},\ B \subseteq \Sigma_J^{\checkmark}, \\ & \mathcal{R}(A) \cap \mathcal{R}(B) = \emptyset,\ sync_{(I \cup J)}(A * B) \\ NIL & \text{otherwise} \end{cases}$$

Scope(1) $NIL \Delta_t^B (F, G, H) = H$

Scope(2) $(E_1 + E_2) \Delta_t^B (F, G, H) = (E_1 \Delta_t^B (F, G, H)) + (E_2 \Delta_t^B (F, G, H))$

Scope(3) $(A : E) \Delta_t^B (F, G, H) = \begin{cases} (A * B : F) + H & \text{if } \checkmark \in A \\ (A : (E \Delta_{t-1}^B (F, G, H))) + H & \text{if } \checkmark \notin A \\ & \text{and } t > 1 \\ (A : G) + H & \text{otherwise} \end{cases}$

Close(1) $[NIL]_I = NIL$

Close(2) $[E + F]_I = [E]_I + [F]_I$

Close(3) $[A : E]_I = \begin{cases} (A \cup (T_I^0 - T_{\mathcal{R}(A)}^0)) : [E]_I & \text{if } A \subseteq \Sigma_I^{\checkmark} \\ NIL & \text{otherwise} \end{cases}$

Table 3: The Axiom System, $\mathcal{A}$

$$\text{Close(4)} \quad [[E]_I]_J = \begin{cases} [E]_J & \text{if } I \subseteq J \\ NIL & \text{otherwise} \end{cases}$$

$$\text{Hide(1)} \quad NIL \backslash B = NIL$$

$$\text{Hide(2)} \quad (E + F) \backslash B = E \backslash B + F \backslash B$$

$$\text{Hide(3)} \quad (A : E) \backslash B = \begin{cases} \phi_{hide(B)}(A) : (E \backslash B) & \text{if } sync(A \cap B) \\ NIL & \text{otherwise} \end{cases}$$

Table 4: The Axiom System, $\mathcal{A}$, cont.

As for the connection sets, let $C_1 = \{i1!, i1?\}$, $C_2 = \{i2!, i2?\}$, $C_3 = \{p1\}$, $C_4 = \{p2\}$, $C_5 = \{p3\}$, $C_6 = \{p4\}$, $C_7 = \{c1\}$, and $C_8 = \{c2\}$. That is, resources 1 and 3 are connected by C_1, resources 2 and 3 are connected by C_2, while all other events are local to the resources that own them. The priorities are the same as before.

The entire system is described as follows:

$$System = [(P1_{\{1\}} \|_{\{2\}} P2)_{\{1,2\}} \|_{\{3\}} (C1_{\{3\}} \|_{\{3\}} C2)]_{\{1,2,3\}}$$

By definition of δ_t, $P1$ and $P2$ are equivalent $(\sim_\pi)$ to $P1'$ and $P2'$ respectively:

$$\begin{aligned}
P1' = (\{p1\} : (&\{i1!\} : \{p3\}^3 : \emptyset^\infty \\
+ &\emptyset : (\{i1!\} : \{p3\}^3 : \emptyset^\infty \\
&+ \emptyset^\infty))) \Delta_6^{\emptyset} (NIL, P1', NIL)
\end{aligned}$$

$$\begin{aligned}
P2' = (\{p2\} : (&\{i2!\} : \{p4\} : \emptyset^\infty \\
+ &\emptyset : (\{i2!\} : \{p4\} : \emptyset^\infty \\
&+ \emptyset : (\{i2!\} : \{p4\} : \emptyset^\infty \\
&+ \emptyset : (\{i2!\} : \{p4\} : \emptyset^\infty \\
&+ \emptyset^\infty))))) \Delta_6^{\emptyset} (NIL, P1', NIL)
\end{aligned}$$

Combining $P1'$ and $P2'$ using repeated applications Par(5) and Choice(5), we get:

$$(P1'_{\{1\}}\|_{\{2\}} P2') \sim_\pi$$
$$\text{fix } X.(\{p1,p2\} : (\{i1!,i2!\} : \{p3,p4\} : \{p3\} : \{p3\} : \emptyset^\infty$$
$$+\{i1!\} : (\ \{p3,i2!\} : \{p3,p4\} : \{p3\} : \emptyset^\infty$$
$$+\{p3\} : (\{p3,i2!\} : \{p3,p4\} : \emptyset^\infty$$
$$+\{p3\} : (\ \{p3,i2!\} : \{p4\} : \emptyset^\infty$$
$$+\{p3\} : \emptyset^\infty)))$$
$$+\{i2!\} : (\{i1!,p4\} : \{p3\} : \{p3\} : \{p3\} : \emptyset^\infty$$
$$+\{p4\} : (\{i1!\} : \{p3\} : \{p3\} : \{p3\} : \emptyset^\infty$$
$$+\emptyset^\infty))$$
$$+\emptyset : (...)) \Delta_6^\emptyset (NIL, X, NIL))$$

Combining $C1$ and $C2$ using repeated applications of Par(5), and noting that the side condition $\mathcal{R}(A) \cap \mathcal{R}(B) = \emptyset$ prevents two events from the same resource appearing in the same action, we get:

$$(C1_{\{3\}}\|_{\{3\}} C2) \sim_\pi$$
$$\text{fix } X.(\emptyset : X + \{i1?\} : (\{c1\})^2 : X + \{i2?\} : (\{c2\})^2 : X)$$

Using the rules for recursion, Par(5), and Choice(5) (noting that the side condition $sync_{(I \cup J)}(A * B)$ forces synchronizing events to occur in the same action), we can formally show that our system is equivalent to the following agent. Note that $P1$ and $P2$ execute p3 and p4 each period.

$$System = [\{p1,p2\} : \textbf{fix}X.(\ \{i1!,i1?\} : \{p3,c1\} : \{p3,c1\} : \{p3,i2!,i2?\} :$$
$$\{p4,c2\} : \{p1,p2,c2\} : X)]_{\{1,2,3\}}$$

SUMMARY AND FUTURE WORK

We developed a resource-based model of computation, in which multiple resources execute synchronously, while processes assigned to the same resource are interleaved according to their priorities. Using this model, we specify the behavior of distributed real-time systems using Communicating Shared Resources. Although CSR is good for specifying distributed real-time systems, it is too complex to be treated as a process algebra, and is therefore not amenable for developing a proof system. We therefore developed a calculus for CSR, CCSR, based on the same resource based computation model. The CCSR syntax includes primitive constructs to express essential real-time functionality, among which are timeouts, interrupts, periodic behaviors and exceptions. Further, there is a single parallel operator that can be used to express both interleaving at the resource level, and "true" concurrency at the system level.

CCSR's proof system derives from a term equivalence based on strong bisimulation, which incorporates a notion of preemption based on priority, synchronization and resource utilization. This prioritized equivalence is also a congruence, which leads to the compositionality of our proof system. Thus we can prove correctness for a real-time system by modularly reasoning about its subsystems, the usefulness of which was shown in [12].

Proving equivalence for two CCSR terms can be a long and laborious process, as it often involves the manipulation of very complex expressions. Thus, we plan to mechanize the procedure using the HOL theorem prover [13], which can assist a human both in structuring these proofs, as well as in verifying their correctness. We are also constructing a reachability analyzer for CCSR terms. This tool will use the transition system to construct a reachability graph for a given program. The generated graph can then provide the foundation for model checking, and can be applied toward decision procedures that distinguish certain properties, such as deadlock, liveness, or the equivalence of two different programs. Finally, we are automating a translation procedure from the CSR programming language [14] to the CCSR process algebra. This translator will preserve the semantic characteristics of CSR programs, and thus, it will enable us to reason about them using the CCSR proof system.

References

[1] C. Huizing, R. Gerth, and W. de Roever, "Full Abstraction of a Denotational Semantics for Real-time Concurrency," in *Proc. 14th ACM Symposium on Principles of Programming Languages*, pp. 223–237, 1987.

[2] R. Koymans, R. Shyamasundar, W. de Roever, R. Gerth, and S. Arun-Kumar, "Compositional Semantics for Real-Time Distributed Computing," *Information and Computation*, vol. 70, 1988.

[3] I. Lee and V. Gehlot, "Language Constructs for Distributed Real-Time Programming," in *Proc. IEEE Real-Time Systems Symposium*, 1985.

[4] R. Milner, "Calculi for synchrony and asynchrony," *Theoretical Computer Science*, vol. 25, pp. 267–310, 1983.

[5] R. Milner, *Communication and Concurrency*. Prentice-Hall, 1989.

[6] R. Koymans, R. Shyamasundar, W. de Roever, R. Gerth, and S. Arun-Kumar, "Compositional Semantics for Real-Time Distributed Computing," in *Logic of Programs Workshop '85, LNCS 193*, 1985.

[7] D. Park, "Concurrency and Automata on Infinite Sequences," in *LNCS 104*, 1981.

[8] C. Hoare, *Communicating Sequential Processes*. Prentice-Hall, 1985.

[9] C. Hoare, "Communicating sequential processes," *Communications of the ACM*, vol. 21, pp. 666–676, August 1978.

[10] G. Plotkin, "A structural approach to operational semantics," Tech. Rep. DAIMI FN-19, Computer Science Dept., Aarhus University, 1981.

[11] R. Cleaveland and M. Hennessy, "Priorities in Process Algebras," *Information and Computation*, vol. 87, pp. 58–77, 1990.

[12] R. Gerber and I. Lee, "A Proof System for Communicating Shared Resource," in *Proc. 11th IEEE Real-Time Systems Symposium*, 1990.

[13] M. Gordon, "HOL – A Proof Generating System for Higher-Order Logic," in *Proc. Hardware Verification Workshop, Calgary, Canada*, 1987.

[14] R. Gerber and I. Lee, "Communicating Shared Resources: A Model for Distributed Real-Time Systems," in *Proc. 10th IEEE Real-Time Systems Symposium*, 1989.

CHAPTER 5

Theory of Real-Time Systems – Project Survey[*]

Hagit Attiya[†]
Nancy A. Lynch
Laboratory for Computer Science
MIT
Cambridge, MA 02139

1 Introduction

An important area of computer applications is real-time process control, in which a computer system interacts with a real-world system in order to guarantee certain desirable real-world behavior. In most interesting cases, the real-world requirements involve timing properties, and so the behavior of the computer system is required to satisfy certain timing constraints. In order to be able to guarantee timing constraints, the computer system must satisfy some assumptions about time—for example, its various components should operate at known speeds.

It is clear that good theoretical work in the area of real-time systems is necessary. In the past few years, several researchers have proposed new frameworks for specifying requirements of such systems, describing implementations, and proving that the implementations satisfy the

---

[*]This work was supported by ONR contract N00014-85-K-0168, by NSF grants CCR-8611442 and CCR-8915206, and by DARPA contracts N00014-89-J-1988 and N00014-87-K-0825.

[†]Current address: Computer Science Department, The Technion, Haifa 32000, Israel.

requirements. These frameworks are based on, among others, state machines ([18, 78, 92]), weakest precondition methods ([43]), first-order logic ([47, 48]), temporal logic ([11]), Petri nets ([17, 62, 91]), and process algebra ([9, 40, 46, 53, 88, 100]). Work is still needed in evaluating and comparing the various models for their usefulness in reasoning about important problems in this area and perhaps in developing new models if these prove to be inadequate.

Work is also needed in developing the complexity theory of such systems; very little work has so far been done in this area. An example of the kind of work needed is provided by the theory of asynchronous concurrent systems.[1] That theory contains many combinatorial results that show what can and cannot be accomplished by asynchronous systems; for tasks that can be accomplished, other combinatorial results determine the inherent costs. In addition to their individual importance, these results also provide a testbed for evaluating modeling decisions and a stimulus for the development of algorithm verification techniques. Similar results should be possible for real-time systems. Some examples of complexity results that have already been obtained for real-time systems are the many results on clock synchronization, including [24, 42, 56, 66, 99] (see [94] for a survey).

In this project, we have embarked on a study of complexity results for real-time systems. We have formulated several abstract problems that seem to be characteristic of real-time computing, and have obtained upper and lower bounds for the time complexity of those problems. The problems we have defined are all variations of problems that have previously been studied for asynchronous concurrent systems; the major differences are that we impose rather stringent timing requirements on the solutions and that we assume that our systems satisfy certain assumptions about the timing of events. The assumptions we make about the timing of events are not exact; rather, we assume that the time required for various events is known to be within certain bounds. For example, in real-time systems, there can be uncertainty in the time required for real-world tasks to be completed, for processors to take steps, for clocks to advance and for messages to be delivered.

We have obtained bounds on the time complexity of solving three fun-

---

[1]Asynchronous systems are those in which processes work at completely independent rates and have no way of estimating time.

damental problems: *mutual exclusion, synchronization* and *agreement,* in a model with inexact timing assumptions. These results are described, respectively, in Sections 2, 3 and 4.

In the course of our work on these problems, we felt a need for a systematic method for reasoning about the correctness and performance of timing based systems. To satisfy this need, we have developed a new assertional method of reasoning about timing based systems.

Assertional reasoning is a very useful technique for proving safety properties of sequential and concurrent algorithms. This proof method involves describing the algorithm of interest as a state machine, and defining a predicate known as an *assertion* on the states of the machine. One proves inductively that the assertion is true of all the states that are reachable in a computation of the machine, i.e., that it is an *invariant* of the machine. The assertion is defined so that it implies the safety property to be proved. Assertional reasoning is a rigorous, simple and general proof technique. Furthermore, the assertions usually provide an intuitively appealing explanation of *why* the algorithm satisfies the property. One kind of assertional reasoning uses a mapping to describe a correspondence between the given algorithm and a higher-level algorithm used as a specification of correctness. (See, for example, [57, 67, 71].)

We have developed an assertional technique based on mappings, for proving correctness and timing properties of timing-based systems. This work is described in Section 5.

The formal model we have used to describe our results is the *timed automaton* model, a slight variant of the *time constrained automaton* model of [78]. We have used this model to state the requirements to be satisfied, to define the basic architectural and timing assumptions, to describe the algorithms, and to prove their correctness and timing properties. We have also used it for describing our mapping proof technique.

The last work described in this survey considers the time complexity of wait-free algorithms in shared-memory distributed systems. In such systems, it is possible for processes to operate at very different speeds, e.g., because of implementation issues such as communication and memory latency, priority-based time-sharing of processors, cache misses and page faults. It is also possible for processes to fail entirely. A *wait-free* algorithm guarantees that each nonfaulty process terminates regardless of the speed and failure of other processes ([44, 58]). Because wait-free algorithms guarantee that fast processes terminate without waiting for slow processes, wait-free algorithms seem to be generally thought of as *fast*. However, while it is obvious from the definition that wait-free algorithms are highly resilient to failures, we believe that the assumption that such algorithms are fast requires more careful examination.

We have addressed this general problem by studying the time complexity of wait-free algorithms for the *approximate agreement problem*. Our results are described in Section 6.

A major emphasis in our project has been on the impact of uncertainty in the system on the time complexity of solving problems. This uncertainty might be due to inexact timing assumptions as described above, to unpredictable inputs, or to failures. More specifically, our work on mutual exclusion involves timing uncertainty and unpredictable inputs, our work on synchronization involves only timing uncertainty, and our work on agreement and wait-free algorithms involves timing uncertainty and failures.

The portion of our work that deals with resource allocation problems is related to prior work in scheduling theory (for example, [40, 65, 86]). Our work on resource allocation is distinguished from the scheduling theory work in its emphasis on distributed algorithms and on timing uncertainties and failures. Also, our emphasis has been on upper and lower bounds for solving particular problems, e.g., mutual exclusion, whereas the emphasis in scheduling theory seems to be on general strategies (e.g., first-come-first-serve) for solving large classes of problems. As the subject matter of scheduling theory broadens, however, we believe that the two areas will become more closely related.

Our work has taken advantage of many of the approaches, techniques and results of distributed computing theory. In particular, our selection of problems, our use of automaton-style formal models and assertional reasoning, the design of our algorithms, and the techniques we use to prove lower bounds (e.g., the perturbation of executions and the use of the limitations of local knowledge) have all been heavily influenced by prior work in distributed computing theory.

2 Mutual Exclusion

We have studied a variant of the *mutual exclusion problem*. This problem is one of the fundamental problems in distributed computing; it serves as an abstraction of a large class of *hazard avoidance* problems. We note that this particular problem appears in the real-time computing literature (cf. [48]) as the "nuclear reactor problem". There, operators push different buttons to request the motion of different control rods in the same nuclear reactor. It is undesirable to have more than one control rod moving at the same time, presumably since in that case the nuclear reaction might be slowed down too much.

More specifically, we have considered a system consisting of some number, n, of identical moving parts (e.g., control rods), no two of which are supposed to move at the same time. An operator associated with each moving part can request permission for the associated part to move by pushing a button that sends a *REQUEST* signal to the control system. The control system responds with *GRANT* signals; each *GRANT* signal gives permission to the designated moving part to move, but such motion is expected to be finished no more than a fixed time, m, later. The control system is only supposed to issue a *GRANT* signal when it knows that it is safe to move the corresponding moving part, i.e., at least real time m has elapsed since the last *GRANT* signal. We assume, for simplicity, that a *REQUEST* signal is only issued by a particular operator if any preceding *REQUEST* by that operator has already been satisfied (by a corresponding *GRANT* signal). Our goal is to minimize the worst-case time between a *REQUEST* signal and the corresponding *GRANT* signal, i.e., the *worst-case response time*.

The control system might consist of a single process running on a dedicated processor or might be a distributed system running on separate processors communicating over a message system. Solving the problem efficiently requires the control system to make accurate estimates of the elapsed time since the last *GRANT* signal; the difficulty, however, is that the control system only has inaccurate information about time, as given by inaccurate clock components within the system and by estimates of the time required for certain events. Specifically, the only information about time that the control system has is the following:

1. the knowledge that a moving part will stop moving within time m

after a $GRANT$ signal,

2. the knowledge that the time between successive ticks of any clock is always in the interval $[c_1, c_2]$, for known constants c_1 and c_2, where $0 < c_1 \leq c_2$,

3. the knowledge that the time between successive steps of any process within the control system is always in the interval $[0, l]$, for a known constant $l, 0 \leq l$, and

4. (if the system is distributed) the knowledge that the time to deliver the oldest message in each channel is no greater than a known constant $d, 0 \leq d$.

In the cases we have in mind, we suppose that $l \ll c_1 < c_2 \ll d \ll m$. We use the notation C to represent the ratio c_2/c_1; C is a useful measure of the timing uncertainty.

We obtain the following results. First, we consider a centralized control system, consisting of just a single process with a local clock. For that case, we show that

$$n \cdot c_2 \left(\lfloor (m + l)/c_1 \rfloor + 1 \right) + l$$

(approximately nmC) is an *exact* bound on the worst-case response time for the timing-based mutual exclusion problem. The upper bound result arises from a careful analysis of a simple FIFO queue algorithm, while the matching lower bound result arises from explicitly constructing and "retiming" executions to obtain a contradiction.

We then consider the distributed case, which is substantially more complicated. For that case, we obtain very close (but not exact) bounds: an upper bound of

$$n \left[c_2 \left(\lfloor (m + l)/c_1 \rfloor + 1 \right) + d + c_2 + 2l \right]$$

(approximately $nmC + nd$) and a lower bound of $nmC + (n - 1)d$. Assuming that the parameters have the relative sizes described earlier, e.g., that d is much larger than l, c_1 and c_2, the gap between these two bounds is just slightly more than a single message delay time. The upper bound arises from a simple token-passing algorithm, while the lower bound proof employs a new technique of shifting some of the events happening at a process while carefully retiming other events.

(The work described in this section appears in [5].)

3 Synchronization

Some problems in real-time computing involve synchronization of several computer system components, in order that they might cooperate in performing a task involving real-world components. For example, multiple robots might cooperate to build a car on an assembly line, with each robot responsible for assembling a small piece of the machinery. Similar synchronization problems arise in distributed computing as well, where the separate components might each be responsible for performing a small part of a computation. We have studied the time complexity of achieving synchronization, in the presence of various assumptions about the timing of basic events.

The particular synchronization problem we have considered is the *session problem*, first defined by Arjomandi, Fischer and Lynch ([2]). Roughly speaking, a *session* is a sequence of events that contains *at least* one step by each process. An algorithm for the *s-session problem* guarantees that each execution of the algorithm includes at least s separate sessions. It was assumed in [2] that processes communicate via *shared variables*, and the time complexity of the session problem was studied in *synchronous* and *asynchronous* models.[2] The results of [2] show that the problem can be solved much faster in the synchronous model than in the asynchronous model.

We have studied the time requirements for the session problem in distributed networks rather than shared memory systems. That is, we have considered a collection of n processes located at the nodes of an undirected communication graph G; communication is assumed to be by messages sent over the edges of G. We have considered both the asynchronous model and a model with inexact timing assumptions (which we call here the *partially synchronous* model).

---

[2]Synchronous systems are those in which processes operate in lock-step, taking steps simultaneously.

Time is measured under the following assumptions on the system. We assume that the delivery time for every message is in the range $[0, d]$, where d is a known nonnegative constant. Instead of assuming explicit clocks (as in the previous section), we assume that the times between successive local steps are in the range $[0, c_2]$ for the asynchronous model, and in the range $[c_1, c_2]$ for the partially synchronous model, where c_1 and c_2 are constants, $0 < c_1 \le c_2$. As before, we define $C = c_2/c_1$.

Our upper bound results are as follows. Our first algorithm relies on explicit communication to ensure that the needed steps have occurred, and does not rely on any timing information. In either the asynchronous model or the partially synchronous model, this algorithm has time complexity $(s - 1)diam(G)(d + c_2)$, where the *diameter* of an undirected graph G, $diam(G)$, is the maximum distance between any two nodes. Our second algorithm does not use any communication and relies only on timing information; this algorithm works only in the partially synchronous model. Its time complexity is $c_2 + (s - 2)(\lfloor C \rfloor + 1)c_2$. These algorithms can be combined to yield a partially synchronous algorithm for the s-session problem whose time complexity is $c_2 + (s-2)\min\{(\lfloor C \rfloor + 1)c_2, diam(G)(d + c_2)\}$.

Our lower bound results are as follows. For the asynchronous model, we prove a lower bound of $(s - 1)diam(G)d$ for the time complexity of any algorithm for the s-session problem; this almost matches our upper bound for that model. For the partially synchronous model, we prove two lower bounds. We first show a simple lower bound of $(s-2)\lfloor C \rfloor c_2$ for the case where communication is not used. We then present our main result: a lower bound of $c_2 + (s - 2)\min\{(\lfloor \frac{C}{2} \rfloor)c_2, diam(G)d\}$ for the time complexity of any partially synchronous algorithm for the s-session problem. For appropriate values of the various parameters, these results imply a time separation between partially synchronous and asynchronous networks.

The lower bounds presented in this paper use the same general approach as in [2]. However, since we assume processes communicate by sending messages while [2] assumes processes communicate via shared memory, the precise details differ substantially. The lower bound proof in [2] uses fan-in arguments, while our lower bounds are based on information propagation arguments using long delays of messages, combined with appropriate selection of processes and careful timing arguments.

Awerbuch ([8]) has introduced the concept of a *synchronizer* as a way to translate algorithms designed for synchronous networks to asynchronous networks. Although the results of [8] may suggest that any synchronous network algorithm can be translated into an asynchronous algorithm with constant time overhead, our results imply that this is *not* the case: for some values of the parameters, any translation of a partially synchronous (and in particular, a synchronous) algorithm for the *s*-session problem to an asynchronous algorithm must incur a nonconstant time overhead.

(The work described in this section appears in [7].)

4 Distributed Agreement

We have also considered the time complexity of the problem of *reaching agreement* among nodes in a distributed system, in the case where some of the nodes are faulty. In the version of the agreement problem we have considered, each of *n* processes starts with an input value. Each process that does not fail must choose a decision value such that (i) no two processes decide differently, and (ii) if any process decides *v* then *v* was the input value of some process. We assume that processes fail only by stopping (without warning). This abstract problem can be used to model agreement on the value of a sensor reading obtained with multiple sensors, or agreement on a course of action such as whether an airplane landing should be completed or aborted.

The time complexity of the distributed agreement problem has been well studied in the synchronous model. In this model, computation proceeds in a sequence of numbered rounds of communication. In each round, each non-failed process sends out messages to all processes, receives all messages sent to it at that round, and carries out some local computation. (See, for example, [60, 82, 21, 32, 19, 59, 29, 41, 76, 28, 79, 13, 80, 10] for results involving time complexity in this model.) The most basic time bound results in these papers are matching upper and lower bounds of $f + 1$ on the number of rounds of communication required for reaching agreement in the presence of at most f faults.

We have considered how these bounds are affected by using, instead of the synchronous model, one in which there are inexact timing assumptions. In particular, we have used the partially synchronous model described in Section 3, assuming that d is an upper bound on message delivery time, c_1 and c_2 are lower and upper bounds, respectively, on process step time, and $C = c_2/c_1$.[3] We have assumed that processes fail only by stopping, so that failures can be detected by "timeouts": if an expected message from some process is not received within a sufficiently long time, then that process is known to have failed.

Initially, we had hoped to be able to adapt known results about the synchronous model to obtain good bounds for the version with inexact timing. Indeed, an $(f+1)$-round algorithm can be adapted in a straightforward way to yield an algorithm for the partially synchronous model that requires time at most $(f+1)dC$ if there are f faults. On the other hand, a simple transformation in the reverse direction, of any partially synchronous algorithm to a synchronous algorithm yields a lower bound of $(f+1)d$. There is a significant gap between these two bounds, namely, a multiplicative factor equal to the timing uncertainty, C. We would like to obtain closer bounds on the time complexity of this problem; in particular, we would like to understand how this complexity depends on C.

Our main result is an agreement algorithm in which the uncertainty factor C is only incurred once, i.e., for one "round" of communication, yielding a running time of approximately $2td + dC$ in the worst case. The term of dC arises from the possible need to time out a failed process; if a process fails, then it stops sending messages, and within time approximately dC, every other process can determine that the failure has occurred. It seems surprising that the overhead for such a timeout need only occur *once* in any execution. The algorithm can be viewed as an asynchronous algorithm which uses a fault detection (e.g., timeout) mechanism. That is, the timing bounds c_1, c_2, d are used only in the fault detection mechanism.

Our second result shows that any agreement algorithm must take time at least $(f-1)d + dC$ in the worst case. The lower bound is unusual in that it combines, in a nontrivial way, three different lower bound techniques: a "chain argument" ([32, 19, 29, 76, 14, 28]), used previously to prove that $f+1$ rounds are required in the synchronous

---

[3]Results of [33, 20] imply that if any one of the bounds c_1, c_2, d does not exist, then there is no agreement algorithm tolerant to even one fault.

rounds model; a "bivalence" argument ([33, 20]) used previously to prove that fault-tolerant agreement is impossible in an asynchronous system; and a "time stretching" argument developed to prove the lower bounds described in Section 2 ([5]). Although these bounds are not completely tight, they do demonstrate that the inherent dependence on C involves just a single term dC; there is no need to multiply C by larger multiples of the message delivery time.

Some prior work on distributed agreement in a model with inexact timing assumptions appears in [27]. The main emphasis in [27] was on determining the maximum fault tolerance possible for various fault models; only rough upper bounds on the time complexity of the algorithms were given, and no lower bounds on time were proved. Related work on the *latency*[4] of reaching agreement when processors are not completely synchronous appears in [12] and [96], although the results are different from ours. These papers assume that process clocks are synchronized to within some fixed additive error. Unlike our results, these results are not stated in terms of absolute real time.

(The work described in this section appears in [4].)

5 A new proof technique for timing-based systems

Assertional reasoning has been used primarily to prove properties of sequential algorithms and synchronous and asynchronous concurrent algorithms. We have developed a way in which assertional reasoning can be used to prove timing properties for algorithms that have timing assumptions of the kind described in the previous sections. Also, the kinds of properties generally proved using assertional reasoning have been "ordinary" safety properties; our method can be used to prove timing properties (upper and lower bounds on time) for algorithms that have timing assumptions. Predictable performance is often a desirable characteristic of real-time systems [95]; assertional techniques could be very helpful in proving such performance properties.

Our method involves constructing a multivalued mapping from an

---

[4]The worst-case elapsed time measured on the clock of any correct process.

automaton representing the given algorithm to another automaton representing the timing requirements. The key to our method is a way of representing a system with timing constraints as an automaton whose state includes predictive timing information. Timing assumptions and timing requirements for the system are both represented in this way, and the mappings we construct map from the "assumptions automaton" to the "requirements automaton".

The formal model used in our work is the *timed automaton* model, adapted from the *time-constrained automaton* model of [78]. A timed automaton is a pair (A, b), consisting of an *I/O automaton A* ([71, 72]), together with a *boundmap b*, which is a formal description of the timing assumptions for the components of the system. We have introduced the notion of a *timing condition* to state upper and lower bounds on the difference between the times at which certain events or states appear in an execution; the conditions imposed by a boundmap are timing conditions of a particular kind. An automaton and a set of timing conditions (in particular, a timed automaton) generate a set of *timed executions* and a corresponding set of *timed behaviors*.

While convenient for specifying timing assumptions and requirements, timed automata are not directly suited for carrying out assertional proofs about timing properties, because timing constraints are described by specially-defined timing conditions and are not part of the automaton itself. We have therefore introduced a way of incorporating timing conditions into an automaton definition. For a given timed automaton A, and a set $\mathcal{U}$ of timing conditions, the automaton $time(A, \mathcal{U})$ is defined to be an ordinary I/O automaton (not a timed automaton) whose state includes predictive information describing the first and last times at which various events can next occur; this information is designed to enforce the timing conditions in $\mathcal{U}$.

The timing requirements to be proved for an algorithm described as a timed automaton, (A, b), are described as a set of timing conditions, $\mathcal{U}$, for A. The *requirements automaton* is defined to be $time(A, \mathcal{U})$. Thus, predictive information about the first and last times at which certain events of interest can next occur are built into the state of the requirements automaton.

The problem of showing that a given algorithm (A, b) satisfies the timing requirements is then reduced to that of showing that any behavior of the automaton $time(A, b)$ is also a behavior of $time(A, \mathcal{U})$. This is done using invariant assertion techniques; in particular, one demonstrates a multivalued mapping from $time(A, b)$ to $time(A, \mathcal{U})$.

We have applied our technique to three examples. The first example is a simplified version of the timing-dependent resource granting system described in Section 2. We have given careful proofs of upper and lower bounds on the amount of time prior to the first *GRANT* event and in between each successive pair of *GRANT* events. The second example is a system consisting of a "line" of processes, in which each process relays a signal received from the process at its left to the process at its right. We have given careful proofs of upper and lower bounds on the time to propagate a signal from the left end to the right end of the line. The third, more complicated example involves one process incrementing a counter until another process modifies a flag, and then decrementing this counter. When the counter reaches 0, a *DONE* action occurs. We have given careful proofs of upper and lower bounds on the time until a *DONE* occurs.

The mappings we provide for all three of these examples have a particularly interesting and simple form—a set of inequalities relating the time bounds to be proved to those that can be computed from the state. These inequalities contain information about how the bounds are to be satisfied.

Technically, mapping techniques of the sort used in this paper are only capable of proving safety properties, but not liveness properties. Timing properties have aspects of both safety and liveness. A timing lower bound asserts that an event cannot occur before a certain amount of time has elapsed; a violation of this property is detectable after a finite prefix of a timed execution, and so a timing lower bound can be regarded as a safety property. A timing upper bound asserts that an event must occur before a certain amount of time has elapsed. This can be regarded as making two separate claims: that the designated amount of time does in fact elapse (a liveness property), and that that amount of time cannot elapse without the event having occurred (a safety property). In our work, we have *assumed* the liveness property that time increases without bound, so that all the remaining properties that need to be proved in order to prove either upper or lower time bounds are safety properties. Thus, our mapping technique provides complete proofs for timing properties without requiring any special techniques (e.g., variant functions or temporal logic methods) for arguing liveness.

We have shown that this method is *complete*: if every behavior of (A, b) is also a behavior of $time(A, \mathcal{U})$ then is there necessarily a strong possibilities mapping (in the form of inequalities) from $time(A, b)$ to $time(A, \mathcal{U})$. Related completeness results for the usage of refinement mappings to prove properties of non timing-based algorithms were proved in [1] and [77].

There has been some prior work on using assertional reasoning to prove timing properties. In particular, Hasse [43], Shankar and Lam [92], Tel [97], Schneider [90], Lewis [63] and Shaw [93] have all developed models for timing-based systems that incorporate time information into the state, and have used invariant assertions to prove timing properties. In [97] and [63], in fact, the information that is included is similar to ours in that it is also predictive timing information (but not exactly the same information as ours). None of this work has been based on mappings, however. Several other, quite different formal approaches to proving timing properties have also been developed. Some representative papers describing these other methods are [11], [52], [48], [45], [100], [49], and [35].

(The work described in this section appears in [68].)

6 Time complexity of asynchronous resilient algorithms

In shared-memory distributed systems, some number n of independent asynchronous processes communicate by reading and writing to shared memory. *Wait-free* algorithms have been proposed as a mechanism for computing in the face of variable speeds and failures: a wait-free algorithm guarantees that each nonfaulty process terminates regardless of the speed and failure of other processes ([44, 58]). The design of wait-free shared-memory algorithms has recently been a very active area of research (see, e.g., [3, 22, 44, 58, 64, 83, 84, 89, 98]).

We have studied the *time complexity* of wait-free and non-wait-free algorithms in "normal" executions, where no failures occur and processes operate at approximately the same speed. We have selected this particular subset of the executions for making the comparison, because it is only reasonable to compare the behavior of the algorithms in cases where both are required to terminate. Since wait-free algorithms terminate even when some processes fail, while non-wait-free algorithms may fail to terminate in this case, the comparison should only be made in executions in which no process fails, i.e., in *failure-free* executions. The time measure we have used is the one introduced in [54, 55], and used to evaluate the time complexity of asynchronous algorithms, in, e.g., [2, 15, 69, 70, 85]. To summarize, we are interested in measuring the time cost imposed by the wait-free property, as measured in terms of extra computation time in the most normal (failure-free) case.

We have addressed the general question by considering a specific problem—the *approximate agreement* problem studied, for example, in [23, 30, 31, 73]; we have studied this problem in the context of a particular shared-memory primitive—single-writer multi-reader atomic registers. In this problem, each process starts with a real-valued input, and (provided it does not fail) must eventually produce a real-valued output. The outputs must all be within a given distance ε of each other, and must be included within the range of the inputs. This problem, a weaker variant of the well-studied problem of distributed consensus (e.g., [33, 60]), is closely related to the important problem of synchronizing local clocks in a distributed system.

Approximate agreement can be achieved very easily if waiting is allowed, by having a designated process write its input to the shared memory; all other processes wait for this value to be written and adopt it as their outputs. In terms of the time measure described above, it is easy to see that the time complexity of this algorithm is constant—independent of n, the range of inputs and ε. On the other hand, there is a relatively simple wait-free algorithm for this problem which is based on successive averaging of intermediate values. The time complexity of this algorithm depends linearly on n, and logarithmically on the size of the range of input values and on $1/\varepsilon$. A natural question to ask is whether the time complexity of this algorithm is optimal for wait-free approximate agreement algorithms.

Our first major result is an algorithm for the special case where $n = 2$, whose time complexity is constant, i.e., it does *not* depend on the range of inputs or on ε. The algorithm uses a novel method of overcoming the uncertainty that is inherent in an asynchronous environment, without resorting to synchronization points (cf. [39]) or other waiting mechanisms (cf. [15]): this method involves ensuring that the two processes base their decisions on information that is approximately, but not exactly, the same.

Next, using a powerful technique of integrating wait-free (but slow) and non-wait-free (but fast) algorithms, together with an $O(\log n)$ wait-free input collection function, we generalize the key ideas of the 2-process algorithm to obtain our second major result: a wait-free algorithm for approximate agreement whose time complexity is $O(\log n)$. Thus, the time complexity of this algorithm does not depend on either the size of the range of input values or on ε, but it still depends on n, the number of processes.

At this point, it was natural to ask whether the logarithmic dependence on n is inherent for wait-free approximate agreement algorithms, or whether, on the other hand, there is a constant-time wait-free algorithm (independent of n). Our third major result shows that the $\log n$ dependency is inherent: any wait-free algorithm for approximate agreement has time complexity at least $\log n$.[5] This implies an $\Omega(\log n)$ time separation between the non-wait-free and wait-free computation models.

We note that the constant time 2-process algorithm behaves rather badly if one of the processes fails. The *work* performed in an execution of an algorithm is the total number of atomic operations performed in that execution by all processes before they decide. We have proved a tradeoff between the time complexity of and the work performed by any wait-free approximate agreement algorithm. We have shown that for *any* wait-free approximate agreement algorithm for 2 processes, there exists an execution in which the work exhibits a nontrivial dependency on ε and the range of inputs.

In practice, the design of distributed systems is often geared towards optimizing the time complexity in "normal executions," i.e., executions where no failures occur and processes run at approximately the same pace, while building in safety provisions to protect against failures (cf. [61]). Our results indicate that, in the asynchronous shared-memory

---

[5]The lower bound is attained in an execution where processes run synchronously and no process fails.

setting, there are problems for which building in such safety provisions *must* result in performance degradation in the normal executions. This situation contrasts with that occurring, for example, in synchronous systems that solve the distributed consensus problem. In that setting, there are *early-stopping* algorithms (e.g., [25, 28, 79]) that tolerate failures, yet still terminate in *constant* time when no failures occur. The exact cost imposed by fault-tolerance on normal executions, was studied, for example, in [14, 28, 79]. It has been shown, for synchronous message passing systems, that non-blocking commit protocols take twice as much time, in failure-free executions, as blocking protocols ([29]).

Recent work has addressed the issue of adapting the usual synchronous shared-memory PRAM model to better reflect implementation issues, by reducing synchrony ([15, 16, 39, 81, 74]) or by requiring fault-tolerance ([50, 51]). To the best of our knowledge, the impact of the *combination* of asynchrony and fault-tolerance (as exemplified by the wait-free model) on the time complexity of shared-memory algorithms has not previously been studied.

(The work described in this section appears in [6].)

7 Further research

Our future research plans include more work on upper and lower bounds for problems of interest in real-time computing. Some specific problems we are currently working on are as follows.

- More complex resource allocation problems than simple mutual exclusion.

- A problem of probabilistic processor fault diagnosis.

- Probabilistic versions of agreement problems.

- Extensions of the consensus problem described in Section 4 to the case where more severe faults than simple stopping faults can occur.

- The problem of determining the power of a bounded capacity link.

We also plan to continue our work on modeling and verification. Specifically, this includes the following.

- An attempt to relate recent work on process algebraic approaches to reasoning about real-time systems to state-machine models such as [78].

- An attempt to develop timing analysis techniques for randomized algorithms.

- An effort to apply the mapping method to verify substantial algorithms of interest in the fields of communication and/or real-time processing. A particular example we are working on is a new link-state packet distribution algorithm proposed as a standard by DEC.

- An effort to simplify our mapping method described in Section 5.

7.0.1 Acknowledgements:

We owe great thanks to the other researchers who worked with us on these papers: Cynthia Dwork, Marios Mavronicolas, Nir Shavit and Larry Stockmeyer. We also thank Nancy Leveson, Michael Merritt, Stephen Ponzio, Mark Tuttle and Jennifer Welch for many helpful discussions and for their reading of drafts of our papers.

References

[1] M. Abadi and L. Lamport, "The existence of refinement mappings," DEC SRC Research Report 29, August 1988.

[2] E. Arjomandi, M. J. Fischer and N. Lynch, "Efficiency of synchronous versus asynchronous distributed systems," *Journal of the ACM,* Vol. 30, No. 3 (July 1983), pp. 449–456.

[3] J. Aspnes and M. Herlihy, "Fast randomized consensus using shared memory," *Journal of Algorithms,* September 1990, to appear.

[4] H. Attiya, C. Dwork, N. .A. Lynch and L. J. Stockmeyer, "Bounds on the time to reach agreement in the presence of timing uncertainty," in preparation.

[5] H. Attiya and N. A. Lynch, "Time bounds for real-time process control in the presence of timing uncertainty," *Proc. 10th IEEE Real-Time Systems Symposium,* 1989, pp. 268–284. Also, Technical Memo MIT/LCS/TM-403, Laboratory for Computer Science, MIT, July 1989.

[6] H. Attiya, N. Lynch and N. Shavit, "Are wait-free algorithms fast?" to appear in *the 31st Annual IEEE Symposium on Foundations of Computer Science (FOCS),* October 1990.

[7] H. Attiya and M. Mavronicolas, "Efficiency of asynchronous vs. semi-synchronous networks," to appear in *the 28th annual Allerton Conference on Communication, Control and Computing,* October 1990.

[8] B. Awerbuch, "The complexity of network synchronization," *Journal of the ACM,* Vol. 32, No. 4 (1985), pp. 804–823.

[9] J. C. M. Baeten and J. A. Bergstra, *Real time process algebra,* Technical Report P8916b, University of Amsterdam, March 1990.

[10] P. Berman, J. A. Garay and K. J. Perry, "Towards optimal distributed consensus," *Proc. 30th IEEE Symp. on Foundations of Computer Science,* 1989, pp. 410–415.

[11] A. Bernstein and P. Harter, Jr. "Proving real-time properties of programs with temporal logic," *Proc. 8th Symp. on Operating System Principles,* Operating Systems Review, Vol. 15, No. 5 (December 1981), pp. 1–11.

[12] F. Cristian, H. Aghili, R. Strong and D. Dolev, "Atomic broadcast: From simple message diffusion to Byzantine agreement," *Proc. 15th Int. Conf. on Fault Tolerant Computing,* 1985, pp. 1–7. Also, IBM Research Report RJ5244, revised October 1989.

[13] B. A. Coan, "A communication-efficient canonical form for fault-tolerant distributed protocols," *Proc. 5th ACM Symp. on Principles of Distributed Computing,* 1986, pp. 63–72.

[14] B. A. Coan and C. Dwork, "Simultaneity is harder than agreement," *Proc. 5th IEEE Symp. on Reliability in Distributed Software and Database Systems*, 1986, pp. 141–150.

[15] R. Cole and O. Zajicek, "The APRAM: Incorporating asynchrony into the PRAM model," *Proc. 1st ACM Symp. on Parallel Algorithms and Architectures*, 1989, pp. 169–178.

[16] R. Cole and O. Zajicek, "The expected advantage of asynchrony," *Proc. 2nd ACM Symp. on Parallel Algorithms and Architectures*, 1990, to appear.

[17] J. E. Coolahan and N. Roussopoulus, "Timing requirements for time-driven systems using augmented Petri nets," *IEEE Transactions on Software Engineering*, Vol. SE-9, No. 5 (September 1983), pp. 603–616.

[18] B. Dasarathy, "Timing constraints of real-time systems: Constructs for expressing them, methods for validating them," *IEEE Transactions on Software Engineering*, Vol. SE-11, No. 1 (January 1985), pp. 80–86.

[19] R. DeMillo, N. A. Lynch and M. Merritt, "Cryptographic protocols," *Proc. 14th Annual ACM Symp. on Theory of Computing*, May 1982, pp. 383–400.

[20] D. Dolev, C. Dwork and L. Stockmeyer, "On the minimal synchronism needed for distributed consensus," *Journal of the ACM*, Vol. 34, No. 1 (January 1987), pp. 77–97.

[21] D. Dolev, M. J. Fischer, R. Fowler, N. A. Lynch and H. R. Strong, "Efficient byzantine agreement without authentication," *Information and Control*, Vol. 52 (1982), pp. 257–274.

[22] D. Dolev, E. Gafni and N. Shavit, "Toward a non-atomic era: ℓ-exclusion as a test case," *Proc. 20th ACM Symp. on the Theory of Computing*, 1988, pp. 78–92.

[23] D. Dolev, N. Lynch, S. Pinter, E. Stark and W. Weihl, "Reaching approximate agreement in the presence of faults," *Journal of the ACM*, Vol. 33, No. 3, 1986, pp. 499–516.

[24] D. Dolev, J. Halpern and H. R. Strong, "On the possibility and impossibility of achieving clock synchronization." *Journal of Computer and Systems Sciences,* Vol. 32, No. 2 (1986) pp. 230–250.

[25] D. Dolev, R. Reischuk, and H. R. Strong, "Eventual is earlier than immediate," *Proc. 23rd IEEE Symp. on Foundations of Computer Science,* 1982, pp. 196–203.

[26] D. Dolev and H. R. Strong, "Authenticated algorithms for byzantine agreement," *SIAM Journal on Computing,* Vol. 12, No. 3 (November 1983), pp. 656–666.

[27] C. Dwork, N. Lynch, and L. Stockmeyer, "Consensus in the presence of partial synchrony," *Journal of the ACM,* Vol. 35 (1988), pp. 288–323.

[28] C. Dwork and Y. Moses, "Knowledge and common knowledge in byzantine environments I: Crash failures," *Proc. 1st Conf. on Theoretical Aspects of Reasoning About Knowledge,* Morgan-Kaufmann, Los Altos, CA, 1986, pp. 149–170; *Information and Computation,* to appear.

[29] C. Dwork and D. Skeen, "The inherent cost of nonblocking commitment," *Proc. 2nd ACM Symp. on Principles of Distributed Computing,* 1983, pp. 1–11.

[30] A. Fekete, "Asymptotically optimal algorithms for approximate agreement," *Proc. 5th ACM Symp. on Principles of Distributed Computing,* 1986, pp. 73–87.

[31] A. Fekete, "Asynchronous approximate agreement," *Proc. 6th ACM Symp. on Principles of Distributed Computing,* 1987, pp. 64–76.

[32] M. Fischer and N. Lynch, "A lower bound for the time to assure interactive consistency," *Information Processing Letters,* Vol. 14, No. 4 (June 1982), pp. 183–186.

[33] M. Fischer, N. Lynch and M. Paterson, "Impossibility of distributed consensus with one faulty process," *Journal of the ACM,* Vol. 32, No. 2 (1985), pp. 374–382.

[34] M. W. Franklin and A. Gabrielian, "A transformational method for verifying safety properties in real-time systems," in *Proc. 10th IEEE Real-Time Systems Symp.*, pp. 112–123, December 1989.

[35] A. Gabrielian and M. W. Franklin, "State-based specification of complex real-time systems," in *Proc. IEEE Real-Time Systems Symp.*, 1988, pp. 2–11.

[36] A. Gabrielian and M. W. Franklin, "Multi-level specification and verification of real-time software," Technical Report 89-14, Tomson-CSF, Inc., July 1989.

[37] R. Gerth and A. Boucher, "A timed failure semantics for extended communicating processes," In *Proc. ICALP '87*, Springer-Verlag Lecture Notes in Computer Science #267, 1987.

[38] R. Gerber and I. Lee, "The formal treatment of priorities in real-time computation." In *Proc. 6th IEEE Workshop on Real-Time Software and Operating Systems*, 1989.

[39] P. Gibbons, "Towards better shared memory programming models," *Proc. 1st ACM Symp. on Parallel Algorithms and Architectures*, 1989, pp. 169–178.

[40] D. W. Gillies and J. W.-S. Liu, "Greed in resource scheduling," *Proc. 10th IEEE Real-Time Systems Symposium*, 1989, pp. 285–294.

[41] V. Hadzilacos, *Issues of fault tolerance in concurrent computations*, Ph.D. Thesis, Harvard University, June 1984. Technical Report TR–11–84, Department of Computer Science, Harvard University.

[42] J. Halpern, N. Megiddo and A. A. Munshi, "Optimal precision in the presence of uncertainty." *Journal of Complexity*, Vol. 1 (1985), pp. 170–196.

[43] V. H. Hasse, "Real-time behavior of programs," *IEEE Transactions on Software Engineering*, Vol. SE-7, No. 5 (September 1981), pp. 494–501.

[44] M. Herlihy, "Wait-free implementations of concurrent objects," *Proc. 7th ACM Symp. on Principles of Distributed Computing*, 1988, pp. 276–290.

[45] J. Hooman, *A compositional proof theory for real-time distributed message passing,* TR. 4-1-1(1), Department of Mathematics and Computer Science, Eindhoven University of technology, March 1987.

[46] C. Huizing, R. Gerth, and W. P. deRoever, "Full abstraction of a real-time denotational semantics for an OCCAM-like language," in *Proc. 14th ACM Symp. on Principles of Programming Languages,* 1987, pp. 223–237.

[47] F. Jahanian and A. Mok, "Safety analysis of timing properties in real-time systems," *IEEE Transactions on Software Engineering,* Vol. SE-12, No. 9 (September 1986), pp. 890–904.

[48] F. Jahanian and A. Mok, "A graph-theoretic approach for timing analysis and its implementation," *IEEE Transactions on Computers,* Vol. C-36, No. 8 (August 1987), pp. 961–975.

[49] F. Jahanian and D. A. Stuart, "A method for verifying properties of Modechart specifications," in *Proc. IEEE Real-Time Systems Symp.,* 1988, pp. 12–21.

[50] P. Kanellakis and A. Shvartsman, "Efficient parallel algorithms can be made robust," *Proc. 8th ACM Symp. on Principles of Distributed Computing,* 1989, pp. 211–221.

[51] Z. Kedem, K. Palem and P. Spirakis, "Efficient robust parallel computations," *Proc. 22nd ACM Symp. on Theory of Computing,* 1990, pp. 138–148.

[52] R. Koymans, J. Vytopil and W. P. deRoever, "Real-time programming and asynchronous message passing," in *Proc. 2nd ACM Symp. on Principles of Distributed Computing,* 1983, pp. 187–197.

[53] R. Koymans, R. K. Shyamasundar, W. P. deRoever, R. Gerth, and S. Arun-Kumar, "Compositional semantics for real-time distributed computing," *Information and Computation,* Vol. 79, No. 3 (December 1988), pp. 210–256.

[54] L. Lamport, "The synchronization of independent processes," *Acta Informatica,* Vol. 7, No, 1 (1976), pp. 15–34.

[55] L. Lamport, "Proving the correctness of multiprocess programs," *IEEE Transactions on Software Engineering*, Vol. SE-3, No. 2 (March 1977) pp. 125–143.

[56] L. Lamport, "Time, clocks and the ordering of events in distributed systems." *Communications of the ACM*, Vol. 21, No. 7 (July 1978), pp. 558–565.

[57] L. Lamport, "Specifying concurrent program modules," *ACM Trans. on Programming Languages and Systems*, Vol. 5, No. 2 (April 1983), pp. 190–222.

[58] L. Lamport, "On interprocess communication. parts I and II" *Distributed Computing 1, 2* 1986, 77–101.

[59] L. Lamport and M. J. Fischer, "Byzantine generals and transaction commit protocols," Tech. Report Op. 62, SRI International, Menlo Park, CA, 1982.

[60] L. Lamport, R. Shostak and M. Pease, "The byzantine generals problem," *ACM Transaction on Prog. Lang. and Sys.*, Vol. 4, No. 3 (July 1982), pp. 382–401.

[61] B. Lampson, "Hints for computer system design", in *Proc. 9th ACM Symposium on Operating Systems Principles*, 1983, pp. 33–48.

[62] N. Leveson and J. Stolzy, "Safety analysis using Petri Nets," *IEEE Transactions on Software Engineering*, Vol. SE-13, No. 3 (March 1987), pp. 386–397.

[63] H. R. Lewis, "Finite-state analysis of asynchronous circuits with bounded temporal uncertainty," Techincal Report TR-15-89, Aiken Computation Laboratory, Harvard University.

[64] M. Li, J. Tromp and P. M.B. Vitanyi, "How to share concurrent wait-free variables," *ICALP 1989*. Expanded version: Report CS-R8916, CWI, Amsterdam, April 1989.

[65] C. L. Liu and J. W. Layland, "Scheduling algorithms for multiprogramming in a hard real time environment," *Journal of the ACM*, Vol. 20, No. 1 (1973), pp. 46-61.

[66] J. Lundelius and N. Lynch, "An upper and lower bound for clock synchronization," *Information and Control,* Vol. 62, Nos. 2/3 (August/September 1984), pp. 190–204.

[67] N. Lynch, "Concurrency control for resilient nested transactions," *Advances in Computing Research,* Vol. 3, 1986, pp. 335–373.

[68] N. A. Lynch and H. Attiya, "Using mappings to prove timing properties," proceedings of *the 9th Annual ACM Symposium on Principles of Distributed Computing (PODC),* 1990, pp. 265–280. Also, Technical Memo MIT/LCS/TM-412.b, Laboratory for Computer Science, MIT, December 1989.

[69] N. Lynch and M. Fischer, "On describing the behavior and implementation of distributed systems," *Theoretical Computer Science,* Vol. 13, No. 1 (January 1981), pp. 17-43.

[70] N. Lynch and K. Goldman, *Lecture notes for 6.852.* MIT/LCS/RSS-5, Laboratory for Computer Science, MIT, 1989.

[71] N. Lynch and M. Tuttle, "Hierarchical correctness proofs for distributed algorithms," in *Proc. 7th ACM symp. on Principles of Distributed Computing,* 1987, pp. 137–151. Expanded version available as Technical Report MIT/LCS/TR-387, Laboratory for Computer Science, MIT, April 1987.

[72] N. Lynch and M. Tuttle, "An introduction to input/output automata," *CWI-Quarterly,* Vol. 2, No. 3, 1989. Also, Technical Memo, MIT/LCS/TM-373, Laboratory for Computer Science Massachusetts Institute of Technology, November 1988.

[73] S. Mahaney and F. Schneider, "Inexact agreement: Accuracy, precision, and graceful degradation," *Proc. 4th ACM Symp. on Principles of Distributed Computing,* 1985, pp. 237–249.

[74] C. Martel, A. Park and R. Subramonian, "Optimal asynchronous algorithms for shared memory parallel computers," Technical Report CSE-89-8, Division of Computer Science, University of California, Davis, July 1989.

[75] C. Martel, R. Subramonian and A. Park, "Asynchronous PRAMs are (almost) as good as synchronous PRAMs," to appear in *the 31st Annual IEEE Symposium on Foundations of Computer Science (FOCS),* October 1990.

[76] M. Merritt, "Notes on the Dolev-Strong Lower Bound for Byzantine Agreement," unpublished manuscript, 1985.

[77] M. Merritt, "Completeness theorems for automata," REX Workshop, May 1989.

[78] M. Merritt, F. Modugno and M. Tuttle, "Time constrained automata," unpublished manuscript, November 1988. Revised: Aguest 1990.

[79] Y. Moses and M. R. Tuttle, "Programming simultaneous actions using common knowledge," *Algorithmica,* Vol. 3 (1988), pp. 121–169.

[80] Y. Moses and O. Waarts, "Coordinated traversal: $(t + 1)$-round byzantine agreement in polynomial time," *Proc. 29th IEEE Symp. on Foundations of Computer Science,* 1988, pp. 246–255.

[81] N. Nishimura, "Asynchronous shared memory parallel computation," *Proc. 2nd ACM Symp. on Parallel Algorithms and Architectures,* 1990, to appear.

[82] M. Pease, R. Shostak and L. Lamport, "Reaching agreement in the presence of faults," *Journal of the ACM,* Vol. 27, No. 2 (1980), pp. 228–234.

[83] G. Peterson, "Concurrent reading while writing," *ACM Transactions on Programming Languages and Systems,* Vol. 5, No. 1 (January 1983), pp. 46–55.

[84] G. Peterson, and J. Burns, "Concurrent reading while writing II: The multi-writer case," *Proc. 28th IEEE Symp. on Foundations of Computer Science,* 1987, pp. 383–392.

[85] G. Peterson and M. Fischer, "Economical solutions for the critical section problem in a distributed system," *Proc. 9th ACM Symp. on Theory of Computing,* 1977, pp. 91–97.

[86] R. Rajkumar, *Task synchronization in real-time systems,* Ph.D. thesis, Carnegie-Mellon University, Augurst 1989.

[87] K. Ramamritham, J. Stankovic and W. Zhao, "Distributed scheduling of tasks with deadlines and resource requirements," *IEEE Transactions on Computers,* Vol. C-38, No. 8 (August 1989), pp. 1110–1123.

[88] G. M. Reed and A. W. Roscoe, "A timed model for communicating sequential processes," in *ICALP '86.*

[89] R. Schaffer, "On the correctness of atomic multi-writer registers," MIT/LCS/TM-364, June 1988.

[90] F. B. Schneider, "Real-time reliable systems project," in *Foundations of Real-Time Computing Research Initiative,* ONR Kickoff Workshop, November 1988, pp. 28–32.

[91] J. Sifakis, "Petri nets for performance evaluation, in measuring, modeling and evaluating computer systems," in *Proc. 3rd Symp. IFIP Working Group 7.3,* H. Beilner and E. Gelenbe (eds.), Amsterdam, The Netherlands, North-Holland, 1977, pp. 75–93.

[92] A. U. Shankar and S. L. Lam, "Time-dependent distributed systems: Proving safety, liveness and real-time properties," *Distributed Computing,* Vol. 2, pp. 61–79, 1987.

[93] A. C. Shaw, "Reasoning about time in higher-level language software," *IEEE Transactions on Software Engineering,* Vol. SE-15, No. 7 (July 1989), pp. 875–889.

[94] B. Simons, J. L. Welch and N. Lynch, "An overview of clock synchronization," IBM Technical Report RJ 6505, October 1988.

[95] J. Stankovic and K. Ramamritham, "The SPRING kernel: A new paradigm for real-time operating systems," *ACM Opertating Systems Reviews,* Vol 23, No. 3 (July 1987), pp. 54–71.

[96] R. Strong, D. Dolev and F. Cristian, "New latency bounds for atomic broadcast," to appear in *11th IEEE Real-Time Systems Symposium,* 1990.

[97] G. Tel, "Assertional verification of a timer based protocol," in *ICALP '88,* Lecture Notes in Computer Science 317, Springer-Verlag, pp. 600–614.

[98] P. Vitanyi and B. Awerbuch, "Atomic shared register access by asynchronous hardware," *Proc. 27th IEEE Symp. on Foundations of Computer Science,* pp. 233–243, 1986.

[99] J. L. Welch and N. Lynch, "A new fault-tolerant algorithm for clock synchronization," *Information and Computation,* Vol. 77, No. 1 (April 1988), pp. 1–36.

[100] A. Zwarico, *Timed acceptence: an algebra of time dependent computing,* Ph.D. thesis, Dept. of Computer and Information Science, University of Pennsylvania, 1988.

[101] A. Zwarico, I. Lee and R. Gerber, "A complete axiomatization of real-time processes," submitted for publication.

CHAPTER 6

HMS Machines: A Unified Framework for Specification, Verification and Reasoning for Real–Time Systems

Armen Gabrielian
Thomson–CSF, Inc.
630 Hansen Way, Suite 250
Palo Alto, CA 94304

Abstract

An overview of research on "hierarchical multi–state (HMS) machines" is presented. HMS machines consist of parallel and hierarchical automata that are integrated with a temporal interval logic called TIL. The underlying automaton model reduces the state space by orders of magnitude compared to traditional automata and TIL provides a uniform method for defining temporal constraints for the past, the present and future in both discrete or continuous time. HMS machines provide a formal and visual framework for the specification of the dynamic behavior and requirements of complex real–time systems. In addition, various forms of reasoning such as planning, situation assessment and scheduling can be performed in the HMS framework. The formal syntax and semantics of TIL and a new non–operational formalization of execution of HMS machines are presented. An overview of the "multi–level" approach to specification is presented that offers a high degree of modularity and reusability of specifications. The application of multi–level specification to planning in real–time domains is also discussed briefly. Two complementary methods of verification of HMS machines are reviewed: (1) model checking for verifying properties expressed in the branching version of TIL and (2) correctness–preserving transformations for verifying safety properties. As an example of reasoning using HMS machines, a method is presented for scheduling *interdependent* activities, leading to a model–based approach to temporal constraint satisfaction.

INTRODUCTION

Various techniques for specification and verification of real–time systems have been proposed over the last few years. At the same time, numerous studies have been performed on reasoning about real–time systems, both in the fields of artificial intelligence and in real–time system theory. While specification and verification efforts have been closely related, very little connection has been established between this body of literature and AI studies on real–time systems or fields like real–time scheduling theory.

The most common specification formalisms for real–time systems have been based on variations of temporal logic [24, 26, 6]. Another approach has been to introduce simple temporal constraints in terms of minimum and maximum delays into fair transition systems [25] Petri nets [18, 16] or a variation of Statecharts [19]. A large body of the AI studies in real–time systems has been concerned with heuristic techniques (e.g., see the survey in [21]) where the guarantee of hard real–time constraints is not a primary concern. On the other hand, the extension of the constraint satisfaction approach to the temporal domain in [8] has begun to address a subclass of problems that is also of interest to the scheduling field, namely, the scheduling of tasks with precedence constraints [5] or synchronization constraints. This suggests a natural connection with specification theory since the definition of behavioral constraints is one of the main goals in the specification of real–time systems.

In this paper, an overview of research on "hierarchical multi–state (HMS)" machines is presented [13, 11, 14, 12, 15]. HMS machines consist of parallel and hierarchical automata in which the transitions are "controlled" by predicates defined in a temporal interval logic called TIL or its variants. This provides a very general and rich framework for specification, verification and model–based reasoning for real–time systems. The specific examples of reasoning to be considered in this paper will be a limited form of planning and the scheduling of logically and temporally interdependent concurrent activities. The constraint networks considered in [8] represent only a subclass of the types of temporal constraints that arise in our study of scheduling. We emphasize, however, that our goal here is not the development of efficient solution algorithms. Rather, it is to derive the mathematical formulation of scheduling problems from specifications in a systematic way.

The following are the key concepts of HMS machines along with some of the associated benefits:

Multi-state Viewpoint and Concurrency. In the underlying automaton model of HMS machines, multiple states may be true at a moment of time. This results in a potentially logarithmic reduction in the number of states compared to traditional automata. In addition, parallelism is modeled through the simultaneous firing of multiple transitions rather than through an interleaving model.

The Temporal Interval Logics TIL and BTIL. TIL and its branching counterpart BTIL provide a uniform treatment of time for all intervals in the time-line from $-\infty$ to $+\infty$. Compared to the usual definition of interval logics where all intervals are relative to the present [7, 23, 26], this makes the manipulation of intervals particularly convenient. Although most of the research on HMS machines has been concerned with discrete time, recent work has extended the time model to the continuous case.

Controls on Transitions. The TIL controls on transitions of HMS machines generalize a number of previous concepts without introducing excessive complexity in the decidability properties of HMS machines. On the one hand, TIL controls generalize propositional logic controls that, for example, are used in Büchi automata [4]. On the other hand, TIL controls generalize a wide class of Petri net and other state-based models in which time delays are introduced on transitions [16, 19]. Specifically, in HMS machines logical and temporal constraints on a transition may depend on states other than the one from which the transition emanates. This provides a convenient method of defining causal interactions among events and synchronization constraints. TIL controls on transitions also simplify the complexity of the state space further in many applications by reducing the need for defining intermediate states to control a system's behavior.

State Hierarchies, Recursion and Granularities of Time. State hierarchies in HMS machines follow the tradition of many other top-down design methodologies, except that the interface between different levels is formalized in terms of ports in the manner of CCS and two extensions are introduced: recursive hierarchies and a clock rate factor at each level of hierarchy. As a result, for example, real-time versions of common abstract data types can be specified precisely in terms of hierarchical HMS machines.

Composition of Asynchronous HMS Machines. By a slight modification of the concept of hierarchy, the composition of asynchronous HMS machines can be defined. This allows the specification of loosely–coupled distributed systems.

Nondeterminism. Nondeterminism plays a key role in the theory of HMS machines since it provides a powerful abstraction principle for defining classes of similar systems and *reusable* specifications through multi–level specification. While the standard notion of nondeterminism common to automata theory and Petri nets can be accommodated in HMS machines, a more liberal "inclusive" notion has generall˙ been adopted in which any subset of eligible nondeterministic transit˙ons may fire at any moment. This allows a higher level of abstraction, wiᵗhout a major increase in the complexity of analysis. We note that both deterministic and nondeterministic transitions may be present in an ᵀHMS machine.

Multi–level Specification. Multi–level spᵉcification is a unique approach for defining modular and reusable HMS machine specifications at multiple levels of abstraction. In contrast to the traditional refinement approach to specification, where a top–level specification is progressively refined to give a detailed specification, the multi–level view provides a mechanism for obtaining a detailed specification by using a hierarchy of interacting HMS machines. Such an approach allows the separation of concerns and reduces the total amount of effort to specify a system significantly.

Objects in States, First–order TIL and Probabilities. Boolean states can be generalized to include complex algebraic objects. In this more general framework, TIL is extended to a many–sorted first–order temporal interval logic and the objects are manipulated by functions associated with transitions. Some preliminary studies on probabilistic HMS machines have also been performed. In this connection, a promising idea is the representation of probabilistic HMS machines in terms of Markov random fields.

The following is a summary of the analysis techniques that have been developed for HMS machines:

Interactive Simulation And Abstract Animation. The most basic analysis tool for HMS machines is interactive simulation. While efficient methods of implementing multi–level specifications have not yet been studied in detail, both general and specific prototype simulation environments that provide a limited abstract animation capability in terms of states have been implemented. Experiments have been performed using these environments in specifying a C^3I system scenario, multiple elevators, several railroad crossing systems, and a robot planner on a grid with barriers.

Model Checking. Standard model checking [6] can be extended to the HMS framework with the following changes: (1) The size of the computation tree may be reduced significantly. (2) Repetitive execution of a set of transitions can be represented in an abbreviated fashion using a parametric notation. (3) An arc may represent the simultaneous firing of several transitions. (4) Properties relating to the past or the future specified in BTIL can be evaluated by forward and reverse traversal of the computation tree in a uniform manner.

Transformational Proof Technique. A correctness–preserving transformation technique for verifying safety properties of HMS machines has been developed [11] that is complementary to model checking. It is essentially a variation of theorem proving that is complete but requires a heuristic choice of rules to be applied at each step. Even for some simple systems, a transformational proof can be much simpler than the more mechanical approach of model checking. Limited versions of model checking and transformations have been implemented in the HMS simulation environment.

Verifying Existence of Schedules. Our scheduling approach [14] can be considered as a limited form of verifying the existence of schedules for plans consisting of potentially concurrent execution paths of a nondeterministic HMS machine. The problem in general reduces to the solution of a set of linear inequalities and is closely related to temporal constraint satisfaction.

In this paper, we first present the basic concepts of HMS machines. We then provide an overview of multi–level specification, along with a brief discussion of its relationship to planning. In the following two sections, we discuss, respectively, methods of verifying properties of HMS machines and an approach to scheduling of concurrent interdependent tasks. In the final section, we present the conclusions.

BASIC CONCEPTS OF HMS MACHINES

In traditional system theory and automata theory, a system is in a single state at a moment of time. Sometimes a fixed state vector is used which in the case of automata theory corresponds to the cartesian product of several automata. Two problems arise from this rigid viewpoint. First, for problems of realistic size, one is quickly confronted with a proliferation of the state space that is difficult to manage unless certain simplifying assumptions are made. Secondly, for many computer science problems, the single–state concept is simply inadequate. For example, for a recursively defined system or even an unbounded queue, it is much more natural to allow multiple or even an unbounded number of simple states rather than insisting on the existence of a single state with a very complicated value. In fact, following [3], in this paper we assume that a state space can be a "non–well–founded set" that may include itself as a member. We also allow multisets, in which multiple copies of a state may be included in the state set. By a simple labeling scheme all confusion about reference to different instances of states can be eliminated.

We begin our formalization of HMS machines by introducing the control language TIL and two of its variants. We then present the definition of HMS machines by first considering non–hierarchical multi–state (MS) machines followed by the generalization to the hierarchical case.

The Propositional Temporal Interval Logic TIL

Traditional temporal logic is obtained by extending propositional logic by the addition of the operators □ (*always*) and ◇ (*sometime*). To deal with finite intervals in a discrete model of time, often the operator **O** (next moment) is used. A number of researchers have considered interval–based logics, where □ and ◇ are replaced with the finite operators [t] and < t >, respectively [7, 23, 26]. Thus, for example, < t > A states that A will be true within t moments. The main difficulty with this definition is that the expression of temporal constraints about arbitrary intervals becomes somewhat cumbersome. Also, traditionally, temporal logic has been concerned with reasoning about the future only. In the HMS framework, we need to reason about both the future and the past.

Definition 1. Given a set S, an "instantaneous marking" or simply "marking" of S at the relative time t is a mapping $M_t: S \rightarrow \{F, T\}$, with F and T representing false and true, respectively.

Definition 2. A sequence ..., M_{-1}, M_0, M_1, ... of markings on a set S is called a "marking sequence" for S over the discrete relative time sequence ..., -1, 0, 1, ..., where 0 represents the "current moment."

We now introduce the propositional temporal interval logic TIL, which consists of a language for defining temporal properties of markings on a set of "states" S over time. TIL is obtained by augmenting standard propositional logic with four temporal operators. In the sequel, given a marking M and a formula ψ, we denote the satisfiability of ψ in M by $M \models \psi$.

Definition 3. Given a set S and a marking sequence ..., M_{t-1}, M_t, M_{t+1}, ... on S, the propositional temporal interval logic TIL on the set of literals S is the minimal set satisfying the following:

Literals For all $s \in S$, s is in TIL. $M_t \models s \Leftrightarrow M_t(s) = T$.

Negation If ψ is a TIL formula, then $\neg\psi$ is in TIL.
$M_t \models \neg\psi \Leftrightarrow (M_t \models \psi)$ is not true.

Disjunction If ψ and ϕ are TIL formulae, then $\psi \vee \phi$ is in TIL.
$M_t \models \psi \vee \phi \Leftrightarrow M_t \models \psi$ or $M_t \models \phi$.

Conjunction If ψ and ϕ are TIL formulae, then $\psi \wedge \phi$ is in TIL.
$M_t \models \psi \wedge \phi \Leftrightarrow M_t \models \psi$ and $M_t \models \phi$.

$O(t')$ *At* relative time t'. If ψ is in TIL, then $O(t')\psi$ is in TIL.
$M_t \models O(t')\psi \Leftrightarrow M_{t+t'} \models \psi$.

$[t_1, t_2]$ *Always* between t_1 and t_2. If ψ is in TIL, then $[t_1, t_2]\psi$ is in TIL. $M_t \models [t_1, t_2]\psi \Leftrightarrow$ for all t', $t_1 \leq t' \leq t_2$ implies $M_t \models O(t')\psi$.

$<t_1, t_2>$ *Sometime* between t_1 and t_2. If ψ is in TIL, then $<t_1, t_2>\psi$ is in TIL. $M_t \models <t_1, t_2>\psi \Leftrightarrow$ there exists a t' such that $t_1 \leq t' \leq t_2 \wedge M_t \models O(t')\psi$.

$<t_1, t_2>!$ *Sometime–change* between t_1 and t_2. If ψ is in TIL, then $<t_1, t_2>!\psi$ is in TIL. $M_t \vDash <t_1, t_2>!\psi \Leftrightarrow$ there exists a t' such that $((t_1-1) \leq t' < t_2) \wedge (M_t \vDash O(t')\neg\psi) \wedge (M_t \vDash <t'+1, t_2>\psi)$.

The first four in the list above are propositional operators and the last four are temporal operators. As an example of a TIL formula, $<-10, 5>[-3, 0]A$, for $A \in S$, is true at time t if for some t' in the period from t–10 to t+5, the state A was (or will have been) true continuously from t'–3 to t'.

We note that standard temporal operators, including the finite versions are special cases of TIL operators. Thus, $\square = [0, \infty]$, $\diamond = <0, \infty>$, and $[t] = [0, t]$. The sometime–change operator $< >!$ is not normally defined in standard temporal logics. It is convenient in specifying certain types of deadlines and it is particularly useful in our transformational proof technique.

As noted earlier, all intervals are treated in a uniform fashion in TIL. As a result, operations on temporal expressions become particularly easy. The following is a subset of the properties of TIL presented in [15]:

$O(t)[t_1, t_2]A \Leftrightarrow [t+t_1, t+t_2]A$

$O(t)<t_1, t_2>A \Leftrightarrow <t+t_1, t+t_2>A$

$<t_1, t_2> <t_3, t_4>A \Leftrightarrow <t_1+t_3, t_2+t_4>A$

$[t_1, t_2][t_3, t_4]A \Leftrightarrow [t_1+t_3, t_2+t_4]A$

We now define a subset of TIL that permits a simple class of HMS machines to be defined that are relatively easy to analyze.

Definition 4. TIL_0 is the subset of TIL, in which disjunctions and nesting of temporal operators are disallowed.

While TIL_0 is a proper subset of TIL, the class of HMS machines defined with TIL_0 is behaviorally equivalent to the class of machines defined with TIL [15]. The main advantage of TIL is that it provides a more compact language for specifying complex temporal constraints.

We now consider a branching time version of TIL, called BTIL, that generalizes a number of existing branching temporal logics such as CTL [6], CTL* [10], RTCTL [9] and the partial order logic POTL of [27].

Definition 5. The branching temporal interval logic BTIL is obtained by extending TIL with the following two "branching operators:"

∃   *There exists an execution.* If ψ is in BTIL, then $\exists\psi$ is in BTIL. $M_t \models \exists\psi \Leftrightarrow$ there exists a marking sequence ..., M_{t-1}, M_t, M_{t+1}, ... such that $M_t \models \psi$.

∀   *For all executions.* If ψ is in BTIL, then $\forall\psi$ is in BTIL. $M_t \models \forall\psi \Leftrightarrow$ for all marking sequences ..., M_{t-1}, M_t, M_{t+1}, ... , we have $M_t \models \psi$.

The languages TIL and TIL_0 will be used in the following two subsections to define constraints on transitions of machines. BTIL will be used later for defining properties to be evaluated by model checking. As noted in [15], it is also possible to use BTIL as a control language for HMS machines. However, because of the close relationship between nondeterminism and the concept of branching or multiple futures, such controls can sometimes be replaced by simpler TIL controls [15].

Multi–State (MS) Machines

We now turn to the definition of the non–hierarchical version of HMS machines and we introduce our visual notation for representing such machines.

Definition 6. For logical language L, a "multi–state" (MS/L) machine, or MS machine when L is understood, is a 5–tuple $H = (S, S_{in}, S_{out}, \Gamma_D, \Gamma_N)$ or a triple $H = (S, \Gamma_D, \Gamma_N)$ if $S_{in} = S_{out} = \{\ \}$ such that

(a) S is a set of "states." In general, if $\{A, B, ...\}$ is a subset of S, we denote it by (A, B, ...).

(b) $S_{in} \subseteq S$ is a set of "input ports" and $S_{out} \subseteq S$ is a set of "output ports."

(c) Γ_D and Γ_N consist, respectively, of "deterministic" and "nondeterministic," transitions of the form

    (PRIMARIES) (CONTROL) → (CONSEQUENTS),

where PRIMARIES $\subseteq$ S - S$_{out}$, CONSEQUENTS $\subseteq$ S - S$_{in}$ and CONTROL is a predicate in L with literals from the set S. For a particular transition γ = (A, B, ...) (P) $\rightarrow$ (E, F, ...) in $\Gamma_D \cup \Gamma_N$, we write PRIMS(γ) = (A, B, ...), CNTRL(γ) = P, and CNSQS(γ) = (E, F, ...).

In this paper, we are particularly interested in the class of MS/TIL. In this case, the enablement conditions or "controls" on transitions are defined in terms of TIL predicates. Figure 2.1 presents our visual notation for representing MS machines. Rectangles represent states and dark arrows denote transitions with nondeterminism indicated by an asterisk. TIL controls are indicated by a combination of VLSI notation and temporal operators next to the symbol ⓣ. Thus, for example, for the nondeterministic transition v and the deterministic transition u in the MS machine of Figure 1, we have

PRIMS(u) = (C, D), CNTRL(u) = T, and CNSQS(u) = A.

PRIMS(v) = (A), CNTRL(v) = [-10, 0]A $\wedge$ <-5, -2>(D $\wedge$ ¬E), and CNSQS(v) = B.

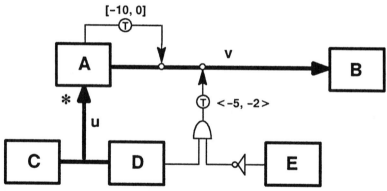

Figure 1. MS Machine with TIL Controls

We consider next the semantics of execution for MS machines. We assume that input ports are controlled externally and output ports become true only when transitions fire into them.

Definition 7. Given an MS machine H = (S, S$_{in}$, S$_{out}$, Γ_D, Γ_N), an "execution of H" is a marking sequence ..., M$_{t-1}$, M$_t$, M$_{t+1}$, ... on S such that

(a) There exists a "firing set" sequence ..., $\Gamma_{t-1}, \Gamma_t, \Gamma_{t+1}, ...,$ where for each i and a transition γ of H

    1.   If $\gamma \in \Gamma_D$ then $\gamma \in \Gamma_i \Leftrightarrow (M_i(s) = T$ for all $s \in PRIMS(\gamma)$ and $M_i \vDash CNTRL(\gamma))$

    2.   If $\gamma \in \Gamma_N$ then $\gamma \in \Gamma_i \Rightarrow (M_i(s) = T$ for all $s \in PRIMS(\gamma)$ and $M_i \vDash CNTRL(\gamma))$

(b) $\forall \gamma \in \Gamma_i$ if $s \in CNSQS(\gamma)$, then $M_{i+1}(s) = T$

(c) $(\forall s \in S_{in}) \; M_{i+1}(s) = T \Leftrightarrow \exists \gamma \in \Gamma_i$ such that $s \in PRIMS(\gamma)$

(d) $(\forall s \in S_{out}) \; M_{i+1}(s) = F$ unless $\exists \gamma \in \Gamma_i$ such that $s \in CNSQS(\gamma)$

(e) $\forall s \in (S - S_{in})$ if $\exists \gamma \in \Gamma_i$ such that $s \in PRIMS(\gamma)$ then $M_{i+1}(s) = F$ if $(\forall \gamma' \in \Gamma_i) \; s \notin CNSQS(\gamma')$

(f) $\forall s \in (S - S_{in} - S_{out}) \; M_{i+1}(s) = T$ if $M_i(s) = T$ and $(\forall \gamma \in \Gamma_i) \; s \notin PRIMS(\gamma)$

Intuitively, during an execution, the marking of the state set of an HMS machine is updated at each discrete moment of time t through the "firing" of the transitions in the firing set Γ_t. Firing of a transition causes its consequent states to become true, while a primary state of a fired transition becomes false unless it is also the consequent state of a fired transition. The firing of a transition does not directly affect the states associated with its control.

A transition γ is said to be "enabled" if all its primary states and its control are true. By our definition, at a time t, only enabled transitions may be in the firing set Γ_t and all enabled deterministic (nondeterministic) transitions must (may) be in Γ_t. This results in an "inclusive" notion of nondeterminism, whereby some or all enabled transitions from a set of primary states may fire simultaneously. This view is also consistent with the Markov random field approach to modeling random processes. The traditional "exclusive" view of nondeterminism can be obtained by (1) adding additional controls in TIL on transitions to limit the number of firings from a state, (2) using a variation of the "choice function" of [17] to determine the type and combination of transitions that can fire simultaneously, or (3) imposing additional problem–oriented constraints at the machine level.

Operational definitions of execution were presented in [11, 14] for MS machines without ports and with TIL_0 "past" controls, i.e., controls that involve only negative or zero time values. An important advantage of Definition 7 is that "future" controls can also be accommodated. Thus, the firing of a transition may depend on future values of states as well as present or past values. This is particularly useful in defining requirements on systems.

Hierarchies and Composition of HMS Machines

In this section, we use three main concepts to generalize MS machines to the hierarchical case. First, we allow a state to be an HMS machine itself. If a machine is a member of its own state set, then a recursive machine is obtained and the state set is a "non–well–founded set" [3]. Secondly, we define how input and output ports can act as vehicles for establishing interfaces between parent and child states. Thirdly, we define a mechanism for machines to operate at different granularities of time. This is important both for making possible the specification of complex systems and from the point of view of efficiency of implementation.

Definition 8. Given a logical language L, a "hierarchical multi–state" (HMS/L) machine, or HMS machine when L is understood, is a 6–tuple $H = (S, S_{in}, S_{out}, \Gamma_D, \Gamma_N, \tau)$ such that

(a) $(S, S_{in}, S_{out}, \Gamma_D, \Gamma_N)$ is an MS/L machine such that each $s \in (S - S_{in} - S_{out})$ is a "primitive" state or a "child" state consisting of another HMS machine, possibly H itself.

(b) If H' is a child state of S, then each output port of H' is an input port of H and each input port of H' an output port of H.

(c) τ is a "clock rate factor" for H relative to the next higher level of hierarchy so that the clock rate of H operates at the speed of $1/\tau$ times that of its parent. We assume that the rate at the top level is established externally.

Similarly, we define next a method of establishing interactions between two independent HMS machines that may operate with asynchronous clocks.

Definition 9. The "composition" of two HMS machines H_1 and H_2 is obtained by equating a certain input (output) port of H_1 with a certain output (input) port of H_2. Composition of an arbitrary number of machines is defined similarly.

Figure 2 presents an example of two disjoint HMS machines H_1 and H_2 that are composed through the ports P and Q. A and C are hierarchical states of H_1, while B, D and E are primitive states in A, C and H_2, respectively. In our visual notation, we draw ports only when necessary. Thus, the transition u really consists of three separate transitions: (1) from B to an output port of A, (2) from the output port of A to the input port of C, and (3) from the input port of C to D. Similarly, the ports P and Q can be eliminated when no confusion can arise (actually, P and Q are by definition identical). The need for explicit representation of ports arises only when there is a need to establish an association between two separate drawings in terms of hierarchies or composition. Ports are, in general, also necessary for recursive hierarchies or when controls on ports are needed. An example of a recursive hierarchical HMS machine specifying a real–time first–in–first–out (FIFO) buffer appears in [15], in which each level of hierarchy operates at twice the speed of its parent and a control on an output port is employed at each level.

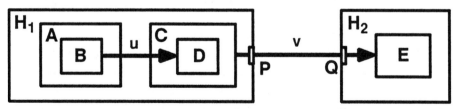

Figure 2. Execution under Hierarchy and Composition

A critical problem in the definition of hierarchy and composition is the need for a consistent definition of (1) machine execution and (2) evaluation of state markings. To guarantee that, for example, a state will never be true and false at the same time, we adopt the following conventions:

A1. Each transition in a sequence of transitions may be controlled at its own level. Thus, separate controls may be defined for the transition u in Figure 2 at the levels of machines A, H_1 and C. All these must be true before u can fire.

A2. The transitions in a sequence through input and output ports fire instantaneously and simultaneously, according to the clock of the eventual consequent state. Therefore, in Figure 2 u fires according to the clock of machine C and v fires according to the clock of machine H_2. This leads to a form of "cycle stealing" that allows a consequent state of a transition to cause a primary state to become false between two consecutive time steps of the primary state machine.

A3. Primary state and control state markings are evaluated at an infinitesimal moment before the firing of transitions actually occur. For discrete clocks one can always find a finite time before a clock tick that will guarantee correctness of marking evaluations. For continuous time HMS machines, this scheme can also be made precise in a manner consistent with the discrete case.

Hierarchies permit the top–down definition of complex specifications, while composition provides the mechanism for specifying loosely–coupled distributed systems. Recursion offers additional facilities for defining, e.g., real–time abstract data types.

MULTI–LEVEL SPECIFICATION AND PLANNING

The value of a formal specification is in its ability to detect inconsistencies in requirements and in providing mechanisms for verifying the correctness of a design at the early stages of a system's life cycle. It is well-known that this can result in a significant reduction in the cost of a system compared to postponing decisions to later stages. Since a change in requirements or design is the rule rather than the exception in the development of most complex real-time systems, systematic techniques are needed in a specification formalism to simplify the process of change. This has also been a major goal in the design of programming languages, resulting in techniques such as data abstraction, object–oriented programming, structured design, and so on. In the HMS machine framework, state hierarchies and composition provide limited forms of abstraction and modularity that can aid the system specification process. In this section, we present an overview of the concept of "multi–level" specification [14] that provides a much more powerful capability in terms of abstraction, generalization, reusability, and separation of concerns.

The key idea behind multi–level specification is *nondeterminism*. Nondeterminism is viewed in this scheme as a mechanism for capturing generalization and abstraction. Our inclusive notion of nondeterminism extends this even further. Thus, an HMS machine with nondeterministic transitions can be construed as representing an entire class of behaviors or, equivalently, specifying a class of related systems. The main goal then is to devise a method of choosing a specific behavior or system in a particular situation. In our approach, this is accomplished by using higher–level "policy HMS machines," that define dynamic goals or requirements, along with heuristic guidelines for achieving them. As a consequence, a unified method is obtained for specifying both requirements and conceptual design of a system. In addition, a significant amount of the details of a specification can be left to an automatic search process. This is somewhat analogous to the use of an expert system, in which the inference engine removes much of the drudgery in defining the control aspects of a rule system. In our framework, policy machines define goals that are to be achieved through "plans," which are sequences of sets of nondeterministic transitions in a basic HMS machine of the type discussed in the previous section. The process of generating such plans has much in common with model-based planning in AI [12]. A formal notion of consistency is the key for establishing a meaningful combination of policy and basic HMS machines for multi–level specification of systems.

The basic idea behind multi–level specification is to consider a list of machines $(H_1, H_2, ..., H_n)$, such that H_1 is a basic nondeterministic HMS machine and each H_i, for $i > 1$, is a high–level "policy HMS machine" (to be defined shortly) that establishes constraints on the behavior of all the H_j, for $1 \leq j < i$. In combination, then $(H_1, H_2, ..., H_n)$ form a multi–level specification, in which separation of concerns can be established and a high degree of modularity and reusability is provided. For example, a lower–level machine can often be modified without affecting higher–level machines, indicating a different design concept for achieving the same requirements. Similarly, higher–level machines can be modified, indicating different requirements on the same conceptual design structure. The modification of an intermediate–level machine corresponds to (1) a change in the strategy for achieving a given goal within a design framework or (2) the imposition of new constraints at a particular level of abstraction. Such a viewpoint is in direct contrast to the "refinement approach" to specification [2] which is commonly used in the field of computer security. In the refinement approach, a top–level specification is gradually refined to provide more detail, finally resulting in a stand–alone detailed specification. In such a scheme, modularity and reusability are much more difficult to achieve as requirements, certain aspects of design or strategies for achieving goals change.

We now turn to the formalization of the main concepts of multi–level specification. In this paper, we consider only the 2–level specification of MS machines without input or output ports. Further details can be found in [14].

Definition 10. Let $H = (S, \Gamma_D, \Gamma_N)$ be an MS machine without ports, then $H' = (S', \Gamma_D', \Gamma_N')$ is a "policy machine" for H if (1) $S' \subseteq S$, and (2) Γ_D' and Γ_N' are, respectively, the sets of deterministic and nondeterministic "policy transitions" of H' of the form

$$\text{(PRIMARIES) (CONTROL}_B, \text{CONTROL}_M, \text{CONTROL}_E) \rightarrow$$
$$\text{(CONSEQUENTS),}$$

where PRIMARIES $\subseteq S$, CONSEQUENTS $\subseteq S$ and each CONTROL_i for $i = B, M$ or E is a predicate in TIL with literals from the set S. For a particular policy transition $\gamma = (A, B, ...)(P, Q, R) \rightarrow (E, F, ...)$ in $\Gamma_D' \cup \Gamma_N'$, we define $\text{PRIMS}(\gamma) = (A, B, ...)$, $\text{CNTRL}_B(\gamma) = P$, $\text{CNTRL}_M(\gamma) = Q$, $\text{CNTRL}_E(\gamma) = R$ and $\text{CNSQS}(\gamma) = (E, F, ...)$. The predicates $\text{CNTRL}_B(\gamma)$, $\text{CNTRL}_M(\gamma)$ and $\text{CNTRL}_E(\gamma)$ are called, respectively, the "beginning control," the "middle control" and the "end control" of γ.

Figure 3 presents an example of our visual notation for policy HMS machines. In this case, u is the only policy transition with

$PRIMS(u) = A$, $CNTRL_B(u) = [-5, 0]C$, $CNTRL_M(u) = C \wedge \neg D$,
$CNTRL_E(u) = <-10, 0> A$ and $CNSQS(u) = B$.

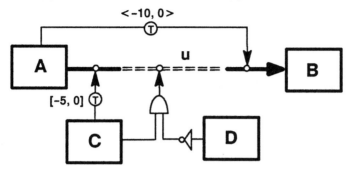

Figure 3. Example of a Policy MS Machine

Only an informal definition of execution of policy machines will be provided in this paper. Note that in a 2–level specification (H_1, H_2), since the states of a policy HMS machine H_2 are also states of H_1, there is a unique evaluation of all predicates. The firing of a transition then is achieved through the firing of a "plan," or a *sequence of sets* of transitions in H_1. The basic machine H_1 normally will be highly nondeterministic, signifying a "generic specification" of a class of related systems or behaviors. The policy machine H_2 imposes dynamic constraints on the behavior of H_1. Thus, the execution of a deterministic policy transition such as u of Figure 3 is achieved through the execution of a lower–level plan $p = \Gamma_1\Gamma_2...\Gamma_n$ in H_1, where each Γ_i is a firing set in H_1. This process goes through the following steps:

(a) u "begins" by the firing of Γ_1 in H_1 if its primary state A and its beginning control are both true

(b) If u has begun firing, it "continues" if its middle control remains true through $\Gamma_2...\Gamma_{(n-1)}$

(c) u "terminates" firing through Γ_n, assuming that its end control is true.

In general, corresponding to a plan $p = \Gamma_1\Gamma_2...\Gamma_n$ for H_1, one can define a "policy plan" for H_2 as $p' = [(\Gamma_1', \mathcal{C}_1', \mathcal{T}_1')(\Gamma_2', \mathcal{C}_2', \mathcal{T}_2')...(\Gamma_n', \mathcal{C}_n', \mathcal{T}_n')]$, where for each i, Γ_i' is the set of policy transitions that *begin* firing, $\mathcal{C}_i'$ is the set of policy transitions that *continue* firing, and $\mathcal{T}_i'$ is the set of policy transitions that *terminate* firing. In [14], an outline of requirements for "consistency" of plans and policy plans for n–level specifications is presented, along with an example of a 3–level specification of a steam generator monitoring system.

The concept of multi–level specification provides a modular approach to specifying real–time systems at multiple levels of abstraction that offers a high degree of reusability and perspicuity. In a recent application of the HMS methodology to the specification of a fragment of a C^3I system, multi–level specification was the key element that simplified the representation and allowed the complexity of the system to be hidden, without jeopardizing the completeness of the representation.

VERIFYING PROPERTIES OF HMS MACHINES

A variety of techniques for verification of specifications have been proposed in the literature. For real–time systems, two common approaches have been based on (1) "model checking" using variations of the branching temporal logic CTL [6, 9] and (2) the comparison of languages accepted by a requirements–oriented automaton and a representation of an implementation [20, 22]. For standard temporal logic, theorem proving methods based on the tableau method and resolution [1] have also been investigated.

An important issue in the verification of properties of specifications is the language in which the properties to be verified are expressed. For example, a simple property such as "state A will be true every n moments (for $n > 1$)" is not expressible in pure temporal logic [27] or CTL, while it is expressible in "extended temporal logic" [27]. Also, CTL–like logics, in general, do not address the verification of properties relating to the past, present and the future in a uniform manner. The method of [20] permits the verification of arbitrary "safety properties," but at the cost of dealing with infinite–state automata.

In [11], a general method of representing and verifying safety properties of MS/TIL_0 machines was presented. In this scheme, the negation of a safety property is represented in terms of an "extended state," and "correctness–preserving" transformations are used to prove that the extended state is unreachable. Since it can be shown that any extended temporal logic formula is representable as an extended state of an MS machine, this results in a verification method for all safety properties of MS machines expressible in extended temporal logic. The key advantage of the HMS machine approach compared to other automata–based methods is that safety properties are expressible *within* the same representation as the specification itself.

In [15], a model checking approach for MS/TIL machines was presented, for which the properties to be evaluated were expressed in BTIL. Clearly model checking can be used to verify BTIL formulae on the extended states of an MS machines as well.

The model checking and transformation techniques for verifying properties of HMS machines are complementary in several respects. Model checking is a mechanical decision procedure, essentially involving a forward branching execution. On the other hand, the transformational approach has much in common with theorem proving, relies on a heuristic choice of transformations to be applied and involves mainly backward execution with occasional forward execution. The availability of both verification methods for HMS machines is particularly important for the following reason. There exist some simple properties that are difficult to verify by model checking, but are extremely easy to prove by transformations. At the same time, there are properties that are difficult to verify by transformations, but are relatively easy to prove using model checking.

In the following two subsections we review the highlights of the model checking and transformational methods for verifying properties of HMS machines. For details, see [15, 11]. In this section, we consider only HMS machines that have a finite set of states and contain controls that use present or finite past TIL operators only. These might be referred as "causal machines" since execution in them does not depend on future markings.

Model checking

In model checking for an MS machine H, we begin with a particular marking sequence ..., M_{-1}, M_0 as the root of a "computation graph" and we designate a possible "future" marking sequence M_1, M_2, ..., as a path of the computation graph starting at the root. Each new marking potentially creates a new node, for which, we record all "relevant" past markings. Any BTIL formula can then be evaluated by the traversal of such a graph in a straightforward manner. The following definition helps limit both the marking history that must be maintained at a node and the size of the computation graph.

Definition 11. The "maximum relevant history" of a state s of an HMS machine H, denoted by MRH(s), is the absolute value of the largest negative temporal parameter for s in all the controls of H.

Thus, for the machine of Figure 2.1, $MRH(A) = 10$, $MRH(D) = MRH(E) = 5$, $MRH(C) = MRH(B) = 0$.

Observation 1. The maximum marking history for a state s that needs to be kept at a node of a computation tree of an MS machine is MRH(s).

This limits the amount of information that needs to be stored at a node. In many cases, even a smaller limit on marking history can be derived.

Observation 2. If two nodes N_1 and N_2 of a computation graph contain identical marking histories, then N_1 and N_2 can be coalesced into a single node.

Observation 3. The number of distinct nodes of the computation graph of an MS machine H with state space S is less than or equal to

$$G(H) = 2^{\sum_{s \in S}(MRH(s) + 1)}$$

This follows from the fact that for each node s, the markings of its relevant past histories can take on only $2^{(MRH(s) + 1)}$ different values. This result also gives an indication of the savings in state space that the HMS machine concept provides compared to traditional automata. It is possible to construct an MS machine H with state space S such that the smallest equivalent traditional automaton would have $G(H)$ states. As noted in [15], logarithmic savings are achieved even compared to cartesian products of traditional automata.

We now introduce a notation that helps simplify the recording of computation graphs significantly.

Notation. The empty firing set of an HMS machine is denoted by ϕ. A plan consisting of the repetition of ϕ over n consecutive time steps is denoted by ϕ^n.

In the recording of a computation graph, we label each arc by the firing set that causes a change in marking. It is often the case that for a large number of consecutive steps no transitions are enabled or because of our inclusive notion of nondeterminism no transitions are actually fired. Such a sequence of steps can be abbreviated by a single arc with the label ϕ^n, for an appropriate fixed or parametric n. Note that for a traditional automaton, each such individual step, in general, would require a separate arc and an associated node. Figure 4 depicts a very simple example of an MS machine and its abbreviated computation graph, in which only histories of states that are true and are needed for execution are recorded at the nodes. Properties of the machine expressed in BTIL can then be evaluated by the traversal of such an abbreviated computation graph. A larger example and further explanation can be found in [15].

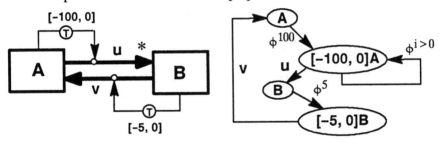

Figure 4. A Simple MS Machine and its Computation Graph

Correctness–Preserving Transformations

A "safety property" for an HMS machine is a behavioral characteristic that must always remain true, and once it is violated it will never become true again. A simple example of safety property is a "deadline property" which indicates that some event must always happen within a particular time. Consider the deadline property "state B will always occur within 20 moments of A." Formally, this can be stated in terms of a past TIL formula as $\Box p$, where $p = (O(-20)A \Rightarrow \ <-20, 0 > B)$. The safety property p holds then if and only if the extended state $\neg p = (O(-20)A \land [-20, 0]\neg B)$ is *unreachable*. Figure 5 presents a graphic view of such an extended state.

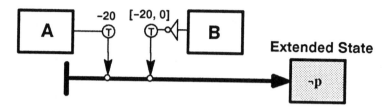

Figure 5. Extended State as a Deadline Safety Property

In this section, we consider only safety properties expressible in extended temporal logic. As noted in [20], the only safety properties that are not expressible in this manner are those definable by automata with infinite states. Preliminary studies have been made on an extension of HMS machines that can accommodate even such properties.

In [11] a set of "correctness–preserving" transformations on MS/TIL$_0$ machines were presented that modify the structure of a machine, without affecting its behavior. The main result of [11] is as follows:

> If a safety property is true for an MS machine, then there exists a sequence of transformations that will demonstrate this by making the associated extended state isolated, thus proving its unreachability.

Figure 6 depicts two examples of transformations from [11]. Such transformations are applied repeatedly until the extended state representing a safety property becomes isolated. Nine transformations were shown to be sufficient in [11] for demonstrating the truth of any safety property definable in terms of an extended state. A larger set of transformations were defined in [11] that can make this process simpler.

The transformational approach of [11] dealt with MS/TIL$_0$ machines only. However, since a behaviorally equivalent MS/TIL$_0$ machine can be derived constructively for every MS/TIL machine [15], the transformational method can also be used to verify safety properties of MS/TIL machines.

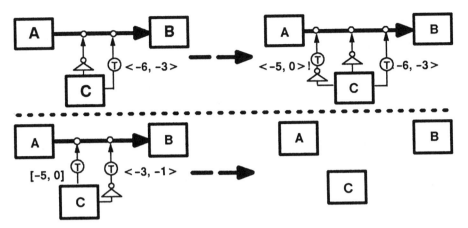

Figure 6 Examples of Correctness–Preserving Transformations

Scheduling of Tasks with Temporal Constraints

Given a multi–level HMS specification, a key problem is the derivation of plans for satisfying policy transitions. While it is often the case that by ignoring controls, a "potential plan" can be derived by a search process over the nondeterministic transitions of a basic HMS machine, it is usually not easy to derive a "schedule" for such a plan. Recall that a plan $p = \Gamma_1 \Gamma_2 ... \Gamma_n$ is a sequence of set of firing sets that implements a policy transition. Thus, firing the set of nondeterministic transitions in Γ_1 followed by the firing of the transitions in Γ_2 and so on through Γ_n is assumed to lead from an initial set of states in an HMS machine to a *desired* set of states. In the presence of controls, however, temporal and logical constraints defined in the HMS machine must be satisfied for the transitions in p. In this section, we review a general method presented in [14] for deriving "delays" between the consecutive steps of p in order to satisfy such constraints. These delays essentially define a schedule for p.

A plan can also be considered as defining the execution of a set of concurrent tasks, for which precedence as well as temporal constraints have been defined. Thus, scheduling of plans in the HMS framework can have applications in the scheduling of concurrent tasks in a multi–processing computer system, manufacturing automation, robotic control and so on.

In order to derive a schedule for a plan $p = \Gamma_1\Gamma_2...\Gamma_n$, we define its associated "variable delay plan" as $p' = \phi^{i_1}\Gamma_1\phi^{i_2}\Gamma_2...\phi^{i_n}\Gamma_n$, where ϕ is the empty set of transitions. In p', a wait of length i_k is interposed before the transitions in Γ_k are fired, for $k = 1,...$, n. If solutions for i_k, for $k = 1, ..., $ n, can be found that cause p' to satisfy all the controls of the associated HMS machine, then a feasible schedule for p will have been found. This can also be considered as a limited verification method for determining the consistency of a multi–level specification.

The key element of our scheduling algorithm is the application of a set of "precondition laws" and a set of "postcondition laws" [14] that allow the symbolic execution of plans and the derivation of linear inequalities in terms of the parameters i_k. This will be illustrated for the example in Figure 7.

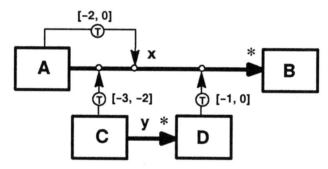

Figure 7. An Example of a Scheduling Problem

In the MS machine of Figure 7 we assume that (1) initially, the states A and C are true, while B and D are false, and (2) the goal is to make state B true. For this purpose, it is clear that the transitions y and x must be fired. The question is "when should y and x be fired?" Formally, we define a potential plan $p = yx$ and an associated variable delay plan $p' = \phi^i y \, \phi^j x$. The parameters i and j define a schedule for plan p. Intuitively, to execute p', we wait i moments and fire y then we wait j moments and fire x. If i and j are chosen in a way that the controls on x are all satisfied, then we have a feasible schedule for p.

We denote the empty plan by [ ] and the marking of the machine after the execution of a plan q as M[q]. Then, for the MS machine in Figure 7, our postcondition laws permit the derivation of the symbolic facts that will be true as the plan p′ is executed. In particular, we can deduce that

$$M[\phi^i y \phi^j] \models [-i-j-1, 0]A \wedge [-i-j-1, -j-1]C \wedge [-j, 0]D \wedge [-j, 0]\neg C.$$

At the same time, our precondition laws allow us to derive the critical fact that *must be true* in order to enable the transition x in p′:

$$M[\phi^i y \phi^j] \models [-2, 0]A \wedge [-3, -2]C \wedge [-1, 0]D$$

From these two sets of facts, we can derive the following set of inequalities:

$$-i-j-1 \le -2, \quad -i-j-1 \le -3, \quad -j-1 \le -2, \quad -j \le -2 \qquad (*)$$

By solving for i and j, we derive the parametric solution $p′ = \phi^{i>0} y \phi x$. Therefore, a feasible schedule for p is to wait one or more moments, fire y, wait one more moment exactly and then fire x.

Our scheduling algorithm has similarities with the method of temporal constraint satisfaction in [8]. The main differences are two–fold: (1) in [8] the inequalities of the form (*) are assumed to be given, while we *derive* them from a model of the system, and (2) only sets of constraints of the form $(a_1 \le X_j - X_i \le b_1) \vee \ldots \vee (a_n \le X_j - X_i \le b_n)$ are considered in [8], whereas much more general types of temporal constraints can be derived in the application of our scheduling method.

CONCLUSIONS

The HMS machine concept has served as a fruitful paradigm for the investigation of a wide class of problems relating to real–time systems. Specifically, (1) highly compact, visual and formal representations of complex real–time systems can be defined in terms of HMS machines, (2) multi–level HMS machines provide a powerful approach to reusability of specifications, (3) model checking and correctness–preserving transformations offer two complementary approaches to verification of safety, deadline and other properties of hard real–time systems, and (4) a model–based framework is provided for investigating problems relating to real–time planning and scheduling. Extensions to the theory hold the promise of providing a formal specification and verification method for real–time databases, and systematic methodologies for reasoning about systems under conditions of uncertainty. Areas of potential application include distributed computer systems, network management, protocols, hardware and software design, command and control systems, and design or decision support for a variety of other systems where complex interactions among subelements occur and time is a critical factor.

ACKNOWLEDGMENTS

The author is indebted to M.K. Franklin for his contributions to the transformational proof method, the scheduling approach, and earlier versions of formalization of HMS machines. He is also indebted to R. Iyer for useful comments on earlier drafts of this paper and his participation in the formulation of the temporal logic TIL and the model checking concepts.

REFERENCES

[1] M. Abadi, "Temporal-logic theorem proving," *Dissertation*, Stanford Univ., March 1987.

[2] M. Abadi, and L. Lamport, "The existence of refinement mappings," *Proc. Logic in Computer Science Conference*, Edinburgh, Scotland, July 1988.

[3] P. Aczel, *Non-Well-Founded Sets*, Lecture Notes 14, Center for the Study of Language and Information, University of Chicago Press, 1988.

[4] J.R. Büchi, "On a decision method in restricted second order arithmetic," *Proc. Int. Cong. Logic, Methodology and Philosophy of Science, 1960*, Stanford Univ. Press, 1962, pp. 1–12.

[5] S.-C. Cheng, J.A. Stankovic and K. Ramamritham, "Scheduling algorithms for hard real-time systems – a brief survey," *Technical Report*, No. 87-55, COINS Dept., University of Massachusetts, 1987.

[6] E.M. Clarke, E.A. Emerson, and A.P. Sistla, "Automatic verification of finite-state concurrent systems using temporal logic," *ACM Trans. on Programming Languages and Systems*, Vol. 8, No. 2, 1986, pp. 244-263.

[7] L. Da-Hai and T.S.E. Maibaum, "Developing a high level specification formalism," in *Formal Methods: Theory and Practice*, P.N. Scharbach (Ed.), CRC Press, Boca Baton, FL, 1988.

[8]   R. Dechter, I. Meiri and J. Pearl, "Temporal constraint networks," *Proc. First Int. Conf. on Principles of Knowledge Representation and Reasoning*, Toronto, Canada, May 1989.

[9]   E.A. Emerson, A.K. Mok, A.P. Sistla, and J. Srinivasan, "Quantitative temporal reasoning," *Manuscript*, University of Texas, Austin, TX, January 1989.

[10] E.A. Emerson and J. Srinivasan, "Branching time temporal logic," *Linear Time Branching Time and Partial Order in Logics and Models of Concurrency*, J.W. de Bakker, W.-P. de Roever and G. Rozenberg (Eds.), LNCS 354, Springer–Verlag, Berlin, 1989, pp. 123–172.

[11] M.K. Franklin and A. Gabrielian, "A transformational method for verifying safety properties in real–time systems," *Proc. 10th Real–Time Systems Symposium*, Santa Monica, CA, December 5–7, 1989, pp. 112–123.

[12] A. Gabrielian, "Reasoning about real–time systems with temporal interval logic constraints on multi–state automata," *Proc. Space Operations, Applications and Research Symposium*, Albuquerque, NM, June 26–28, 1990, pp. 368–374.

[13] A. Gabrielian and M. K. Franklin, "State–based specification of complex real–time systems," *Proc. IEEE Real–Time Systems Symposium*, 1988, pp. 2–11.

[14] A. Gabrielian and M.K. Franklin, "Multi–level specification and verification of real–time software," *Proc. 12th Int. Conf. on Software Engineering*, March 26–30, 1990, Nice, France, pp. 52–62. Revised version to appear in *Communications of the ACM*, May 1991.

[15] A. Gabrielian and R. Iyer, "Integrating automata and temporal logic: a framework for specification of real–time systems and software," *The Unified Computation Laboratory*, C.M. Rattray and R.G. Clark (editors), Institute of Mathematics and its Applications, Oxford University Press, 1991.

[16] C. Ghezzi, D. Madrioli, et al., "A general way to put time in Petri nets," *Proc. Fifth Int. Workshop on Software Specification and Design*, Pittsburgh, PA, May 1989, pp. 60–67.

[17] A. Gabrielian and M.E. Stickney, "Hierarchical representation of causal knowledge," *Proc. WESTEX–87 IEEE Expert Systems Conference*, June 1987, pp. 82–89.

[18] *International Workshop on Timed Petri Nets*, Torino, Italy, July 1–3, 1985, IEEE Computer Society Press, 1985.

[19] F. Jahanian and D.A. Stuart, "A method for verifying properties of Modechart specifications," *Proc. IEEE Real–Time Systems Symposium*, 1988, pp. 12–21.

[20] N. Klarlund and F.B. Schneider, "Verifying safety properties using non–deterministic infinite–state automata," *Tech. Report TR–89–1036*, Cornell Univ., Ithaca, N.Y., Sept. 1989.

[21] T.J. Laffey, et al., "Real–time knowledge based systems," *AI Magazine*, Vol.9, No.1, Spring 1988, pp.27–45.

[22] N.A. Lynch and H. Attiya, "Using mappings to prove timing properties," *ACM Symposium on Principles of Distributed Computing*, 1990, pp. 265–280.

[23] P.M. Melliar–Smith, "A graphical representation of interval logic," in *Proc. Concurrency 88*, LNCS 335, Springer–Verlag, 1988, pp, 106–120.

[24] Z. Manna and A. Pnueli, "The anchored version of the temporal framework," *Proc. Linear Time, Branching Time and Partial Order in Logics and Models for Concurrency*, LNCS 354, Springer–Verlag, 1989, pp. 201–284.

[25] J.S. Ostroff, "Deciding properties of timed transition models," *IEEE Trans. on Parallel and Distributed Systems*, Vol. 1, No. 2, April 1990, pp. 170–183.

[26] A. Pnueli and E. Harel, "Applications of temporal logic to the specification of real–time systems (extended abstract)," *Proc. Symp. Formal Techniques in Real–Time and Fault–Tolerant Systems*, LNCS 331, Springer–Verlag, 1988, pp. 84–98.

[27] P. Wolper, "Temporal logic can be more expressive," *Information and Control*, Vol. 56, 1983, pp. 72–99.

CHAPTER 7

Concepts and Models for Real-Time Concurrency[1]

Eric Shade
Department of Computer Science
Whitmore Laboratory
The Pennsylvania State University
University Park, Pa 16802

K.T. Narayana
ORA Corporation
(Odyssey Research Associates, Inc.)
301A Harris B Dates Drive
Ithaca, NY 14850

Abstract

We give a compositional denotational semantics for components of a small low level language. The semantics is given in a limited parallelism model with realistic assumptions about the execution environment. Among the modeling issues considered are:

- The semantics of the individual program segments.
- The number of physical processors.
- The relative speeds of the processors, i.e. local clocks.
- The manner in which processors are assigned to processes.
- Constraints on shared memeory access.
- Scheduling disciplines.

The model can be extended to account for the real-time programming concepts such as those being defined in the Ada 9X revision effort. The semantic model serves as a basis for correctness theories of real-time programs in a limited parallelism model.

INTRODUCTION

A real-time program is a concurrent program which must meet certain time constraints. It consists of one or more sequential *processes* which are run in parallel, *i.e.* multiple physical processors are used so that the executions of the processes will overlap in time. Processes have the ability to cooperate with one other. Cooperation between processes consists

---

[1]Work reported in this paper has been partially supported by the Office of Naval Research under the grant number #N00014-89-J-1171. Any opinions, findings, conclusions, or recommendations contained herein are those of the authors and not of the department of defense.

of a combination of synchronization, communication, and mutual exclusion. Real-time programs are mostly written in imperative programming languages such as Modula-2, Ada, CHILL, etc.

Concurrent programs alone are difficult to reason about. Real-time constraints add another level of complexity. Consider the program

$$S_1; y := y + 5 \parallel S_2; y := y * 3,$$

where the initial value of y is zero. Assume that there are two physical processors available, statements S_1 and S_2 do not modify y, and that the assignments to y are mutually exclusive. When the program terminates, y will be equal to 5 or 15. If the program must deliver the value 15 to be correct, it must be possible to prove that S_1 will finish before S_2. Abstractly, such a proof depends on the statements S_1 and S_2. In practice, it also depends on the relative speeds of the processors which are executing those statements.

Real-time programs are orders of magnitude more complex to reason about than sequential programs. Unfortunately, they are used in the most critical of applications, such as navigation systems, patient monitoring systems, etc., where failure to meet the time constraints can be costly or fatal. Further, the real-time behavior of such systems is highly dependent of the physical execution environment. Therefore we need formal methods for reasoning about real-time programs which reflect this dependence. To be of any practical value, a formal analysis must take into account at least the following factors:

- The semantics of the individual program statements.

- The number of physical processors available.

- The relative speeds of the processors.

- The manner in which processors are assigned to processes.

- Constraints on access to the shared memory.

In this paper we provide a denotational semantics for components of a representative real-time programming language L which takes all of these factors into account. The semantics incorporates the notion of time and makes local assumptions about the execution environment, and then applies global verification conditions to ensure that the assumptions are correct. The accuracy and complexity of the semantic model is directly proportional to the strength of the assumptions. In order to develop a computationally tractable theory it is necessary to weaken the assumptions as much as possible. One of the purposes of this research is to identify how to weaken the assumptions while retaining the ability to prove strong temporal properties of programs.

The work reported in this paper is part of an attempt to study semantic models, language concepts, and proof theories for real-time concurrency under the program *Fundamental Initiatives in Real-Time Computing* conducted by the Office of Naval Research.

TIME, ENVIRONMENTS AND LANGUAGES

In this section, we define our notion of time, describe the physical programming environment we will consider, introduce the language L and its informal semantics, and define the basic execution models.

Time

We distinguish between *real* time, which is measured in seconds, and *conceptual* time, which is measured in discrete units called "ticks". Since real time is continuous, it can be difficult to measure, and intervals may have irrational length which can be computationally troublesome. Thus we assume that all time is conceptual. Provided we assume that the grain of time is small enough to distinguish temporally distinct events, this view of time is sufficient. Formal analysis thus occurs in the conceptual time domain, and if necessary conceptual time can be mapped back to real-time.

The Physical Environment

Real-time programs are mostly executed on a MIMD (multiple-instruction, multiple-data) *shared-memory machine* which consists of one or more physical processors running concurrently. We will always assume that there are ρ processors, numbered from 1 to ρ. The value of ρ is fixed for a given program, but need not be the same for all programs. Each physical processor has its own local memory, and in addition there is a single shared memory which can be accessed by any processor.

We assume that there is a conceptual global clock which acts as a standard for measurement. Each physical processor has its own conceptual local clock which runs at a fixed speed relative to the global clock. Each "tick" of a local clock takes a discrete non-zero amount of global time, which is the *speed* of the processor. The function θ maps processors to their speeds. For example, if $\theta(4) = 3$ and $\theta(1) = 2$, then processor 4 runs 50% more slowly than processor 1. Execution of a machine instruction takes one "tick" of the local clock.

Many different schemes have been devised to control access to the shared memory. For simplicity we assume that each shared variable in a program occupies one location in the shared memory. We will consider the following models:

- CREW (concurrent read, exclusive write). Any number of processes may read from a single variable simultaneously. If a variable is being written to, no other read or write of that variable can occur simultaneously.

- EREW (exclusive read, exclusive write). There can be at most one read or write access of a variable at a time.

- Bus-arbitration. Access to the shared-memory is controlled by a single bus which can only service one request at a time. No simultaneous accesses of any kind are permitted, even of different variables.

In all of the models, a processor can only access one variable at a time, although it could conceivably be *waiting* to access more than one variable. We assume that all memory accesses will be resolved within a finite period of time. δ denotes the maximum amount of global time that a process must wait before it is granted access to a variable. The function δ is a parameter of the model, and is obviously dependent on ρ.

The Language L

Most standard concurrent programming languages have a cumbersome syntax and a large number of constructs which are important in practice but of no theoretical interest. Therefore we will define a language L which captures all of the essential features of existing languages but avoids any unnecessary baggage. The syntax of L is shown in figure .

A program Π is the parallel composition of one or more sequential processes. We do not consider nested parallelism, in which a process may contain parallel subprocesses. A process consists of one or more statements $S_1; S_2; \ldots; S_k$, where ";" denotes sequential composition.

The assignment statement $v := E$ has the usual operational meaning: the expression E is fully evaluated and the resulting value is assigned to the variable v. Expressions and variables can take on any values from the domain C; we assume that all expressions and assignments are type-correct. We use $\otimes$ and $\ominus$ to denote arbitrary binary and unary operations over C, respectively. All shared variable accesses are atomic. To avoid having to deal with blocks and scope, we assume that the local variables of distinct processes are disjoint.

The delay E command is an uninterruptible instruction which consumes $n + e$ local time units, where e is the value of the expression E and n is the amount of time required to evaluate E.

sync ℓ is a synchronization command; when executed by a process P it forces P to wait until some other process Q executes a sync ℓ command. At that point both processes proceed independently.

The statement $I \equiv [\parallel_{i=1}^{n} G_i \rightarrow S_i]$ is an *alternative (guarded) command*. In general each guard G_i has the form $E; C$, where E is a Boolean expression and C is either a sync or delay command. A guard $E; C$ is *open* if E is true and C succeeds. Note that a delay command always succeeds, but a sync command need not. I is executed by evaluating all of the guards G_i *simultaneously*. If none of the guards are open, then the alternative command fails and the program aborts. Otherwise, the first guard G_j to become open is selected and the corresponding statement S_j is executed. If two or more guards become open simultaneously, a nondeterministic choice is made.

$*I$ is a repetitive command. The statement I is repeatedly executed as described above, with the exception that if no guards are open, the command terminates rather than abort.

$\ll_\ell S \gg$ is an indexed atomic action, where ℓ is the index. It enforces a limited form of mutual exclusion. For all distinct pairs of indexed atomic actions $(\ll_\ell S_1 \gg, \ll_\ell S_2 \gg)$ appearing in a program, the executions of S_1

Domains

$$c \in \mathcal{C} \quad \equiv \quad \text{constants}$$
$$\ell \in \mathcal{L} \quad \equiv \quad \text{synchronization labels}$$
$$x \in \mathcal{V}_L \quad \equiv \quad \text{local variables}$$
$$y \in \mathcal{V}_S \quad \equiv \quad \text{shared variables}$$
$$v \in \mathcal{V} = \mathcal{V}_L \cup \mathcal{V}_S \quad \equiv \quad \text{variables}$$

Syntactic Categories

$$\Pi \quad \in \quad \text{programs}$$
$$C \quad \in \quad \text{guard components}$$
$$E \quad \in \quad \text{expressions}$$
$$G \quad \in \quad \text{guards}$$
$$I \quad \in \quad \text{if-commands}$$
$$S \quad \in \quad \text{sequential processes}$$

Language Syntax

$$\Pi \quad ::= \quad \|_{i=1}^{n} S_i$$
$$S \quad ::= \quad v := E \mid C \mid I \mid *I \mid S; S \mid \ll_\ell S \gg$$
$$I \quad ::= \quad [\,\|_{i=1}^{n} G_i \to S_i\,]$$
$$G \quad ::= \quad E \mid C \mid E; C$$
$$C \quad ::= \quad \text{sync } \ell \mid \text{delay } E$$
$$E \quad ::= \quad (E \otimes E) \mid (\ominus E) \mid v \mid c$$

Figure 1: The Language L

and S_2 must be disjoint, *i.e.* they may not overlap in time.

Execution Models

In order to be able to reason about concurrent programs, it is necessary to make assumptions about the number of available processors, their speeds, and the manner in which processes are executed. These assumptions collectively form the *execution model*. There are three basic models.

Interleaving

The interleaving model is the weakest (least restrictive) of the execution models. Processor speeds are ignored. The only restriction enforced is that the relative order of actions within a process is preserved. Conceptually, the actions of the individual processes are "shuffled" together in all possible ways. Any of these shuffles is a legal execution of the program. This model is useful because it imposes minimal implementation restrictions. A legal program execution in any other model will also be legal in the interleaving model. A program which is proven correct with respect to the interleaving model will therefore run correctly on *any* physical implementation.

The difficulty is that it is not possible to prove strong temporal properties in the interleaving model. For example, in the program $S_1; S_2$, the strongest property that one can hope to prove in general is "if S_1 terminates then S_2 will *eventually* be executed." There is usually no way to infer how much time it will take.

Maximal Parallelism

In the maximal parallelism model [9,18], the number of processors, ρ, is equal to the number of processes. Each process is allocated a processor which it uses until program termination. The local clocks of the processors are all synchronized with the global clock. During one "tick" of the clock, all of the processors simultaneously perform one machine instruction. In addition, *maximal throughput* is enforced. Given a choice between executing an action or idling (possibly waiting for some event to occur), a processor must always choose to perform an action as soon as possible. This *locally* maximizes processor utilization, but does not guarantee that the global execution time of the program will be minimal.

This is the strongest model. The actions of a process will not be delayed or interrupted except as explicitly programmed. Unfortunately, it is not a practical model. In large systems which consist of hundreds or thousands of processes it is not feasible to have one processor per process. Further, system hardware often consists of collection of computers and physical devices from a variety of different manufacturers, and it is optimistic to expect that they all run at the same speed.

Limited Parallelism

Limited parallelism models [16], are a compromise between interleaving and maximal parallelism. ρ may be less than the number of processes. Maximal throughput is enforced, with the added constraint that processors may not go unused if there is a process waiting for execution. Since there may not be enough processors to go around, process *scheduling* is required to make good use of the available processors. In order to make our semantic model as general as possible, we will make minimal assumptions about the scheduler. As long as it does not violate the program semantics, the scheduler is free to move processes between processors at will. However we do require that there be a delay of at least one global time unit before a process is switched from one processor to another. This is to prevent pointless process swapping. We call such a scheduler an *instantaneous* scheduler. Of course, real schedulers are far more complex than this, but it provides an excellent basis for a formal model which can easily be enhanced to account for more realistic systems.

It is important to note that limited parallelism and *interleaving* are very distinct models. Interleaving models represent the minimal assumptions necessary to ensure qualitatively correct execution of concurrent programs. They impose the least possible implementation restrictions. Limited parallelism, on the other hand, is a real-time model which enforces maximal throughput, and makes the processor resources explicit. By choosing ρ to equal the number of processes and choosing $\theta(i)$ to be one for $1 \leq i \leq \rho$, maximal parallelism is just a special case of limited parallelism.

LINEAR-HISTORY SEMANTICS

In order to be able to reason about programs, we must have a formal understanding of them. The approach that we will use is to formally define the semantics of L denotationally. There are a number of different techniques which could be employed, but we have adopted the linear-history style semantics of [5]. In this section we provide a general discussion of linear-history semantics.

In the denotational approach to semantics, the idea is to define the meaning of a program as a continuous function on a suitable domain. In a linear-history style semantics, the semantic domain $\mathcal{D}$ consists of non-empty, prefix-closed sets of state-history pairs. A state-history pair is written $\langle s, h \rangle$, where s is the *state* and h is the *history*. The pair $\langle s, h \rangle$ denotes a computation: intuitively, s is the state at the end of the computation and h is the sequence of actions which led to s.

The state domain is denoted by $\mathcal{S}$. It can be partitioned into a set $\mathcal{S}_P$ of *proper* states, and a set $\mathcal{S}_I$ of *improper* states. Usually, a proper state is a "snapshot" of program memory which records the values of the variables at a given instant of time. For simple languages, a proper state may simply indicate successful termination. The improper states $\mathcal{S}_I$ will always contain $\perp$, which denotes an incomplete computation. Another common improper state is ∇, used to denote nondeterministic failure. Naturally, the precise choice of $\mathcal{S}$ depends on the language being modeled.

A history records a sequence of abstract actions. The ith element of a history h contains the observable actions of a program at time unit i. Typical *observables* include waiting for synchronization, accessing a shared variable, and executing an atomic action. The set of all observables is denoted by O. Since a program may contain two or more processes running in parallel, it is possible that two different processes may be simultaneously performing actions which are denoted by the same observable. Therefore, the history elements are modeled by *bags* (or *multisets*).

Intuitively, a bag is a "set" in which there may be multiple copies of an element. A bag is denoted by $\{x_1, \ldots, x_n\}$, where the x_i need not be distinct. Formally, for any set X, a *bag* over X is a function $f: X \to \mathcal{N}$ which maps elements of X to natural numbers; $f(x)$ represents the number of occurrences of x in f. We extend the set membership operator "$\in$" to bags by defining $x \in f$ to mean $f(x) > 0$. $\mathcal{B}(X)$ denotes the set of all bags over X.

A history element is a member of $\mathcal{O} = \mathcal{B}(O)$, and the history domain $\mathcal{H}$ equals $\mathcal{P}(\mathcal{O}^*)$. A history is a finite sequence of the form $o_1 o_2 \ldots o_n$, where $o_i \in \mathcal{O}$. The empty history is denoted by ϵ. Since time is discrete, each element of a history corresponds to one "tick" of the clock, and the length of a history is equal to the duration of the computation.

Let h, h' be histories and H be a non-empty set of histories. $|h|$ denotes the length of h, and hh' denotes the usual concatenation of h and h'. If $1 \leq i \leq |h|$ then $h[i]$ denotes the ith element of h, otherwise $h[i] = \{\!\!\{\}\!\!\}$. Some additional operations on histories are defined below.

- $h^n = \textbf{if } n \leq 0 \textbf{ then } \epsilon \textbf{ else } hh^{n-1}$.

- $h[i..j] = \textbf{if } 1 \leq i \leq |h| \wedge i \leq j \textbf{ then } h[i] \ldots h[j] \textbf{ else } \epsilon$.

- $h[i..] = h[i..|h|]$.

- $H[i] = \bigcup_{h \in H} h[i]$.

- $h \prec h' \iff |h| < |h'| \wedge h = h'[1..|h|]$.

- $Cmb(h_1, \ldots, h_n) = H[1] \ldots H[\max\{|h| \mid h \in H\}]$, where $H = \{h_1, \ldots, h_n\}$.

A set $X \subseteq \mathcal{S} \times \mathcal{H}$ is *prefix closed* if $\langle s, h \rangle \in X$ and $h' \prec h$ imply $\langle \perp, h' \rangle \in X$. The *prefix closure* of X is denoted $Cls(X)$ and is given by

$$Cls(X) = X \cup \{\langle \perp, h' \rangle \mid \langle s, h \rangle \in X \wedge h \prec h'\}.$$

The semantic domain $\mathcal{D}$ consists of sets of prefix-closed state-history pairs. Formally,

$$\mathcal{D} = \{Cls(X) \mid X \subseteq (\mathcal{S} \times \mathcal{H}) \wedge X \neq \emptyset\}.$$

$\mathcal{D}$ can be partially ordered by subset inclusion, where the minimal element is $\{\langle \perp, \epsilon \rangle\}$. For $D \in \mathcal{D}$, the natural projections are given by

$$
\begin{aligned}
\pi_{\mathcal{S}}(D) &= \{s \mid \exists h.\langle s, h \rangle \in D\} \\
\pi_{\mathcal{H}}(D) &= \{h \mid \exists s.\langle s, h \rangle \in D\}.
\end{aligned}
$$

For every valid program Π of a given language, we define a function $\mathcal{M}[\![\Pi]\!]: \mathcal{S}_P \to \mathcal{D}$ such that $\mathcal{M}[\![\Pi]\!]s$ denotes the behavior of Π starting from the initial proper state s. The semantics should be compositional; for example, $\mathcal{M}[\![S_1; S_2]\!]s$ (where ";" denotes sequential composition) should be the functional "composition" of $\mathcal{M}[\![S_2]\!]$ and $\mathcal{M}[\![S_1]\!]s$. Unfortunately, such functions cannot be composed in the usual sense because their domain and range are disjoint. To avoid this problem, we introduce the following definitions. Let f be a function from $\mathcal{S}_P$ to $\mathcal{D}$. Then $\tilde{f}: \mathcal{S} \to \mathcal{D}$ and $\hat{f}: \mathcal{D} \to \mathcal{D}$ are given by

$$\tilde{f}(s) = \text{if } s \in \mathcal{S}_P \text{ then } f(s) \text{ else } Cls\{\langle s, \epsilon \rangle\}$$
$$\hat{f}(D) = \{\langle s', hh' \rangle \mid \langle s, h \rangle \in D \land \langle s', h' \rangle \in \tilde{f}(s)\}.$$

We can now write $\mathcal{M}[\![S_1; S_2]\!]s = \widehat{\mathcal{M}}[\![S_2]\!](\mathcal{M}[\![S_1]\!]s)$.

A state-history pair $\langle s, h \rangle$, where $s \in \mathcal{S}_P$, denotes a successful terminating computation with history h. The pair $\langle \perp, h \rangle$ denotes an incomplete computation which is either an approximation of a terminating computation $\langle s, hh' \rangle$, or an element of an infinite sequence of incomplete computations. Thus, if $D \in \mathcal{D}$ is the meaning of a program Π, Π terminates if there exists $\langle s, h \rangle \in D$ such that $s \in \mathcal{S}_P$, and diverges if D contains an infinite set $\{\langle \perp, h_i \rangle \mid i \geq 0\}$ such that $h_i \prec h_{i+1}$. Note that more than one of these possibilities may hold for a nondeterministic program.

FORMAL SEMANTICS OF COMPONENTS OF L

It order to simplify the discussion, we will define the semantics incrementally by considering two sublanguages of L. The modelling of these sublanguages captures most of the important semantic issues associated with real-time programming. Of primary importance are the verification conditions which need to be imposed at parallel composition. The structure of these verification conditions and the difficulties associated with their imposition provide us a significant insight into the complexity of the correctness problem for real-time computing. The sublanguages we consider do not even include alternative and repetitive constructs, so they have little computational power and are basically "toy" languages. However, the full language L is quite realistic and is treated in [16].

Shared Variables: The Language L_A

We consider a small language $L_A \subseteq L$ which contains sequential composition, parallel composition, and assignment. For now we only consider the maximal parallelism model. The main purpose of this section is to illustrate how the shared memory is modeled. The language L_A is defined as follows:

$$
\begin{aligned}
\Pi &::= \quad \|_{i=1}^{n} S_i \\
S &::= \quad v := E \mid S; S \\
E &::= \quad (E \otimes E) \mid (\ominus E) \mid v \mid c
\end{aligned}
$$

$\mathcal{S}_P$, the proper states, is the set of all partial functions $s: \mathcal{V} \to \mathcal{C}$. $s[c/v]$ denotes the state s' which agrees with s except that $s'(v) = c$. For $V \subseteq \mathcal{V}$, $s|V$ denotes the restriction of s to the variables in V. As observables we take the set

$$
O = \{A_{y \to c}, A_{c \to y}, I, W_y \mid c \in \mathcal{C} \wedge y \in \mathcal{V}_S\}.
$$

I denotes a local internal action of a process, a computation which does not involve the shared memory. W_y indicates that a process has requested (or is currently requesting) access to shared variable y but has not yet been granted access. $A_{y \to c}$ indicates that a process is reading the value c from shared variable y, and $A_{c \to y}$ indicates that c is being written to y. The following definitions will be useful, where $o \in \mathcal{O}$:

$$
\begin{aligned}
Reads(y, o) &= \sum_{c \in \mathcal{C}} o(A_{y \to c}) \\
Writes(y, o) &= \sum_{c \in \mathcal{C}} o(A_{c \to y}) \\
Accesses(y, o) &= Reads(y, o) + Writes(y, o).
\end{aligned}
$$

The semantics of an expression E is defined as a function $\mathcal{E}[\![E]\!]: \mathcal{S}_P \to \mathcal{C} \times \mathcal{H}$ as shown below. The presence of (c, h) in $\mathcal{E}[\![E]\!]s$ indicates that one possible evaluation of E starting from the proper state s produces the history h and yields the value c. Note that if an expression E contains a reference to a shared variable, it is impossible to locally determine the value of E, because other processes may modify the shared variable while the evaluation of E is taking place. For example, before evaluating $(x+3)*y$ the variable y may have the value 0, but while the subexpression

$(x + 3)$ is evaluated another process might overwrite y with some non-zero value. The solution is to assume that a shared variable can have *any* value, and then reject all incorrect assumptions at the time of parallel composition, when all activity involving the shared variable is known. This "assume-reject" strategy is used repeatedly in the sequel. The formal definitions are as follows:

$$\mathcal{E}[\![(E_1 \otimes E_2)]\!]s = \{(c_1 \otimes c_2, h_1 h_2 \{\!|I|\!\}) \mid$$
$$(c_1, h_1) \in \mathcal{E}[\![E_1]\!]s \wedge (c_2, h_2) \in \mathcal{E}[\![E_2]\!]s\}$$
$$\mathcal{E}[\![(\ominus E)]\!]s = \{(\ominus c, h\{\!|I|\!\}) \mid (c, h) \in \mathcal{E}[\![E]\!]s\}$$
$$\mathcal{E}[\![c]\!]s = \{(c, \{\!|I|\!\})\}$$
$$\mathcal{E}[\![x]\!]s = \{(s(x), \{\!|I|\!\})\}$$
$$\mathcal{E}[\![y]\!]s = \{(c, \{\!|W_y|\!\}^i \{\!|A_{y \to c}|\!\}) \mid 0 \le i \le \delta \wedge c \in \mathcal{C}\}.$$

The denotation of $(\ominus E)$ indicates that first the expression E is evaluated, where h is the sequence of steps performed and c is the resulting value; the application of $\ominus$ to c requires one internal action, and the result is $\ominus c$. The other definitions are similar.

The semantics of the primitive commands are given by

$$\mathcal{M}[\![x := E]\!]s = Cls\{\langle s[c/x], h\{\!|I|\!\}\rangle \mid (c, h) \in \mathcal{E}[\![E]\!]s\}$$
$$\mathcal{M}[\![y := E]\!]s = Cls\{\langle s, h\{\!|W_y|\!\}^i\{\!|A_{c \to y}|\!\}\rangle \mid (c, h) \in \mathcal{E}[\![E]\!]s \wedge 0 \le i \le \delta\}$$
$$\mathcal{M}[\![S_1; S_2]\!]s = \widehat{\mathcal{M}[\![S_2]\!]}(\mathcal{M}[\![S_1]\!]s).$$

The internal action in the history of $\mathcal{M}[\![x := E]\!]s$ represents the actual assignment of the value c to x. Note that the state s is updated to reflect the new value of x, but no such update is performed in the assignment $y := E$. There are two reasons for this. First, as indicated above, the global state may be changed at any time by another process. Second, a complete record of all shared-variable accesses is kept in the histories.

The meaning of a program $\|_{i=1}^{n} S_i$ is obtained by *merging* the denotations of the S_i. Intuitively, each process must make assumptions about the value of a shared variable at a given time instant, since the variable may have been changed by another process. Thus, it is possible that different processes may make contradictory assumptions. Merging consists of detecting such inconsistencies and combining consistent state-history pairs from each process. Let $\mathcal{V}_L(S_i)$ denote the set of all local variables accessed by S_i, and for $D \in \mathcal{D}$, let h_D denote the history $Cmb(\pi_{\mathcal{H}}(D))$. Then

$$\mathcal{M}[\![\|_{i=1}^{n} S_i]\!]s = \{Merge(s, \bigcup_{i=1}^{n}\{\langle s_i | \mathcal{V}_L(S_i), h_i \rangle\}) \mid \langle s_i, h_i \rangle \in \mathcal{M}[\![S_i]\!]s\},$$

where

$$
\begin{aligned}
Merge(s, D) &= \text{if } Comp(D) \wedge Cons_A(s, D) \text{ then } \langle SM_A(s, D), h_D \rangle \\
&\quad \text{else } \langle \bot, \epsilon \rangle \\
Comp(D) &= \forall \langle s, h \rangle \in D(s = \bot \Rightarrow |h| = |h_D|) \\
Cons_A(s, D) &= Mem(h_D) \wedge NoWait(h_D) \wedge Verify(s, h_D)
\end{aligned}
$$

The arguments to the *Merge* function are the initial state s, and a set D which contains one state-history pair from each process. *Comp* is the *compatibility* predicate, which enforces the technical requirement that histories whose corresponding state is $\bot$ are not merged with longer histories. (Intuitively, it would make no sense to merge a long completed history with a short incomplete one.) *Cons* is the *consistency* predicate; consistent histories are merged by simply combining them element-wise into a single history. SM_A is the state merge function. *Cons* and SM_A are defined below.

To guarantee consistency, three properties must be satisfied. First, the value read from a shared variable must be the same as the value most recently written to it. This is ensured by the *Verify* predicate, where

$$Verify(s, h) = \forall i (A_{y \to c} \in h[i] \Rightarrow LastWr(y, s, h[1..i-1], c))$$

and the predicate $LastWr(y, s, h, c)$ is true iff

$$(\sum_i Writes(y, h[i]) = 0 \wedge s(y) = c) \vee$$

$$\exists j (A_{c \to y} \in h[j] \wedge \sum_{k=j+1}^{|h|} Writes(y, h[k]) = 0)$$

LastWr says that if y had the value c at time i, then the last value written to y *before* time i was the value c.

Second, there must be no memory conflicts, and finally, there must be no unnecessary waiting to access a shared variable. These conditions are enforced by the *Mem* and *NoWait* predicates, respectively:

$$Mem(h) \quad = \quad \forall i, y(Accesses(y, h[i]) > 1 \Rightarrow Writes(y, h[i]) = 0)$$
$$NoWait(h) \quad = \quad \forall i, y(W_y \in h[i] \Rightarrow Writes(y, h[i]) > 0)$$

These definitions are for the CREW model. *Mem* says that at every time instant i, if more than one process is accessing the shared variable y, then they are all read accesses. *NoWait* ensures that if a process is waiting to access y, it is because some other process is currently writing to y. Other models can be handled in a similar way. Making a small change yields the EREW model:

$$Mem(h) \quad = \quad \forall i, y(Accesses(y, h[i]) \leq 1)$$
$$NoWait(h) \quad = \quad \forall i, y(W_y \in h[i] \Rightarrow Accesses(y, h[i]) > 0),$$

and bus-arbitration is enforced by:

$$Mem(h) \quad = \quad \forall i(\sum_y Accesses(y, h[i]) \leq 1)$$
$$NoWait(h) \quad = \quad \forall i(W_y \in h[i] \Rightarrow \exists z(Accesses(z, h[i]) > 0)).$$

Merging states is performed as follows. First, if any of the states is $\perp$, then the combined state is $\perp$ since at least one of the processes has not completed its computation. Now assume that all states are proper. Note that proper states are restricted to their local components at parallel composition, and the local variables of each process are disjoint. Changes to the global state are recorded only in the histories. It therefore suffices to form the union of the local states and compute the global state using the initial state s and any changes recorded in the associated histories:

$$SMA_A(s, D) \quad = \quad \text{if } \perp \in \pi_S(D) \text{ then } \perp \text{ else } Global(s, h_D) \cup \bigcup \pi_S(D)$$
$$Global(s, h) \quad = \quad \{(y, c) \mid y \in \text{dom}(s) \wedge LastWr(y, s, h, c)\}.$$

Example 1

Consider the program $y := y + 1 \parallel y := y - 1$. Assuming CREW memory, we compute

$$\mathcal{M}[\![y := y + 1]\!]s \quad = \quad Cls\{\langle s, \{W_y\}^i \{A_{y \to c}\} \{I\} \{I\} \{W_y\}^j \{A_{c+1 \to y}\} \rangle \mid$$

$$c \in C \wedge 0 \le i, j \le \delta\}$$
$$\mathcal{M}[\![y := y - 1]\!]s = Cls\{\langle s, \{\!|W_y|\!\}^i \{\!|A_{y \to d}|\!\} \{\!|I|\!\} \{\!|I|\!\} \{\!|W_y|\!\}^j \{\!|A_{d-1 \to y}|\!\} \rangle \mid$$
$$d \in C \wedge 0 \le i, j \le \delta\}.$$

If we assume that $s(y) = 5$, the parallel composition is

$$Cls\{\langle y = 4, \{\!|A_{y \to 5}, A_{y \to 5}|\!\} \{\!|I, I|\!\} \{\!|I, I|\!\} \{\!|A_{6 \to y}, W_y|\!\} \{\!|A_{4 \to y}|\!\} \rangle,$$
$$\langle y = 6, \{\!|A_{y \to 5}, A_{y \to 5}|\!\} \{\!|I, I|\!\} \{\!|I, I|\!\} \{\!|W_y, A_{4 \to y}|\!\} \{\!|A_{6 \to y}|\!\} \rangle\}$$

Synchronization and Mutual Exclusion: The Language L_S

The sublanguage L_S contains parallel and sequential composition, delay and synchronization commands, and indexed atomic actions. Unlike the previous section we consider the limited parallelism model, so there are a fixed number ρ of processors whose speeds are defined by θ. This language is somewhat useless because it has no variables, but it illustrates how limited parallelism, synchronization and mutual exclusion are handled. The syntax of L_S is as follows:

$$\begin{aligned} P &::= \|_{i=1}^{n} S_i \\ S &::= \texttt{delay } c \mid \texttt{sync } \ell \mid S; S \mid \ll_\ell S \gg \end{aligned}$$

We take S_p to be the singleton $\{\mathsf{T}\}$, where T denotes successful termination. The set O of observables is defined in the table below, where $\ell \in \mathcal{L}$ and $1 \le i \le \rho$:

B_ℓ:	waiting to execute an atomic action indexed by ℓ
I :	an internal action
Q :	waiting for a processor
R_ℓ:	waiting for synchronization on ℓ
S_ℓ:	synchronization on ℓ
U_i:	processor i is in use
X_ℓ:	execution within an atomic action indexed by ℓ
Z :	delay (sleep) for one local time unit.

Conceptually, the semantics can be split into two levels: the *a priori* semantics, which gives the denotation of the primitive commands independent of the execution environment, and the parallel composition, which computes the full meaning of the program, taking all execution details into account. The *a priori* semantics is straightforward:

$$\mathcal{M}[\![\text{delay } c]\!]s = Cls\{\langle s, \{Z\}^c\rangle)\}$$
$$\mathcal{M}[\![\text{sync } \ell]\!]s = Cls\{\langle s, \{R_\ell\}^i\{S_\ell\}\rangle) \mid i \geq 0\}$$
$$\mathcal{M}[\![S_1; S_2]\!]s = \widehat{\mathcal{M}[\![S_2]\!]}(\mathcal{M}[\![S_1]\!]s)$$
$$\mathcal{M}[\![\ll_\ell S\gg]\!]s = Cls\{\langle s', \{B_\ell\}^i\{X_\ell\}Cmb(h, \{X_\ell\}^{|h|})\rangle) \mid$$
$$i \geq 0 \wedge \langle s', h\rangle \in \mathcal{M}[\![S]\!]s\}$$

Prefix closure ensures that the set $\{\langle\perp, \{R_\ell\}^i\rangle) \mid i \geq 0\}$ is contained in the denotation of sync ℓ. This models the case when the process waits forever to synchronize. Similar remarks apply to the denotation of $\ll_\ell S\gg$. In $\mathcal{M}[\![\ll_\ell S\gg]\!]s$, we are assuming that the process waits for an unspecified duration, then *holds* ℓ (denoted by the single action $\{X_\ell\}$), and then begins atomic execution of S. X_ℓ is added to all of the elements in h to indicate that the execution is atomic.

The basic strategy for computing $\mathcal{M}[\![\|_{i=1}^n S_i]\!]s$ is as follows. Let $D_i = \mathcal{M}[\![S_i]\!]s$. Figure out all of the different ways that the histories in D_i could be executed in a limited parallelism environment with ρ processors, taking the processor speeds into account, but ignoring the other processes. We assume instantaneous scheduling, as discussed in section 3. Let this *scheduled* meaning be D_i'. Merge all of the D_i' as usual and then reject inconsistent histories, *i.e.* those in which the maximal throughput constraints are violated.

Scheduling consists of three distinct phases. Let h be a history to be scheduled.

Phase 1: Interleave Q elements. Since there are fewer processors than processes (in general), it is possible that actions of h may be delayed due to the lack of an available processor. This is modeled by interleaving arbitrarily long sequences of Q elements with the actions of h. There is one restriction: Q's cannot be inserted between elements denoting an uninterruptible action, such as the Z elements denoting a delay command. This phase will produce a set H_1 of histories.

Phase 2: Add U_i elements. Each executable action (not Q) must be executed on *some* processor. There is no local way to decide which processor is used. So for each history $h_1 \in H_1$, and for each executable action in h_1, generate ρ different histories, each corresponding to the assumption that the action was executed on processor i. To record this assumption, add the element U_i to the action. Again, there is a restriction: contiguous sequences of executable actions must all run on the same processor, since a context-switch must be preceded by at least one Q action.

Phase 3: Expand the executable actions. The processor speeds must be taken into account. If an action is executed on processor i, there must be some way to indicate that execution of that action takes $\theta(i)$ units of global time. The idea is to expand the action into an appropriate subhistory of length $\theta(i)$. How should the expansion be performed? For purely local actions, such as the Z action denoting a delay, repetition is sufficient. For example, if $\theta(3) = 4$, the expansion of $\{U_3, Z\}$ would be $\{U_3, Z\}^4$. However, some actions are measured against the global clock. For example, the exact moment that a synchronization occurs or an indexed atomic action is released must be measured in global time, and could therefore occur in the middle of a local processor cycle. The action must be recorded in global time, so the expansion consists of an appropriately chosen prefix and suffix which "pad" the computation so that it is of the proper duration. These are defined below in the Exp function.

Scheduling is formally handled by the function Sch, which takes three arguments: h, the history to be scheduled; o, the previous action; and p, the processor on which o was executed. As a base case, $Sch(\epsilon, o, p) = \{\epsilon\}$, and for $h \neq \epsilon$, $Sch(h, o, p)$ is defined recursively as follows:

$$\{h_1 h_2 \mid h_1 \in Exp(h[1], p) \land h_2 \in Sch(h[2..], h[1], p)\} \cup$$
$$\{\{Q\}^i h_1 h_2 \mid i \geq 1 \land 1 \leq p' \leq \rho \land h_1 \in Exp(h[1], p') \land$$
$$h_2 \in Sch(h[2..], h[1], p') \land Intr(h[1], o) \land \neg excl(h[1], o)\} \cup$$
$$\{\{Q, X_\ell\}^i h_1 h_2 \mid i \geq 1 \land 1 \leq p' \leq \rho \land h_1 \in Exp(h[1], p')$$
$$\land h_2 \in Sch(h[2..], h[1], p') \land Intr(h[1], o) \land excl(h[1], o)\}$$

where
$$Intr(x, o) = \neg(Z \in x \land Z \in o),$$
$$excl(x, o) = (X_\ell \in o \land X_\ell \in x)$$

and

$$Exp(p,x) = \begin{cases} \{\!\{R_\ell, U_p\}\!\}^i \{\!\{S_\ell, U_p\}\!\} \{\!\{I, U_p\}\!\}^j \mid i+j+1 = \theta(p)\} & \text{if } x = \{\!\{S_\ell\}\!\}, \\ \{\!\{B_\ell, U_p\}\!\}^i \{\!\{U_p, X_\ell\}\!\}^j \mid i+j = \theta(p)\} & \text{if } x = \{\!\{X_\ell\}\!\}, \\ \{(x \cup \{\!\{U_p\}\!\})^{\theta(p)}\} & \text{otherwise.} \end{cases}$$

Intr defines those actions which are interruptable. *excl* records the occurrence of two consecutive X_ℓ actions.

The clauses in the *Sch* function can be explained as follows. The first clause gives the process behavior when the scheduler does not intervene at the current observation. The second clause records that the process can unconditionally wait on the scheduler when its current action is an interruptable one and is not the continuation of an initiated atomic action. The third clause records that the proces can conditionally wait on the scheduler, denoted by $\{\!\{Q, X_\ell\}\!\}^i$, when its current action is the continuation of an initiated atomic action with label ℓ.

Exp performs the necessary expansion of global actions.

Definition 1 *A history h is* **legal** *if for all $1 \le i \le |h|$ exactly one of the following is true: either 1) $Q \in h[i]$, or 2) $U_p \in h[i]$ for some unique p, $1 \le p \le \rho$.*

Lemma 2 *Let $\langle s', h\rangle = \mathcal{M}[\![S]\!]s$. If $h' \in Sch(h, o, p)$, then h' is legal.*

Formally, parallel composition is handled in much the same way as it was in the previous section. The only major change is the use of the scheduling function *Sch*. We also assume that for each S_i, $Init(S_i)$ is the processor on which process S_i will initially run. It is possible that $Init(S_i) = Init(S_j)$ for $i \ne j$, in which case processes S_i and S_j will compete for the processor. However, we insist that $Init$ fully utilize the available processors, *i.e.* it cannot map two processes to the same processor unless there is at least one process mapped to every processor. The function $Init$ can be viewed as a part of the program (although it depends on ρ). $Init$ was not required in the previous section since all processors were identical.

$$\mathcal{M}[\![\,\|_{i=1}^n S_i]\!]s = Cls\{Merge(s, \bigcup_{i=1}^n \{\langle s_i, h_i\rangle\}) \mid$$
$$\langle s_i, h\rangle \in \mathcal{M}[\![S_i]\!]s \wedge h_i \in Sch(h, \{\!\{\}\!\}, Init(S_i))\},$$

where

$$
\begin{aligned}
Merge(s, D) &= \text{if } Comp(D) \wedge Cons(s, D) \text{ then } \langle SM(s, D), h_D \rangle \\
&\quad \text{else } \langle \bot, \epsilon \rangle \\
Comp(D) &= \forall \langle s, h \rangle \in D(s = \bot \Rightarrow |h| = |h_D|) \\
Cons(s, D) &= MaxTPut(D) \wedge Mutex(h_D) \wedge Sync(h_D) \\
SM(s, D) &= \text{if } \bot \in \pi_S(D) \text{ then } \bot \text{ else } \top.
\end{aligned}
$$

Since there is only one proper state, the SM function is simple: if all processes have terminated, so has the parallel composition, and *vice versa*. The compatibility predicate $Comp$ is unchanged. The consistency predicate $Cons$ plays the same role as before, although the details have changed.

To guarantee consistency, three properties must be satisfied. First, processors must execute at most one process, and processes must not wait for a processor unless all processors are in use. Second, indexed atomic actions must be mutually exclusive and there must be no unnecessary waiting to begin an atomic action. Third, all synchronizations must occur in pairs, and a process must not wait for synchronization if another process is ready. These properties are enforced by the $MaxTPut$, $Mutex$ and $Sync$ predicates, respectively:

$$
\begin{aligned}
MaxTPut(h) &= \forall i((Q \in h[i] \Rightarrow Usage(h[i]) = \rho) \wedge \forall j(h[i](U_j) \le 1)) \\
Usage(o) &= \sum_{j=1}^{\rho} h[i](U_j) \\
Mutex(h) &= \forall i(h[i](X_\ell) \le 1 \wedge (B_\ell \in h[i] \Rightarrow X_\ell \in h[i])) \\
Sync(h) &= \forall i, \ell(h[i](R_\ell) \le 1 \wedge h[i](S_\ell) \bmod 2 = 0).
\end{aligned}
$$

Theorem 3 *If $\rho = n$, then no Q elements will appear in $\mathcal{M}[\![\,\|_{i=1}^{n} S_i]\!]s$.*

Corollary 4 *If $\rho = n$, then no process switching occurs.*

Thus if there are a sufficient number of processors, the scheduler does nothing. If the processors are also synchronous, then (except for U_i elements) our limited parallelism model reduces to maximal parallelism.

Abbreviations

If r is a regular expression, then $\langle s, r \rangle$ denotes the set $\{\langle s, h \rangle \mid h \in L(r)\}$. The regular expression $x^{\le n}$ denotes between zero and n repetitions of x, inclusive. The symbol "?" is used as a placeholder for an arbitrary or unknown value. We will often drop U_i elements when all processors are in use. We will also implicitly use theorem 3 and ignore Q elements when ρ equals the number of processes. These abbreviations are somewhat informal, but the increased clarity more than makes up for the technical imprecision.

Example 2

Suppose that $\rho = 2$, $\theta(1) = 2$ and $\theta(2) = 3$. Consider the following program:

$$S_1 :: [\text{delay } 2; \text{sync } \ell_1] \parallel S_2 :: [\text{sync } \ell_2] \parallel S_3 :: [\text{sync } \ell_1; \text{sync } \ell_2]$$

The S_i labels are for convenience only. We compute

$$
\begin{aligned}
\mathcal{M}[\![S_1]\!]s &= Cls\{\langle s, \{\!|Z|\!\}^2\{\!|R_{\ell_1}|\!\}^i\{\!|S_{\ell_1}|\!\}\rangle \mid i \geq 0\} \\
\mathcal{M}[\![S_2]\!]s &= Cls\{\langle s, \{\!|R_{\ell_2}|\!\}^i\{\!|S_{\ell_2}|\!\}\rangle \mid i \geq 0\} \\
\mathcal{M}[\![S_3]\!]s &= Cls\{\langle s, \{\!|R_{\ell_1}|\!\}^i\{\!|S_{\ell_1}|\!\}\{\!|R_{\ell_2}|\!\}^j\{\!|S_{\ell_2}|\!\}\rangle \mid i,j \geq 0\}.
\end{aligned}
$$

Suppose that $Init(S_1) = 1$, and $Init(S_2) = Init(S_3) = 2$. The parallel composition contains infinitely many different computations. The shortest terminating computation is given by:

$$
\begin{aligned}
Cls\langle \top, (\{\!|R_{\ell_1}, Z, Q|\!\}^3 + \{\!|R_{\ell_2}, Z, Q|\!\}^3)\{\!|R_{\ell_1}, Z, Q|\!\} \\
\{\!|S_{\ell_1}, S_{\ell_1}, Q|\!\}\{\!|I, I, Q|\!\}\{\!|S_{\ell_2}, S_{\ell_2}|\!\}\{\!|I, I|\!\}\{\!|I|\!\}\rangle.
\end{aligned}
$$

The remaining computations are of the following form:

$$
\begin{aligned}
Cls\langle \top, (\{\!|R_{\ell_1}, Z, Q|\!\}^3 + \{\!|R_{\ell_2}, Z, Q|\!\}^3)\{\!|R_{\ell_2}, Z, Q|\!\} \\
\{\!|R_{\ell_1}, R_{\ell_2}, Q|\!\}^2(\{\!|R_{\ell_1}, R_{\ell_2}, Q|\!\}^6)^*(h_1 + h_2 + h_3 + h_4)\rangle,
\end{aligned}
$$

where

$$
\begin{aligned}
h_1 &= \{\!|S_{\ell_1}, S_{\ell_1}, Q|\!\}\{\!|I, I, Q|\!\}\{\!|I, R_{\ell_2}, Q|\!\}\{\!|S_{\ell_2}, S_{\ell_2}|\!\}\{\!|I, I|\!\}\{\!|I|\!\} \\
h_2 &= \{\!|R_{\ell_1}, R_{\ell_2}, Q|\!\}^2\{\!|S_{\ell_1}, S_{\ell_1}, Q|\!\}\{\!|I, R_{\ell_2}|\!\}\{\!|S_{\ell_2}, S_{\ell_2}|\!\}\{\!|I, I|\!\}\{\!|I|\!\} \\
h_3 &= \{\!|R_{\ell_1}, R_{\ell_2}, Q|\!\}^3\{\!|S_{\ell_1}, S_{\ell_1}, Q|\!\}\{\!|I, R_{\ell_2}, Q|\!\}^2\{\!|S_{\ell_2}, S_{\ell_2}|\!\}\{\!|I, I|\!\}\{\!|I|\!\} \\
h_4 &= \{\!|R_{\ell_1}, R_{\ell_2}, Q|\!\}^4\{\!|S_{\ell_1}, S_{\ell_1}, Q|\!\}\{\!|I, I, Q|\!\}\{\!|S_{\ell_2}, S_{\ell_2}|\!\}\{\!|I, I|\!\}\{\!|I|\!\}.
\end{aligned}
$$

Note that because of the starred expression $(\{R_{\ell_1}, R_{\ell_2}, Q\})^*$, each of these computations has the possibility of starvation. Remember, an instantaneous scheduler is not necessarily fair, so it is possible that two processes will be permanently allocated processors even though they cannot synchronize.

Scheduling

The notion of an instantaneous scheduler is a convenient one because it is mathematically simple and is the least restrictive scheduler which enforces maximal throughput and yet does not violate the semantics of L_S. However, it is not very practical. In this section we show a few simple examples of how more sophisticated scheduling schemes can be modeled.

Placed Processes

The *Init* function specifies where a process should begin execution. However, after the initial action of the process is executed the scheduler is free to move the process around. It may be desirable to restrict a process to run only on a particular set of processors for the duration of the computation. This is a generalization of the placed processes of occam [13], which are primarily used to map device processes to the processors associated with those devices. It is easily handled in our framework. Let *Run* be a function which maps each process to the set of processors it should use; like *Init*, *Run* should be considered a part of the program. When calculating the scheduled meaning of a process S_i, simply include $Run(S_i)$ as a fourth parameter to the *Sch* function, and replace the condition $1 \leq p' \leq \rho$ in the definition of *Sch* by $p' \in Run(S_i)$.

Non-idle Waiting

The current semantics forces a process to *busy-wait* before entering an indexed atomic action. This wastefully consumes computing resources which could be more profitably spent elsewhere. A realistic implementation might remove the process from its processor until access to the atomic action is permitted. This can be modeled by including the following set in the *Sch* function:

$$\{(h[1] \cup \{\!\!\{Q\}\!\!\})h_2 \mid h_2 \in Sch(h[2..], h[1], p) \wedge B_\ell \in h[1]\}.$$

This requires changing the *MaxTPut* predicate so that a Q element is considered to denote an idle process only if there is no corresponding B_ℓ element:

$$MaxTPut(h) \;=\; \forall i((h[i](Q) > \textstyle\sum_\ell h[i](B_\ell) \Rightarrow Usage(h[i]) = \rho)$$
$$\wedge \forall j(h[i](U_j) \leq 1)).$$

Notice that imposing non-idle waiting requires changes locally and globally. The change in the function *Sch* affects the semantics of the process prior to parallel composition, and the change in the *MaxTPut* predicate affects the semantics globally.

Static Priority Models

In a static priority model, each process has associated with it a fixed *priority*, which reflects its relative "importance" with respect to the other processes. The sole restriction enforced is that, at any given time, a process may execute only if there is no higher-priority process which is waiting for a processor.

The easiest way to handle this is to label each process, as was done in example 2. If the set of process labels is partially ordered by the relation $\sqsubseteq$, we can take the priority of a process to be its label. High priority processes have large labels (in the sense of $\sqsubseteq$). The observable Q_j can be used to indicate that process j is currently waiting for a processor. Enforcing the priority restrictions is accomplished by adding the conjunct $Priority(h_D)$ to the *Cons* predicate, where

$$Priority(h) = \forall i(Q_j \in h[i] \wedge Q_k \notin h[i] \Rightarrow j \sqsubseteq k).$$

It is important to note that although it is simple to model a static priority discipline when given the partial order $\sqsubseteq$, it may be very difficult for a programmer to *derive* a priority which guarantees the timing constraints for a given program.

It is possible to extend this technique to handle dynamic priorities, but in this case priority information must be maintained and updated at every time instant. Mathematically, it requires that another universal quantifier (over priorities) be added to the *Priority* predicate.

DISCUSSION

In the paper, we have shown how the linear history semantics of [5] can be extended to model real-time computations. Currently we do not distinguish between deadlock and nontermination, although it is possible to do so.

The semantics imposes prohibition of unnecessary waiting of processes and of processors. The former yields an upper bound on how long a process must wait before it can synchronization with another. The bound becomes deterministic when we note that the partner will not be ready to synchronize before the established bound. The nonidling of processors is imposed by the $MaxTPut$ predicate. Nonidling of processors is a necessary operational regime for justifying prohibition of unnecessary waiting of processes. Thus $MaxTPut$ provides the required operational basis. In the maximal parallelism model [9], $MaxTPut$ is implicit. It must be explicit in a limited parallelism model.

The model [16] addresses a variety of semantic issues concerning timed execution of concurrent programs in a limited parallelism model. The model and the techniques developed in this paper are being extended to obtain a formal semantic model of real-time concurrency for components of the Ada 9X language. The Ada 9X revision [8] provides *protected records* as a structuring mechanism for programming real-time systems. The mechanism is similar in spirit to Hoare's monitor concept though some of the details vary. Further the Ada 9X revision provides primitives for supporting dynamic priorities. A set of axioms define implicit changes to the priorities of processes caused by the interaction between the language concepts. Defining a formal semantic model will have the consequence of increasing the precision in the language reference manual with regard to real-time aspects.

Real-time models are inherently more complex than their interleaving counterparts. We cannot avoid this complexity if our central concern is the introduction of the time metric into the semantic models and the reasoning of the time behavior of the program.

We have used as an *operational basis* the justifiable criterion that *processors do not idle*. This in turn requires that the scheduler cannot idle in an arbitrary way. However for reasons of realism, we can admit uncertain idling by the scheduler as long as the uncertainity is bounded a priori. In such a case any resulting idling of the processors will be legitimately accounted for in the semantic model. The semantic model in the paper admits a number of idealizations for reasons of simplicity of presentation.

The complexity of the model when scheduling disciplines are imposed is substantial. Often the execution environment plays a key role in the semantic model. From a real-time programming point of view, the simpler the model the better it is; the programmer will then be able to reason about his program in a simple way. However we have to ask the question, "is there a way in the which the programmer need not be concerned about the scheduling policy (beyond the prohibition of unnecessary waiting of processes) and hence avoid the complexity associated with the semantic models?" The maximal parallelism model, though strong, is a simpler model. If we can construct regions of maximally parallel execution in an otherwise limited parallelism execution model, then within those regions we can achieve a simpler semantic characterization. This is achieved by the language concept of *tri-sections* defined in [12]. The concept combines nondeterministic multi-way synchronization and processor holding in a simple way. Using the notion of a *tri-section*, we can define a hybrid model which interleaves maximally parallel computations into an otherwise timeless model [17].

Relation to Other Work

Semantic models for real-time concurrency have been explored in a process-algebraic framework by Milner in [10]. SCCS does not enforce maximal throughput, so the waiting behavior of processes must be *a priori* programmed and cannot be inferred from the context as in our model or that of [9]. In [14], a topological semantic model for real-time concurrency is introduced, based on the theory of complete metric spaces. The model is restrictive and does not impose prohibition of unnecessary waiting of processes.

Future Work

We are investigating assertional proof theories for real-time concurrency in a variety of models. A number of proof theories [2,11,19,21] are available in the literature and can be suitably extended to cater to real-time models. Because real-time proof theory is still in its infancy, it is difficult to say in a qualitative sense that one methodology is superior to another. Thus each must be explored independently. We think that specifying real-time systems using maximal parallelism model with an abstract notion of time is simpler. However their implementations need not be so constrained. If it is possible to observe a set of design rules, then one can implement the specification in a limited parallelism model, or in a hybrid model. Then it is responsibility of the programmer to show that the implementation satisfies the specification. This calls for refinement calculi across models. We are exploring these issues too.

References

[1] "The Programming Language Ada Reference Manual," *Lecture Notes in Comput. Sci.* **155**, Springer-Verlag, Berlin, (1983).

[2] Apt, K.R., de Roever, W.P., and Francez, N.: "A Proof System for Communicating Sequential Processes," *Trans. on Programming Lang. and Systems* **2** (3), 359–385 (1980).

[3] Branquart, P., Louis, G., and Wodon, P.: "An Analytical Description of CHILL, the CCITT High-Level Language VI," *Lecture Notes in Comput. Sci.* **128**, Springer-Verlag, Berlin, (1982).

[4] Dijkstra, E.W.: "Cooperating Sequential Processes," *in* "Programming Languages," Academic Press, New York, (1968).

[5] Francez, N., Lehman, D., and Pneuli, A.: "A Linear-history Semantics for Languages for Distributed Programming," *Theoret. Comput. Sci.* **32**, 25–46, (1984).

[6] Hoare, C.A.R.: "Communicating Sequential Processes," sl Comm. ACM **21** (8), 666–676, (1978).

[7] Huizing, C., Gerth R., de Roever, W.P.: "Full Abstraction of a Real-Time Denotational Semantics for an OCCAM-like Language," *Proc. 14th ACM Symposium on Principles of Programming Languages*, 223–238 (1987).

[8] "Ada 9X Mapping Issues, Version 2.0," *Intermetrics Inc.*, December 1990.

[9] Koymans, R., Shyamasundar, R.K., de Roever, W.P., Gerth, R., and Arun-Kumar, S.: "Compositional Denotational Semantics for Real-time Distributed Computing," *Information and Control* **79** (3), 210–256 (1988).

[10] Milner, R.: "Calculi for Synchrony and Asynchrony," *Theoretical Computer Science* **25**, 267–310 (1983).

[11] Misra, J., and Chandy, K.M.: "Proofs of Networks of Processes," *IEEE TSE* **7** (7), 412–426 (1981).

[12] Narayana, K.T., Shade, E.: "Language Concepts for Real-Time Concurrency," *Research Report #CS-89-23*, Dept. of Computer Science, The Pennsylvania State University, (Subimitted for Publication), (1989).

[13] "The Occam Language Reference Manual," Prentice-Hall, Englewood Cliffs, NJ (1984).

[14] Reed, G.M., and Roscoe, A.W.: "A Timed Model for Communicating Sequential Processes," *Lecture Notes in Comput. Sci.* **226**, 314–323 (1986).

[15] Salwicki, A., Müldner, T.: "On the Algorithmic Properties of Concurrent Programs," *LNCS* **125**, 169–197 (1981).

[16] Shade, E., Narayana, K.T.: "Real-Time Semantics for Shared-variable Concurrency," *Research Report #CS-88-28*, Dept. of Computer Science, The Pennsylvania State University, *To Appear in Information and Computation.*

[17] Shade, E., Narayana, K.T.: "Tri-Sections and an Interleaving Maximal Parallelism Model," Technical Report, ORA Corporation, Ithaca, NY 14850, Feb 1991.

[18] Shyamasundar, R.K., Narayana, K.T., and Pitassi, T.: "A Semantics for Nondeterministic Asynchronous Broadcast Networks," *Lecture Notes in Comput. Sci.* **267**, 72–83 (1987).

[19] Soundararajan, N.: "Axiomatic Semantics of Communicating Sequential Processes," *ACM Trans. on Programming Lang. and Systems* **6** (4), 647–662 (1984).

[20] Widom, J., Gries, D., and Schneider, F.B.: "Completeness and Incompleteness of Trace-Based Network Proof Systems," *in Proc. 14th ACM Symp. on Principles of Programming Lang.*, 27–38 (1987).

[21] Zwiers, J., de Roever, W.P., and van Emde Boas, P.: "Compositionality and Concurrent Networks: Soundness and Completeness of a Proof System," *Lecture Notes in Comput. Sci.* **194**, 509–519 (1985).

CHAPTER 8

Automated Analysis of Concurrent and Real-Time Software

George S. Avrunin*
Department of Mathematics and Statistics
University of Massachusetts
Amherst, MA 01003

Jack C. Wileden*,†
Department of Computer and Information Science
University of Massachusetts
Amherst, MA 01003

Abstract

This paper surveys the current status of our work on automated analysis of the logical and timing properties of concurrent software based on the constrained expression approach. It describes our analysis toolset, reports some extremely encouraging results of using the toolset to analyze logical properties of nontrivial concurrent systems, and discusses the modifications we have made to the toolset to apply it to analyzing timing properties. It then outlines ongoing and planned research directed at further improving these methods.

INTRODUCTION

Software systems can only be made truly robust and reliable if sufficiently powerful analysis techniques are made available to software developers and maintainers. Ideally, such analysis techniques should be applicable throughout the development of a software system, from its initial specification through its

*Research partially supported by NSF grant CCR-8806970 and ONR grant N00014-89-J-1064.

†Research partially supported by NSF grant CCR-8704478 with cooperation from DARPA (ARPA order 6104).

design and coding, and also during its subsequent lifetime, when they would greatly aid its maintenance and modification. Therefore, these analysis techniques should be applicable to a wide range of software system descriptions, not just a single specification, design or programming language. Obviously, to be of the greatest value, the techniques should also be applicable to the broadest possible range of program structures and organizations. Finally, the techniques must be able to analyze systems of realistic size in a reasonable amount of time. This almost certainly requires that the techniques be automatable and computationally tractable.

Traditionally, the primary analysis problem for software developers and maintainers has been to assess *logical properties* of a software system. These logical properties include such things as whether the system will compute the intended results and whether the system's computation will terminate. A variety of analysis techniques, ranging from program testing to program proving, have been proposed and used, with greater or lesser success, to assess logical properties of software. Most programs represent a very large number of distinct possible sequences of statement executions, and most of these analysis techniques depend upon reasoning about or examining as many of those distinct sequences as possible. Generally speaking, they have suffered from limited applicability, computational intractability, or both.

Difficult though it is to assess the logical properties of a single, sequential program running on a single processor, it is significantly more difficult to assess the logical properties of *concurrent* or *distributed* software systems. Such systems consist of several programs running simultaneously, either in a logical sense, by having their executions interleaved on a single processor, or by actually executing on several interconnected computers running in parallel. Moreover, the behavior of such systems is often nondeterministic. As a result, concurrent or distributed software systems typically represent even larger numbers of distinct possible sequences of statement executions than do sequential programs. Furthermore, concurrent programs have additional logical correctness properties, such as freedom from deadlock or mutually exclusive use of shared resources, that must be assessed. It is these attributes that make analyzing concurrent or distributed software even more difficult than analyzing sequential software. Not surprisingly, the analysis techniques that have been proposed for concurrent and distributed software have suffered heavily from limited applicability and computational intractability.

Several years ago, we set out to develop analysis techniques for concurrent and distributed software systems that would be as broadly applicable as possible and that would be sufficiently computationally tractable that they could be used to analyze realistic problems concerning realistic software systems. The result of that effort is a collection of analysis techniques based on the *constrained expression* formalism. These techniques have recently been automated in the form of a prototype toolset, and we have begun to achieve some very encouraging results from applying the toolset to various standard concurrent system problems. Most notably, the toolset demonstrates impressive performance on nontrivial problems and the degradation in its performance as the size of the system being analyzed increases is much less than that of most other approaches. This suggests that analysis of realistic problems and systems using our techniques may be a real possibility.

Real-time software systems, which are those software systems whose correctness depends upon timing properties as well as logical properties, pose an additional set of challenges for software analysis techniques. A central requirement for correct operation of a real-time software system is that the software have predictable timing properties. Of course, the traditional concern for logical correctness (i.e., that the software will compute the intended results) applies to real-time software as well. However, the additional property characterizing correctness for real-time software is that the maximum time required to produce the intended results can be guaranteed to be within some specified bound. The requirement of predictable timing properties implies a need for analysis techniques that can accurately assess the timing, and timing-related (e.g., resource demands), properties of software systems. As with logical properties, analyzing timing properties of concurrent or distributed software is even more difficult than performing similar analysis of sequential software.

We have recently developed and begun experimenting with a technique for assessing timing properties of concurrent, real-time software. This technique is an outgrowth of our work on the constrained expression techniques for analyzing logical properties of concurrent software systems. The results of our initial efforts to apply our constrained expression analysis techniques to real-time system analysis problems have been very encouraging. By extending the constrained expression formalism slightly and modifying parts of the prototype toolset we are now able to carry out an automated derivation of an upper bound on the time that can elapse between the occurrence of any designated pair of events in a concurrent system's behavior. Since the constrained expression techniques were explicitly tailored to be applicable to a wide range of software descriptions, program structures and organizations, techniques and tools resulting from extending them to real-time systems should have those same desirable attributes.

In this paper, we begin by briefly describing the constrained expression formalism and analysis techniques. We then sketch the prototype toolset that automates the analysis techniques and give some representative highlights from our experimentation with the use of the toolset in analyzing logical properties of concurrent systems. Next we explain the modifications and extensions required to apply the constrained expression techniques and toolset to the analysis of timing properties. Finally, we discuss ongoing research aimed at improving our abilities to analyze both logical and timing properties of concurrent systems.

CONSTRAINED EXPRESSIONS

In the constrained expression approach to analysis of concurrent systems, the system descriptions produced during software development (e.g., designs in some design notation) are translated into formal representations, called *constrained expression representations*, to which a variety of analysis methods are then applied. This approach allows developers to work in the design notations and implementation languages most appropriate to their tasks. Rigorous analysis is based on the constrained expression representations that are mechanically generated from the system descriptions created by software developers.

This section contains a brief overview of the constrained expression formalism. Detailed and rigorous presentations of the formalism appear in [12] and in the appendix to [14], while less formal treatments intended to provide a more intuitive understanding of the features of the formalism appear in [7] and [4]. The use of constrained expressions with a variety of development notations is illustrated in [7] and [14]. A detailed discussion of the relation between constrained expressions and a variety of other methods for describing and analyzing concurrent software systems can be found in [7] and [17].

The constrained expression formalism treats the behaviors of a concurrent system as sequences of events. These events can be of arbitrary complexity, depending on the system characteristics of interest and the level of system description under consideration. Associating an *event symbol* to each event, we can regard each possible behavior of the system as a string over the alphabet of event symbols. While this suggests that behaviors must be viewed as total orders on events, in fact the constrained expression formalism is consistent with viewing concurrent system behaviors either as total orders or as partial orders on events, as discussed in [4].

We use interleaving to represent concurrency. Thus, a string representing a possible behavior of a system that consists of several concurrently executing components is obtained by interleaving strings representing the behaviors of the components. The events themselves are assumed to be atomic and indivisible. "Events" that are to be explicitly regarded as overlapping in time are represented by treating their initiation and termination as distinct atomic events.

The set of strings representing behaviors of a particular concurrent system is obtained by a two-step process. First, a regular expression, called the *system expression*, is derived from a description of the system in some notation such as a design or programming language. The language of this expression includes strings representing all possible behaviors of the system. It may, however, also include strings that do not represent possible behaviors, as the system expression does not encode the full semantics of the system description. This language is then "filtered" to remove such strings, using other expressions, called *constraints*, which are also derived from the original system description. A string survives this filtering process if its projections on the alphabets of the constraints lie in the languages of the constraints. The constraints (which need not be regular) enforce those aspects of the semantics of the design or programming language, such as the appropriate synchronization of rendezvous between different tasks or the consistent use of data, that are not captured in the system expression. The reasons for this two-step process, which might not seem as straightforward as generating behaviors directly from a single expression, are discussed in [14], while an equivalent and more uniform interpretation process for constrained expressions is presented in [4].

Our main constrained expression analysis techniques require that questions about the behavior of a concurrent system be formulated in terms of whether a particular event symbol, or pattern of event symbols, occurs in a string representing a possible behavior of the system. For example, questions about whether the system can deadlock might be phrased in terms of the occurrence of symbols representing the permanent blocking of components (e.g., processes or tasks) of the system.

Starting from the assumption that the specified symbol, or pattern of symbols, does occur in such a string, we use the form of the system expression and the constraints to generate inequalities involving the numbers of occurrences of various event symbols in segments of the string. If the system of inequalities thus generated is inconsistent, the original assumption is incorrect and the specified symbol or pattern of symbols does not occur in a string corresponding to a behavior of the system. If the inequalities are consistent, we use them in attempting to construct a string containing the specified pattern.

In summary, the constrained expression approach is applicable to systems expressed in a variety of notations and languages. It offers a focused approach to analysis, which, by keeping the amount of uninteresting information produced to a minimum, can be very efficient. Over the last several years, we have developed a set of tools automating various aspects of constrained expression analysis and have achieved very good results in using them to analyze logical properties of a range of concurrent system examples [4]. We briefly describe the current version of the prototype toolset before discussing the application of the formalism, analysis techniques and toolset to analyzing both concurrent and real-time systems.

THE CONSTRAINED EXPRESSION TOOLS

The prototype toolset (see Figure 1) consists of five major components: a *deriver* that produces constrained expression representations from concurrent system designs in a particular design language; a *constraint eliminator* that replaces a constrained expression with an equivalent one involving fewer constraints; an *inequality generator* that generates a system of inequalities from the constrained expression representation of a concurrent system; an *integer programming package* for determining whether this system of inequalities is consistent or inconsistent, and, if the system is consistent, for finding a solution with appropriate properties; and a *behavior generator* that uses the constrained expression produced by the constraint eliminator plus the solution found by the integer programming package (when the inequalities are consistent) to try to produce a string of event symbols corresponding to a system behavior with the desired properties. The organization of the toolset is illustrated in the figure. We give brief descriptions of the tools and their use below. A more detailed discussion of the toolset and its implementation appears in [4].

The current toolset is intended for use with designs written in the Ada-based design language CEDL (Constrained Expression Design Language) [13]. CEDL focuses on the expression of communication and synchronization among the tasks in a distributed system, and language features not related to concur-

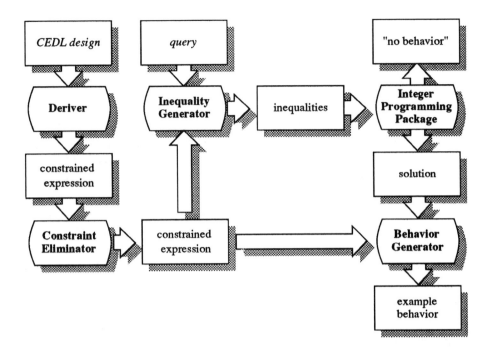

Figure 1: Diagram of Constrained Expression Toolset

rency are kept to a minimum. Thus, for example, data types are limited, but most of the Ada control-flow constructs have correspondents in CEDL. We originally chose to work with a design notation based on Ada because Ada is one of the few programming languages in relatively widespread use that explicitly provides for concurrency, and because we expect our work on analysis of designs to contribute to and benefit from the Arcadia Consortium's work on Ada software development environments [16]. Despite Ada's shortcomings as a language for real-time software [1], we have used CEDL and the existing deriver in our initial experiments with analysis of timing properties.

The deriver [2] produces constrained expression representations from CEDL system designs. The system expressions it produces consist of the interleave of regular expressions, called *task expressions*, representing the behavior of the various components (called *tasks* in Ada, and hence in CEDL, terminology) of the concurrent system. The deriver also generates all required constraints.

The constraint eliminator [10] takes a subexpression of the system expression and certain constraints, and produces a new expression whose language is the set of strings in the language of the subexpression that satisfy the constraints. It requires that the subexpression and the constraints be regular and not involve the interleave operator. We typically use the constraint eliminator with a task expression and constraints that enforce correct dataflow within that task. The constraint eliminator converts the task expression and constraints into deterministic finite state automata (DFAs), and uses a procedure based on standard DFA intersection algorithms to produce a new automaton accepting only that subset of the language of the task expression that also satisfies the constraints. In earlier versions of the toolset, the new automaton was converted back into a regular expression, and the original task expression and constraints were eliminated from the constrained expression and replaced by this new task expression. Although very compact systems of inequalities can be generated from regular expressions, the conversion of the DFA resulting from constraint elimination into a regular expression sometimes results in enormous regular expressions. Our student, James Corbett, investigated this problem [9], and determined that, in certain cases, a more compact system of inequalities can be generated from the DFA representation of a task than from the regular expression into which that DFA would be converted. (In addition, this eliminates the cost of converting the DFA into a regular expression.) He also introduced a hybrid form we call REDFAs. We have found that, in general, it is best to work from the REDFA representation of tasks. The current implementation of the constraint eliminator, therefore, can replace the eliminated task expression with a regular expression, a DFA, or an REDFA, as specified by the user.

The inequality generator [3] takes a constrained expression representation as input. For each task, the inequality generator produces a collection of linear equations involving variables representing the number of times a node in a parse-tree of the task expression (or an arc in a DFA or REDFA representation of the task) is traversed in a behavior of the system. It then generates linear inequalities in these variables reflecting part of the semantics of certain of the constraints. The generation of equations for the tasks depends only on the basic structure of regular expressions and finite state automata, but, for reasons of efficiency, the generation of inequalities from constraints depends on features of CEDL.

The constraints impose restrictions on the order and number of occurrences of event symbols in behaviors of the system. The integer programming variables we use represent only the total numbers of occurrences of symbols (or, more precisely, of traversals of nodes in the parse-trees or arcs in finite state automata) and do not reflect the order in which those symbols occur. The inequalities we generate therefore do not directly reflect information about the order in which the various symbols occur. Similarly, the fact that we restrict ourselves to linear systems of equations and inequalities (in order to avoid the much more difficult computational problems of nonlinear systems) means that our systems do not fully reflect the semantics of the Kleene star operator (or, equivalently, of cycles in task DFAs). For these reasons, which are discussed more fully in [4], our systems of inequalities should be regarded as expressing necessary conditions that must be satisfied by any behavior of the concurrent system.

The inequality generator also provides an interactive facility allowing the analyst to add additional inequalities representing assumptions or queries about the behavior of the system and a reporting facility for use by a human analyst interpreting output of the integer programming package.

The integer programming package, called IMINOS [8], is a branch-and-bound integer linear programming system that we have implemented on top of the MINOS optimization package [15]. When the generated system of inequalities is consistent, the integer programming package produces a solution giving counts for the number of occurrences of the various event symbols. The behavior generator [11] uses heuristic search techniques to find a string of event symbols having the given counts and corresponding to a system behavior, helping the analyst to understand the solution found by the integer programming package. The behavior generator may also be used by the analyst for interactive exploration of the system.

ANALYSIS OF LOGICAL PROPERTIES

We have used the prototype constrained expression toolset to analyze a number of standard problems from the concurrent systems literature. We report here the results of analysis of several versions of the dining philosophers problem in order to give some idea of the capabilities and performance of the toolset. Additional results on these problems and others, together with a more detailed and complete discussion, appear in [4].

Perhaps the most widely known example in the concurrent systems litera-

phils	tasks	deriv	elim	ineq	IMINOS	behav	size	total
60	120	298	21	158	74	78	1141×960	629
80	160	403	35	248	75	122	1521×1280	883
100	200	501	60	399	120	169	1901×1600	1249
20	41	140	105	157	65		603×1261	467
30	61	190	437	538	58		903×2491	1223
40	81	265	1079	1516	81		1203×4121	2941
20	41	141	128	171	222	54	607×1305	716
30	61	196	392	537	296	119	905×2523	1540
40	81	259	1104	1603	865	239	1205×4163	4070

Figure 2: Toolset Performance on Versions of the Dining Philosophers Problem

ture is Dijkstra's dining philosophers problem, in which a group of philosophers sit at a round table with one seat for each philosopher and one fork between each pair of philosophers. The philosophers alternately think and eat. A philosopher requires two forks to eat, and each philosopher who wants to eat attempts to pick up one fork, say the one on the left, and then the other. Having acquired both forks, the philosopher eats and then puts the forks down. The system is interesting because of the possibility of deadlock caused by all the philosophers picking up the forks on their left, leaving each of them unable to pick up a second fork. Various approaches can be used to prevent the deadlock.

We have analyzed several variations of this system. In the basic one, we model each fork by a task with two entries. Calls to the "up" entry represent the fork being picked up by a philosopher and calls to the "down" entry represent the fork being put down. Each fork task loops forever, accepting calls first at its up entry and then at its down entry. Each philosopher is represented by a task that repeatedly calls the up entry of the fork to its "left", the up entry of the fork to its "right", and then the down entries of the two forks. A system with n philosophers thus has $2n$ tasks. Our analysis is intended to detect the possibility of deadlock.

One of the standard ways to prevent deadlock in the dining philosophers system is to introduce a "host" or "butler" who ensures that all the philosophers do not attempt to eat at the same time. We have modeled this by introducing an additional host task and modifying the philosopher tasks. The host task has two entries, "enter" and "leave", and a philosopher must rendezvous with the host at "enter" before attempting to pick up the first fork. After putting down the second fork, the philosopher calls the "leave" entry. The host keeps track of the number of philosophers in the dining room (the number of rendezvous that have occurred at "enter" minus the number at "leave") and repeatedly accepts calls at "enter" as long as no more than $n - 2$ philosophers are in the dining room. The "leave" entry is unguarded, so calls at that entry can be accepted at any time.

Although the dining philosophers system with host and n philosophers involves only one more task than the basic system with the same number of philosophers, control flow in the host task depends on the value of the variable counting the number of philosophers in the dining room. The constraint eliminator intersects the task expression for the host with the constraint involving this variable, so that the system of inequalities properly reflects the dependence of control flow on the number of philosophers in the dining room and the analysis does not spuriously report deadlock. This process, however, together with the additional entry calls in the philosopher tasks, results in significantly bigger systems of inequalities.

In Figure 2, we show the performance of the constrained expression toolset in analyzing these dining philosophers problems. The columns in the table give, respectively, the number of philosophers, the number of tasks in the system, the time in seconds used by the deriver, the eliminator, the inequality generator, IMINOS, and the behavior generator, the size of the system of inequalities (number of inequalities × number of variables), and the total time used by the toolset. All the experiments reported in this paper were run on a DECstation 3100 with 24 MB of memory; times given are in CPU seconds on that machine and include both user and system time. The first three lines of the table give results for versions of the basic dining philosophers system with 60, 80, and 100 philosophers, respectively. In these examples, the toolset produces a behavior displaying the deadlock. The next three lines of the table give results for versions of the dining philosophers problem with a host task and 20, 30, and 40 philosophers respectively. In these examples, IMINOS correctly reports that deadlock is impossible and it is not necessary to run the behavior generator. The last three lines of the table give times for 20-, 30-, and 40-philosopher examples with host in which an erroneous bound in the host task allows all the philosophers into the room at the same time. In these cases, the toolset produces a behavior displaying the deadlock.

As the results in Figure 2 illustrate, the constrained expression toolset is capable of analyzing large systems. The toolset carries out a complete analysis of the basic dining philosophers problem with 100 philosopher tasks and 100 fork tasks, starting from the CEDL code and producing a behavior displaying deadlock, in less than 21 minutes. When the behavior of the individual tasks is more complex, the toolset cannot handle quite so many tasks, but it is clear that it can be used with at least some systems that approach, or even exceed, realistic sizes for concurrent system designs. By way of comparison, we know of few other automated analysis techniques that are capable of handling versions of the basic dining philosophers problem with as many as 10 philosophers, and their execution time typically increases exponentially with the number of philosophers.

With some other examples, however, the integer programming component of the toolset finds solutions that do not correspond to behaviors of the concurrent system being analyzed. This is due to the fact that our systems of inequalities do not fully reflect the semantics of the constrained expression representation of that concurrent system, giving instead only necessary conditions for a sequence of events to correspond to a system behavior. In these cases, the behavior generator reports that the solution does not correspond to a behavior, but the analysis is inconclusive because there may be other solutions to the system of inequalities that do correspond to behaviors. In some cases, it is possible to deal with these problems in an *ad hoc* manner.

The current implementation of the toolset is not able to address questions involving fairness and can address certain questions about the order of event occurrences only indirectly by transforming the question into one involving the number of occurrences of other events. These problems are the subject of ongoing research.

ANALYSIS OF TIMING PROPERTIES

The constrained expression formalism and the toolset described in the preceding sections were originally developed to analyze logical properties of behaviors of concurrent or distributed systems. As a result, the formalism models computation as a stream of non-overlapping atomic events, with no notion of time, and the toolset is oriented toward finding (or disproving the existence of) complete behaviors that have some specified property, such as deadlock.

To apply the constrained expression analysis techniques to real-time systems, the formalism must first be extended to account for time. This can be done straightforwardly by assigning a duration to each event. The time required for a sequence of events is then just the sum of the durations of the individual events in the sequence. However, such an interpretation only makes sense when the events are non-overlapping, as would be the case if the concurrent system being analyzed were to be run on a single processor. We adopt this straightforward extension to the formalism, and the corresponding limitation on the class of concurrent systems whose timing properties we can analyze, as a first step toward applying our constrained expression techniques to the analysis of real-time systems. Ongoing research is directed toward applying our techniques to "truly concurrent" (i.e., multiprocessor) systems.

We are interested in answering questions of the form "What is the longest time that can elapse between an occurrence of event A and the next occurrence of event B in a behavior of the system?" Such questions involve subsequences of events that might occur within the full sequences that correspond to complete system behaviors. (Of course, sometimes the subsequence of interest is the full sequence.) Our initial approach to applying the constrained expression toolset to the analysis of timing properties [6] was to manually modify the constrained expression generated by the deriver and constraint eliminator so that it represented (approximately) the subsequences of interest. In effect, this transformed questions about partial behaviors of the system into questions about complete behaviors of the system represented by the modified constrained expression. We then used the inequality generator and the integer programming package to find a bound on the duration of these behaviors.

The investigation of the DFA and REDFA forms for representing task expressions, however, suggested an approach that has allowed us to generate inequalities describing subsequences of behaviors directly from the original constrained expression, and we have extended the toolset to implement it. We now give an outline of this new approach. Details of our method and an example of its application can be found in [5]. We note that, although these extensions to the toolset were motivated by our interest in analyzing timing properties, they will also be valuable for analyses of logical properties that involve consideration of partial behaviors, such as detecting violations of mutual exclusion.

To explain our method for generating inequalities describing subsequences of behaviors, it is helpful to begin by discussing how we generate inequalities describing complete behaviors from DFA representations of tasks. Given a

DFA accepting the language of a task expression, the basic approach is to assign a variable to each arc of the DFA. The value of the variable associated with an arc gives the number of times that arc is traversed in a particular behavior of the system. We then generate a "flow equation" for each state other than the initial and accepting states. This equation says that the sum of the variables associated with arcs into that state must equal the sum of the variables associated with arcs leaving the state. The initial state and the accepting states must be treated specially, of course. For the initial state, we set the sum of the variables associated with arcs leaving the state to 1, representing fact that the task is activated once and begins its computation in the initial state of the DFA. The flow equations then imply that the sum of the variables associated with arcs into the accepting states is 1, corresponding to the fact that the task ends its computation in exactly one accepting state.

In a subsequence of an event sequence corresponding to a complete behavior of a concurrent system, of course, the state of a particular task DFA at the beginning of the subsequence need not be its initial state and its state at the end of the subsequence need not be an accepting state. So we need to add an extra "flow in" at any state in which the DFA could be at the start of the subsequence, and an extra "flow out" at any state in which the DFA could be at the end of the subsequence. We do this by introducing additional variables representing the state of the DFA at the start and end of the subsequence, and generating additional equations reflecting the fact that the DFA is in exactly one state at each of those times.

The idea is as follows. Assume that each of the tasks of the concurrent system is represented by a task DFA, and that we are interested in finding an upper bound on the time between the occurrence of an event A in one task and the next occurrence of event B, possibly in a different task. For simplicity, we will restrict our attention to subsequences in which A does not occur again before B; we are thus asking for an upper bound on the duration of the subsequences of behaviors beginning with A and ending with B, and having no other occurrences of A or B. We will also assume that the events A and B each occur in exactly one task. This can easily be arranged by using unique names for event symbols corresponding to the events in different tasks.

We generate equations for each task DFA. As in the analysis of complete behaviors, we assign a variable x_a to each arc a in the task DFAs. We then assign a *start variable* s_i to each state i. This variable will be 1 if the task is in state i at the beginning of the subsequence, and 0 otherwise. If the symbol corresponding to A appears as a label on an arc in the DFA, we omit the start variables on all states except those with an outgoing arc labeled by the symbol corresponding to A, since we want the first event in the subsequence to be A. Similarly, we assign a *halt variable* h_i to each state i, but in the DFA in which the symbol corresponding to B occurs, we omit the halt variables for states not having an incoming arc with this symbol. The variable h_i will be 1 if the task is in state i at the end of the subsequence, and 0 otherwise.

We then write flow equations for each state, counting s_i as flow into state i and h_i as flow out. These equations have the form

$$s_i + \sum_{a \in \mathrm{In}(i)} x_a = h_i + \sum_{a' \in \mathrm{Out}(i)} x_{a'},$$

where $\mathrm{In}(i)$ is the set of arcs into state i and $\mathrm{Out}(i)$ is the set of arcs out of state i. We then write equations stating that the sum of the start variables in each task DFA is equal to one. As before, the flow equations then imply that the sum of the halt variables in each task DFA is one.

Finally, we generate an additional equation for each pair consisting of an entry in the concurrent system and a task calling that entry. This equation expresses the fact that the number of times the given task calls that entry must be equal to the number of times a rendezvous with that task is accepted at the entry. This equation involves the variables corresponding to arcs labeled by symbols representing calls to the entry (in the DFA of the calling task) and acceptances of calls at that entry (in the DFA of the accepting task).

The system of equations we have generated expresses a large part of the semantics of the constrained expression representing the behavior of the concurrent system. It states that a DFA representing a task must be in a single state at the start and end of the subsequence, that the number of times the DFA enters any other state must equal the number of times it leaves that state, and that the events corresponding to rendezvous of two tasks must occur the same number of times in the behavior of each of the two tasks. Any subsequence of an actual behavior starting with A and ending with B must satisfy the system of equations. Furthermore, if we were interested in subsequences satisfying some additional condition involving the occurrence of other events, we could easily augment the system of equations to express this. For example, if we wanted a bound on the duration of subsequences starting with A, ending with B, and containing no occurrences of event C, we would add equations stating that the arc variables labeled by the symbol corresponding to C must all be 0.

The total duration of a set of events corresponding to a solution of this system of equations is simply the sum of the arc variables, weighted by the durations of the events whose symbols label the arcs. Taking this weighted sum as the objective function, the integer programming component of our toolset will find a solution to the system of equations, assuming they are consistent, giving the maximum possible value for the total duration. (If there is no maximum value, IMINOS will report that the duration is unbounded. In practice, for reasons discussed below, we usually impose some relatively large upper bound on the variables, thus ensuring that the duration is bounded.) This maximum possible duration reported by IMINOS is a bound on the total duration of the subsequences we are considering.

Because the system of equations represents only necessary conditions that must be satisfied by the subsequences of behaviors and does not completely characterize those subsequences, the solution found by the integer programming package may not correspond to a subsequence of a behavior. In that case, while the maximum value of the objective function found by the integer programming package is an upper bound on the durations of the subsequences in question, it need not be the least upper bound. There are two reasons that solutions to the system of equations may not correspond to subsequences of behaviors.

The first reason is that the equations represent most, but not all, of the semantics of constrained expressions. The equations do not guarantee that events will occur in the order required by the concurrent program, and it may be the case that this order is not consistent with the solution found by IMINOS. Furthermore, the system of equations does not completely constrain the number of occurrences of events labeling arcs forming a cycle in a task DFA. Consider a state i with an arc a from i to itself. The corresponding variable, x_a, will occur on both sides of the flow equation generated for i, since a will belong to both $In(i)$ and $Out(i)$. The flow equation thus does not restrict the value of x_a at all. Indeed, there may be solutions to the system of flow equations in which the variable x_a has a nonzero value but the variables corresponding to the other arcs entering and leaving state i are all zero. Such a solution cannot correspond to a subsequence of a behavior because it does not describe a path through each DFA. The equations saying that the number of calls from a task to an entry must equal the number of times those calls are accepted add enough additional restrictions to eliminate such solutions in many, but not all, cases.

The second reason that a solution to the equations may not correspond to a subsequence of a behavior is that it may not be possible to reach all of the start states in that solution at the same time in any actual behavior of the concurrent system. The equations do not impose any restrictions on the start states of the various DFAs, and therefore do not exclude solutions that are inconsistent with the behavior of the concurrent system.

In some cases, it is possible to tighten the bound obtained by integer linear programming through procedures that overcome some of the problems associated with cycles and with solutions whose initial states are not simultaneously reachable in an actual behavior. We now briefly describe a marking algorithm that reduces the problems due to cycles in DFAs and a procedure for generating additional equations to eliminate many solutions with unreachable initial states. Detailed descriptions of these methods are given in [5].

If upper bounds for all variables are introduced into the integer linear programming problem, the variables associated with cycles that can occur arbitrarily often will all take the maximum value in a solution to the equations giving an upper bound on durations. Such variables can be easily detected by inspection of the solution, and it might seem that a valid upper bound could be obtained by simply subtracting those variables from the solution. This is not the case, however, since the cycle may contain an event that occurs in the subsequence attaining the true maximum duration and eliminating the events in the cycle would eliminate this subsequence. Our marking algorithm removes certain cycles from the DFAs without eliminating any actual subsequences of behaviors. The idea is essentially to mark only those transitions in a task DFA that can be reached from a transition corresponding to the event starting the subsequences (or any other event that the analyst has indicated must occur in the subsequences). Any other transitions cannot occur in any subsequence starting with the specified event and can thus be removed (equivalently, one can think of setting the corresponding arc variables to zero).

The problem with unreachable start states can be addressed by introducing additional variables and generating equations representing conditions that must be satisfied by the initial segment of a behavior containing the subsequence of interest. Essentially, we use the equations to simultaneously find a subsequence starting with A and ending with B and an initial segment that would make that subsequence possible.

We have modified the constrained expression toolset to implement these methods and applied them to several examples with very encouraging results. The upper bounds found by the modified toolset are generally quite good, and frequently are indeed attained by subsequences of behaviors. Detailed discussion of the methods and an illustration of their application are given in [5].

CONCLUSIONS AND FUTURE DIRECTIONS

In this paper, we have given a brief, high-level description of the current status of our work on automated analysis of concurrent and real-time software. Results obtained from applying our automated constrained expression analysis techniques to a range of representative, nontrivial concurrent and real-time programming problems suggest that these techniques have the potential to be of significant value for realistic analysis applications. Our experiments have also suggested a number of directions for further improvements to the techniques and the tools that automate them. We outline a few of these here; more detailed discussions appear in [4] and [5].

The performance of our constrained expression toolset on a range of concurrent system analysis problems is already quite impressive. Various changes to the toolset's components could make its performance even better, however, and changes to its user interface could make it much easier and more convenient to use. We plan, for example, to improve the deriver by removing some of the minor restrictions that it currently imposes on CEDL programs, such as a prohibition on global variables, and by replacing its semantic analysis phase with a better and faster one. We plan to improve the toolset's integer programming component by introducing new and better branch-and-bound strategies making use of semantic information from the CEDL design in choosing a branching variable. We are also exploring alternative approaches to solving inequalities that can take advantage of the special structure of the inequality systems generated by our analysis techniques. We also expect to expand the capabilities of the behavior generator, such as its ability to help an analyst add inequalities that eliminate spurious ILP solutions, and to improve its heuristics so as to reduce its search times. Finally, we plan to add a uniform and friendly user interface, as well as improving the interfaces between the tools.

We also plan to extend the constrained expression formalism and analysis techniques so that we can use them to address a wider range of analysis problems. Among the topics that we are investigating are methods for directly handling more complex queries, such as "Can event A occur between event B and event C?", which are needed to directly analyze such logical properties as mutually exclusive use of resources. We are also looking at ways to express infinite behaviors, so that questions of fairness and starvation can be addressed by our analysis techniques. Another very important concern is with approaches to decomposing analysis problems into smaller parts, and then recombining the results of analyzing those smaller parts in a way that gives accurate analyses of the full system. Finally, we are interested in developing both formal and empirical characterizations of the range of analysis problems and classes of concurrent systems to which constrained expression analysis techniques can fruitfully be applied.

Our application of the constrained expression analysis techniques and tools to real-time problems is still in the early stages. One immediate goal for our work in this area is an extensive experimental evaluation of our current automated analysis of timing properties, similar to the experimentation we have done with our automated analysis of logical properties of concurrent systems. We are also investigating several extensions to our real-time analysis techniques, including approaches to representing "truly concurrent" events, such as would occur in a multiprocessor or distributed real-time system, and methods for describing the effects of various scheduling mechanisms on real-time system behavior. Our preliminary efforts in both of these areas involve extensions to both the constrained expression formalism and the toolset, whose impacts have yet to be assessed.

Extensive experimentation with the constrained expression toolset has shown it to be very effective for performing automated analysis of logical properties of a range of concurrent system examples of realistic size and non-trivial complexity. Preliminary experimentation with applying the toolset to analysis of timing properties has yielded promising results. We expect that further experimentation and improvements along the lines suggested above will lead to automated analysis techniques for concurrent and real-time software that can contribute significantly to the robustness and reliability of this class of software systems.

Acknowledgements

The work described here has benefited immensely from our long-term collaboration with Dr. Laura Dillon. Ugo Buy and James Corbett have also made major contributions to this work. Susan Avery, Michael Greenberg, RenHung Hwang, G. Allyn Polk, and Peri Tarr have all contributed to the toolset implementation or experimentation activities described in this paper.

REFERENCES

[1] *Proceedings of the International Workshop on Real-Time Ada Issues,* sponsored by Ada UK and ACM SIGAda, May 1987. Appeared as *Ada Letters*, 7(6), Fall 1987.

[2] S. Avery. A tool for producing constrained expression representations of CEDL designs. Software Development Laboratory Memo 89-2, Department of Computer and Information Science, University of Massachusetts, 1989.

[3] G. S. Avrunin, U. Buy, and J. Corbett. Automatic generation of inequality systems for constrained expression analysis. Technical Report 90-32, Department of Computer and Information Science, University of Massachusetts, Amherst, 1990.

[4] G. S. Avrunin, U. A. Buy, J. C. Corbett, L. K. Dillon, and J. C. Wileden. Automated analysis of concurrent systems with the constrained expression toolset. Submitted for publication. Available as Technical Report 90-116, Department of Computer and Information Science, University of Massachusetts, Amherst.

[5] G. S. Avrunin, J. C. Corbett, L. K. Dillon, and J. C. Wileden. Automated constrained expression analysis of real-time software. Submitted for publication. Available as Technical Report 90-117, Department of Computer and Information Science, University of Massachusetts, Amherst.

[6] G. S. Avrunin, L. K. Dillon, and J. C. Wileden. Constrained expression analysis of real-time systems. Technical Report 89-50, Department of Computer and Information Science, University of Massachusetts, Amherst, 1989.

[7] G. S. Avrunin, L. K. Dillon, J. C. Wileden, and W. E. Riddle. Constrained expressions: Adding analysis capabilities to design methods for concurrent software systems. *IEEE Trans. Softw. Eng.*, SE-12(2):278–292, 1986.

[8] U. A. Buy. Solving integer programming problems using the IMINOS prototype. In preparation.

[9] J. C. Corbett. On selecting a form for inequality generation in the constrained expression toolset. Constrained Expression Memorandum 90-1. Department of Computer and Information Science, University of Massachusetts, Amherst, 1990.

[10] J. C. Corbett. A tool for automatic elimination of constraints in constrained expression analysis. Constrained Expression Memorandum 90-2. Department of Computer and Information Science, University of Massachusetts, Amherst, 1990.

[11] J. C. Corbett and G. A. Polk. A tool for automatic generation of behaviors for constrained expression analysis. In preparation.

[12] L. K. Dillon. *Analysis of Distributed Systems Using Constrained Expressions*. PhD thesis, University of Massachusetts, Amherst, 1984.

[13] L. K. Dillon. Overview of the constrained expression design language. Technical Report TRCS86-21, Department of Computer Science, University of California, Santa Barbara, October 1986.

[14] L. K. Dillon, G. S. Avrunin, and J. C. Wileden. Constrained expressions: Toward broad applicability of analysis methods for distributed software systems. *ACM Trans. Prog. Lang. Syst.*, 10(3):374–402, July 1988.

[15] M. A. Saunders. MINOS system manual. Technical Report SOL 77-31, Stanford University, Department of Operations Research, 1977.

[16] R. N. Taylor, F. C. Belz, L. A. Clarke, L. J. Osterweil, R. W. Selby, J. C. Wileden, A. L. Wolf, and M. Young. Foundations for the Arcadia environment architecture. In *Proceedings SIGSOFT '88: Third Symposium on Software Development Environments*, pages 1–13, December 1988.

[17] J. C. Wileden and G. S. Avrunin. Toward automating analysis support for developers of distributed software. In *Proceedings of the Eighth International Conference on Distributed Computing Systems*, pages 350–357. IEEE Computer Society Press, June 1988.

CHAPTER 9

TOWARDS A TIMING SEMANTICS FOR PROGRAMMING LANGUAGES

Alan C. Shaw
Department of Computer Science and Engineering
University of Washington
Seattle, WA 98195

Abstract

To provide a basis for predicting and reasoning about the deterministic timing properties of programs, we have developed the notion of *timing schema* which are simply formula for computing the best and worst case execution times of programs and their components. Schema are derived for common sequential and concurrent programming constructs. These schema are independent of particular implementations (e.g. machine, compiler, operating system) and are meant to define a timing semantics for the programming language. The practicality of the approach has been demonstrated with many experiments on sequential C programs and with some initial experiments on parallel code on a multiprocessor. We conclude that the methodology does indeed work, but that many interesting research problems remain.

INTRODUCTION

Our goal is to develop techniques and tools for predicting and reasoning about the *deterministic* timing behavior of programs. Applications include hard real-time systems that must satisfy strict timing constraints, systems where *a priori* guarantees on performance bounds are desired, and software that involves programming with and about time. Our emphasis is on analysis methods that are useable at the *source* program level.

The approach is to define a timing semantics for a programming language in the form of *timing schema* for the constructs of the language. A schema for a construct is an expression that represents the best and worst case times over all possible executions of the construct. The execution time of a particular program is predicted by instantiating the schema for the program's components.

These ideas were first developed in [12] for sequential programs and several examples in concurrent software. A more comprehensive set of deterministic timing schema for parallel programs, suitable for both multiprocessor and distributed target systems, was proposed later [13]. An implementation and extensive validation experiments for sequential programs were reported in [8] and [9]. Some initial experiments with parallel programs have also been completed [5]. Our purpose here is to survey and synthesize the results from the above works.

There is some, but not a great deal, of related research. Both sequential and parallel languages are treated formally by Haase [4], but control costs and many types of parallel interaction, such as critical sections, are not included. [7] presents schema for sequential programs in the form of "cost predicate transformers", that are very similar in spirit to ours - particularly because they also include control costs. Neither of these two efforts seem to have been developed further after the initial papers.

Puschner and Koza [10] describe an implemented method for computing worst case execution times for a restricted subset of C, augmented by declarative constructs for bounding loops and other entities. They use timing formulae for sequential statement constructs, which have some of the same flavor as our schema but ignore control costs. Other related works involving implementations include the time tool development of Mok et al. [6] and the schedulability analyzer of Real-Time Euclid [14]. The time tool analyzes an assembly language stream by graph methods to produce a worst case path and computes execution times by simulating the machine. The system was also expanded to analyze a higher-level language program through the use of annotations that are carried down into the assembly language level, but it still relies on target hardware simulation and extensive analysis of assembly language streams. In the schedulability analyzer, a program is decomposed into a tree of segments, the time of each segment is computed, and finally worst case program execution time is determined from the segment tree. The analyzer also works in some processor sharing and distributed environments with interprocess communication and resource sharing; blocking times of processes are predicted by simulating all possible paths and resource contentions.

All of the above studies attempt to bound the worst case execution time. Our work differs in one or more of the following ways: we employ analytic methods at the *source* language level using *formal* timing schema that include *control* costs, handle hardware interferences such as interrupts, produce *guaranteed* best and worst case bounds, and subject the ideas to validation experiments on real machines.

COMPUTERS AND TIME

Two generic hardware architectures are assumed as possible underlying implementation targets for our higher-level abstractions. One architectural type is a *multiprocessor* shared-memory system. Communications between the processors and shared memory (i.e., reads and writes) occur *deterministically* through some switching device such as a cross-bar switch or bus structure. A similar mechanism may be used for processor-to-processor signalling. Each processor may also have its own private storage. The second generic organization is a *distributed* system. Here, each node may be a single or multiprocessor system and nodes communicate with each other through statically-defined connections, such as a shared communications bus, a local area network, or separate point-to-point "wires". Communication paths are defined statically so that message passing times are predictable.

Each process runs on its *own* (dedicated) *processor*, giving maximal parallelism. The 1:1 process-processor relationship applies to all systems activities including input-output and timers. Processes may interact through shared variables or via message passing, supported by the multiprocessor and distributed architectures, respectively. The effects of *hardware resource contentions*, such as processor sharing, bus and memory contention, communications line collisions, and interrupts, are discussed and factored into the analysis to some extent in a later section of this paper. Initially, both interacting and non-interacting processes are assumed to execute free from any of these interferences.

The "time" in our schema refers to an idealization of real-time as realized by a perfect global clock. This real-time is denoted by rt. Computer time is the discrete approximation to real-time implemented on machines by a variety of hardware and software methods.

Many versions of computer time can coexist in a system. We will assume that each version is approximately synchronized with perfect real-time as follows. If ct represents a computer time, then $ct = rt + \delta$ where $|\delta| \leq \epsilon$ and the bound ϵ is determined by the accuracy of the hardware clock, tick interval, synchronization interval, and synchronization method. This relation does not include the access time to obtain or compute ct.

In this view, our abstract real-time rt is represented by a real number and each ct is a computer approximation to a real number. However, ct is normally a more complex data structure, with separate components designating, for example, the year, month, day, hour, minutes, and seconds. Updating a clock, computing with time as a variable, or even reading a computer clock can consume a significant amount of time, which must be taken into account in many analyses.

THE TIMING SCHEMA APPROACH

The timing schema idea is quite straightforward. Execution time bounds $T(S)$ for a source language construct S are given or derived as a pair, representing an interval:

$$T(S) = [t_{min}(S), t_{max}(S)]$$

where t_{min} denotes the best case execution time for S and t_{max} is the worst case time. A particular execution of S has time $t(S)$ such

$$t_{min}(S) \leq t(S) \leq t_{max}(S)$$

$t(S)$ is the time between the *start event* and *end event* which delimit the execution. Generally, $T(S)$ is given for the atomic elements of a language (as a function of the compiler, run-time system, machine, and other implementation factors), and derived or computed for higher-level objects using the schema.

For example, a conventional conditional construct:

$$S = \textbf{if } B \textbf{ then } S1 \textbf{ else } S2$$

may have the schema:

$$T(S) = [\min(t1_{low}, t2_{low}), \max(t1_{high}, t2_{high})]$$

where $[t1_{low}, t1_{high}] = T(B) + T(S1) + T(\text{then})$, $[t2_{low}, t2_{high}] = T(B) + T(S2) + T(\text{else})$, and $T(\text{then})$ and $T(\text{else})$ denote control flow times, i.e. the times to transfer to and from $S1$ and $S2$.[1] This formula is the result of taking the best and worst case paths through the construct.

Deterministic performance analysis for a program is accomplished by predicting the execution time for each statement S according to the following steps:

1. Decompose S into its primitive or basic components, as defined by the timing schema for S. These basic components are called *atomic blocks*.

2. Predict the implementation (for example, the object code generated by the compiler) of each atomic block.

3. Determine the execution times of the atomic blocks from the times of the machine instructions produced by the implementation.

4. Compute the execution time of S, using the times of the atomic blocks and the timing schema for S.

Using this approach, the execution time of statement
$$S1: \quad a := b + c;$$
could be computed in the following way. A timing schema corresponding to $S1$ could be
$$T(S1) = T(b) + T(+) + T(c) + T(a) + T(:=)$$
The statement is decomposed into 5 atomic blocks, corresponding to b, $+$, c, a, and $:=$. Object code for each atomic block could be predicted:

```
b :    mov M,R    /* mov b,d0 */
+:     add M,R    /* add c,d0 */
c :    none
a :    none
:=     mov R,M    /* mov d0,a */
```

The predicted execution time of $S1$ becomes the sum of the times of the three instructions above.

---

[1]The interval [a,b] can be interpreted as a set of numbers x such that $a \leq x \leq b$. In interval arithmetic, [a,b] *op* [c,d], for any binary operator *op*, has the meaning: [a,b] *op* [c,d] = { x = y *op* z : y *in* [a,b] and z *in* [c,d]}. Thus, [a,b] + [c,d] = [a+c, b+d].

For more complex reasoning about time, we extend standard assertional program logic to include a real-time clock variable rt that is updated at each statement execution. Standard Hoare logic uses assertions P and Q, respectively before and after a statement S, with the notation

$$\{P\} \, S \, \{Q\}.$$

The interpretation is: if P is true before the execution of S and S is executed, then Q will be true after S (assuming that S terminates).

With perfect knowledge of timing, we would augment the above form to:

$$\{P\} < S; rt := rt + t(S) > \{Q\}$$

where P and Q could now include relations involving real-time (rt) before and after execution of S, i.e., at the start and end events, respectively, of S, and the brackets ($<>$) indicate that the execution of S and incrementing of rt occur at the same time. The axiom of assignment can then be used in P and Q for assertions about rt. For example, if $P = P(rt, \cdots)$, then one can assert either

$$\{P(rt, \cdots)\} \, S \, \{P(rt - t(S), \cdots)\}$$

or

$$\{P(rt + t(S), \cdots)\} \, S \, \{P(rt, \cdots)\}.$$

Our approximation to this unrealizable ideal is the rule:

$$\{P\} < S; RT := RT + T(S) > \{Q\}$$

where RT is a pair $[rt_{min}, rt_{max}]$ such that at any time, the perfect real-time rt is in the interval defined by rt_{min} and rt_{max}. P and Q may now include assertions about the elements of RT.

This logic can be used, for example, to specify *deadlines* in a natural way. Let $RT_{dl} = [t_{dlmin}, t_{dlmax}]$ be deadlines such that a program S must be completed no *earlier* than t_{dlmin} and no later than t_{dlmax}. This general deadline problem can be expressed:

$$\{RT + T(S) = RT_{dl}\} \, S \, \{RT = RT_{dl}\}$$

i.e., at the start event of S, real-time must be bounded

$$t_{dlmin} - t_{min}(S) \le rt \le t_{dlmax} - t_{max}(S).$$

It is impossible to meet this constraint if

$$t_{dlmin} - t_{min}(S) > t_{dlmax} - t_{max}(S).$$

From the above (letting $t_{dlmin} = -\infty$) or directly, it is easy to specify a conventional deadline constraint:

$$\{rt \le t_{dlmax} - t_{max}(S)\} \, S \, \{rt \le t_{dlmax}\}.$$

SOURCE LANGUAGE TIMING SCHEMA
Sequential Constructs

A timing formula for a conditional if/then/else statement was given as an example in the last section. Other timing schema for typical constructs in sequential imperative programming languages are presented in Table 1.

For the looping statement, **while** B **do** S, it is assumed that the loop bounds N are obtained using some external means, for example, from user input or as a result of a loop termination proof. Usually, N is a function of the input data. The particular loop schema is just one of several possibilities, depending on the host compiler and target architecture. For example, in our experiments, the schema is parameterized to

$$(N + 1) \times T(B) + N \times T(S) + T(\text{while},N)$$

where the parametrized part $T(\text{while}, N)$ is a function of the hardware M68000 instruction times as follows:

$$T(\text{while},N) = N \times T(\text{JRF\_fail}) + T(\text{JRF\_succ}) + N \times T(\text{JRA})$$

Here, JRA is the "jump_relative always" instruction, JRF_fail is the "jump_relative if false" instruction when the branch is not taken, and JRF_succ is the "jump_relative if false" instruction when the branch is taken.

Our schema for the delay construct yields an upper bound on the delay, something that few if any systems do; for example, the Ada delay statement only specifies a lower bound. However, we feel strongly that such timing-related statements *must* have guaranteed bounds if they are to be used in real-time programs and that the (timing) semantics must include these bounds explicitly. Such bounds can be realized in practice by using dedicated timers or by limiting the amount of sharing of clocks and processors.

Parallel Constructs

The traditional *process* is the basic software unit of concurrency. Processes cannot be nested, and are created statically and pre-loaded. More dynamic generation is deliberately excluded since it would complicate

Construct S	Schema T(S)
$(expr_1 \ op \ expr_2)$ where op is a binary operator such as $+$ or $\times$	$T(expr_1) + T(op) + T(expr_2)$
$v := expr$	$T(.v) + T(:=) + T(expr)$ where $T(.v)$ is the time to obtain the address of a variable v
$S_1 \ ; \ S_2$	$T(S_1) + T(S_2)$
while B **do** S	$(N+1) \times T(B) + N \times T(S) + (2N+1) \times T(\text{while})$ where $T(\text{while})$ is the control cost of the statement (e.g. branches) and N is a given set of loop bounds $N = [n_{min}, n_{max}]$
proc_name$(e_1,...,e_n)$ where proc_name is a procedure name and $e_1, ..., e_n$ are the parameters of the call	$T(\text{call/return}) + T(e_1) + ... + T(e_n) + n \times T(\text{par}) + T(\text{proc\_name\_body})$ where $T(\text{call/return})$ is the procedure call and return time, $T(e_i)$ is the time to evaluate parameter e_i, $T(\text{par})$ is the parameter passing cost, and $T(\text{proc\_name\_body})$ is the time to execute the procedure body
delay(dt)	$dt + [-\epsilon,\epsilon] + T_{oh}$ where ϵ is a bound on the accuracy of the computer clock with respect to real-time and T_{oh} is the software overhead of the delay statement

Table 1: Some Possible Timing Schema for Sequential Constructs

the deterministic prediction of execution times and is not necessary for most applications, especially in real-time systems.

A system S of n parallel programs or processes is represented by the form:
$$S = S_1 \parallel S_2 \parallel ... \parallel S_n$$
where each S_i is a separate program or process and the symbol "$\parallel$" denotes parallelism. To assure that the start and end of concurrent execution are synchronized, each S_i will contain start and final synchronization code (possibly empty) as follows:

S_i = <wait for "start">$_i$; C_i ; < signal "end">$_i$;

Here, C_i is the "normal" sequential code for the process.

Process Initiation and Termination. The following schema is proposed for starting n processes by a broadcast mechanism and synchronizing their termination:
$$T(S) = T(\parallel_n) + \max_i (T(S_i))^2$$
The time for the <wait for "start">$_i$ component of S_i used for defining $T(S_i)$ does *not* include any waiting time but is the time for processing a received "start" signal. The time for <signal "end">$_i$ includes the time to transmit the signal to its receiver. $T(\parallel_n)$ is the additional cost incurred for initiating the n processes and subsequently synchronizing their termination.

A generic *controller* for the system performs the following two functions in sequence:

β : < Broadcast "start" signals to all S_i >;

ρ : < Receive "end" signals from each S_i >;

First, consider a *busy-wait* implementation on a shared-memory multiprocessor. We use two shared variables: a Boolean variable *start* and an integer counting variable *end*, initialized to *false* and 0 respectively. The controller code is:

β: start := true;

ρ: **while** end < n **do** {null statement};

The wait and signal for each process S_i are programmed:

ω_i: **while** $\neg$ start **do** {null statement};

σ_i: [end := end + 1];

---

[2]Define $\max_i(T(S_i)) = [\max_i(t_{min}(S_i)), \max_i(t_{max}(S_i))]$.

The square brackets surrounding the σ_i code indicate that the statement must be atomic or indivisible[3].

The busy-wait solution has some memory and/or bus contention that can result if either of the shared variables are accessed simultaneously. Most of this can be avoided with an *interrupt*-based solution. Here, the controller initiates each process by interrupting its processor; on completion, each process interrupts the controller.

$T(\|_n)$ is derived from the busy-wait form. The second term in the expression below results from the best and worst case paths through the last pass of the **while** loop of the controller's ρ code, when the variable *end* reaches n.

$$T(\|_n) = T(\text{start} := \text{true}) + [t_{min}(\text{while}) + t_{min}(\text{end} < \text{n}),$$
$$2\, t_{max}(\text{while}) + t_{max}(\text{end} < \text{n})]$$
$$= T(\text{start} := \text{true}) + T(\text{while}) + T(\text{end} < \text{n}) + [0, t_{max}(\text{while})]$$

$T(\|_n)$ is not dependent on the number of processes. If interferences due to memory contention ($[end := end + 1]$) are factored in, $T(\|_n)$ would be a function of n for the worst case. The solution using interrupts also has an upper time bound which is a (linear) function of n.

One realization for a distributed system resembles the interrupt-based version mentioned above. We assume non-blocking broadcast (alternatively, multi-cast) and send message commands, and a blocking, buffered receive message command. The controller could then work as follows:

```
β: Broadcast("start");
ρ: while k < n do {k initialized to 0}
        Receive(message); {message = "end" assumed}
        k := k + 1;
    end
```

The wait and signal for each process S_i are simply:

```
ωᵢ: Receive(message); {message = "start" assumed}
σᵢ: Send("end", Controller);
```

For this implementation, we have

---

[3]Many machines have an atomic increment-and-store instruction. If such an instruction is not available, a test-and-set (or similar instruction) can be employed in the standard way to ensure indivisibility.

$$t_{min}(\|_n) = t_{min}(\text{Broadcast(``start'')}) +$$
$$t_{min}(\text{Receive(message)}) + t_{min}(\text{k} := \text{k} + 1)$$
$$+ 2t_{min}(\text{while}) + t_{min}(\text{k} < \text{n})$$

which represents the "start" message transmission to the closest S_i plus the fastest time to handle one (the last) Receive(message) and exit the loop. For the worst case, the expression is:

$$t_{max}(\|_n) = t_{max}(\text{Broadcast(``start'')}) +$$
$$n(t_{max}(\text{Receive(message)}) + t_{max}(\text{k} := \text{k} +1))$$
$$+ (n + 1)\, t_{max}(\text{k} < \text{n}) + (2n + 1)\, t_{max}(\text{while})$$

This corresponds to the situation where the slowest S_i is farthest from the controller and where all the "end" messages arrive simultaneously.

Network message transmission times are included in the time for a Broadcast, and $t_{min}(\text{Broadcast(message)})$ denotes here both CPU processing and the shortest time to reach *any* (not all) S_i. Similarly, we are assuming implicitly that $T(\text{Send(``end'', Controller)})$ also includes message transmission times, and that $T(\text{Receive(message)})$ does *not* include waiting times when no messages have been received.

A second general way to start and end the parallel execution of n processes is through a sequence of "forks" and "joins". This alternative is developed in [13].

Shared Variable Interactions. Timing schema and their practical realizations are provided for two standard mechanisms for controlling access to shared variables: critical section locks and semaphores. The general strategy is to separate processing times from waiting or blocking times, so then the schema for a synchronization construct C takes the form:

$$T(C) = T(C_{no\_wait}) + T(C_{wait})$$

The jth critical section (lexicographically) in a process S_i protected by the shared lock r is designated:

$$S_{ij}^r = \textbf{lock } r \,;\, C_{ij}^r \,;\, \textbf{unlock } r \,;$$

where C_{ij}^r is the actual code. Entry and exit to C_{ij}^r is controlled by the primitive locking commands r_{entry} and r_{exit}, respectively. Given the system $S = S_1 \|...\| S_n$ with critical sections interspersed within each S_i and assuming that entry is allocated fairly on a first-in/first-out (FIFO) basis, the execution times $T(S_{ij}^r)$ are given by

$$T(S_{ij}^r) = T(r_{entry_i}) + T(r_{exit_i}) + T(C_{ij}^r) +$$
$$[0, \sum_{\substack{k=1 \\ k \neq i}}^{n} (t_{max}(r_{entry_k}) + t_{max}(r_{exit_k}) + \max_l(t_{max}(C_{kl}^r)))]^4$$

The last term gives the worst case waiting time, which is the time for all the other S_k ($k \neq i$) to execute their slowest critical section. $T(r_{entry})$ does not include any waiting time. $T(r_{exit})$ includes the time to "wakeup" a waiting process, if there is one.

A clever implementation of the locking protocol that meets our requirements was devised for a different application by Anderson [1]. It assumes an atomic read-and-increment instruction. FIFO service is obtained by maintaining a circular queue for each lock. Anderson's algorithm is:

r_{entry} : myplace := read_and_increment(next) **mod** n; {r1}
        while status[myplace] = "blocked" **do** {spin}; {r2}
        status[myplace] := "blocked"; {r3}

r_{exit} : status[(myplace + 1) **mod** n] := "free";

The variables *status*[ ] and *next* are shared. *myplace* is private; i.e., each S_i has its own *myplace*. Each lock has its own instances of the variables. Initial values are:

status[0] := "free"; status[1 .. n − 1] := "blocked"; next := 0;

The only way that a timing analysis could produce results that were tighter than those generated by our schema is by analyzing explicitly the control flow through each of the S_i *and* through the system, and proving that the best case is impossible (in order to get a tighter lower bound) or that the worst case is impossible (in order to obtain a tighter upper bound). The first case is unlikely since this would indicate that a particular lock is *always* busy when requested by some process. In the second case, it may well be that one could prove that worst case critical section activity cannot exist; for example, a short critical section in one process could imply a long one at the same time in another.

---

[4] r_{entry} and r_{exit} are subscripted by i to indicate that the time depends on the particular process i that the lock is associated with. r may be implemented differently on different processors, and processor execution speeds may be different.

Consider next the behavior of *general* semaphores initialized to zero. The operations P and V are defined:

$P(S)$: [**await** $S > 0 \rightarrow S := S - 1$]

$V(S)$: [$S := S + 1$]

The execution time of the V operation will be described by the schema:

$$T(V(S)) = T(V_{entry}) + T(S := S + 1) + T(V_{exit})$$

For the P operation, we include a separate term for blocked or waiting time (when $S = 0$):

$$T(P(S)) = T(P_{wait}) + T(P_{entry}) + T(S := S - 1) + T(P_{exit})$$

$T(P_{entry})$ and $T(V_{entry})$ will also cover the potential waiting times when several simultaneous calls are made on P and/or V but $S > 0$; i.e. contention for the small critical sections surrounding the P and V, that are required to make them atomic.

Given a system of n processes that communicate only through general semaphores, it is first necessary to prove that the system cannot deadlock on one or more semaphores. Otherwise $t_{max}(P_{wait}) = \infty$. At the other extreme, notice that we have not provided for a *timeout* on a P operation, as defined commonly in many commercial realizations in order to bound explicitly the waiting time; with a timeout, the schema is much simpler but often not too useful. For example, if $P(S, t)$ is a P operation with timeout t (waiting_time $\leq t$, theoretically), then

$$T(P(S,t)) = [0, \max(0, t + \gamma)] + T(P_{entry}) + T(S := S - 1) + T(P_{exit})$$

where $|\gamma|$ is bounded and accounts for the software overhead related to waiting and timeout wakeup and for the difference between computer time and real time [12].

It is useful to view the semaphore "abstract data type" as a *server* that manages requests from n client processes for P and V operations. Then, in order to bound the waiting time on a P operation, it is sufficient to know the maximum interarrival time $t_{max}(\Delta V)$ of V requests. (Note that $(t_{max}(\Delta V))$ may be less than the maximum time between the start events of two successive V's because of contention for the P and V operations.)

The worst case blocking for a process p_i occurs when $(n - 2)$ other processes are also blocked on the same semaphore and p_i made the last P request, assuming a FIFO policy for wakeups. This yields the following expression for $T(P_{wait})$:

$$T(P_{wait}) = [0, (n-1)\, t_{max}(\Delta V)] + [0,(n-1) \max_{j\neq i}(t_{max}(V^j(S)))]^{\,5}$$
$$= (n-1)\, [0,\, t_{max}(\Delta V) + \max_{j\neq i}(t_{max}(V^j(S)))]$$

Of course, one could do better than the above with further information about particular *sequences* of interarrival times, since we have assumed that *all* blocked processes wait for $t_{max}(\Delta V)$ time units. Similarly, further knowledge might indicate that the particular wakeup V's were not the ones associated with the maximum execution time (i.e. not the V^j such that $\max_{j\neq i}(t_{max}(V^j(S)))$). The analysis of semaphore execution times for a producer-consumer pair of processes communicating through a bounded buffer, that appears in [12], essentially derives $t_{max}(\Delta V)$ for a particular case example.

A first-come first-served implementation using *binary* semaphores can be coded with the lock entry and exit programs (r_{entry} and r_{exit}).

Message Passing Interactions. A distributed system is assumed, with each process residing in a separate node and using message passing for interprocess communications. We discuss and analyze remote procedure call interactions and then examine more general forms of communication. As in the shared variable case, the schema consist of the sum of two subschema, one giving processing times and the other expressing waiting or blocking times.

First, consider an environment where a *server* process S receives and handles requests from a set of n *client* processes $C_1, C_2, ..., C_n$ ($n \geq 1$). Requests are issued in the form of a procedure call:

remote_call pname(input_params, results)

where the procedure name *pname* is the name of the request, *input_params* is a list of input values that are also transmitted to the server, and *results* is an output list containing the results of the call as communicated from the server to the client.

The server is a cyclic process that just invokes a local procedure call to handle each request:

---

[5]The superscript j on the V denotes the particular process p_j that issued the V, and is used because the same code may be executed at different speeds by different processes.

```
S: loop
        receive (pname, input_params) from ?client;
        local_call (pname, input_params, results);
        send (results) to client;
    end loop
```

The **receive** primitive is a "blocking" receive with buffering. It has the general form:

receive <message> **from** <object>

The <object> field can be a process name, indicating that the invoking process waits until any message is received from a particular named process. Alternatively, the <object> field may be a "?" followed by a variable, which causes a potential wait until any message is received; the name of the sender process is stored in the variable. The **send** is asynchronous:

send <message> **to** <object>

The sender continues immediately after sending the message.[6] Here, <object> is a process name.

The remote procedure call, **remote_call**, is implemented as a **send/receive** pair:

send (pname, input_params) **to** server; **receive** (results) **from** server;

The timing schema for a **send** is defined:

$$T(\textbf{send } m \textbf{ to } p) = T(\text{Encode}(m,p)) + T(\text{Transmit}(mp))$$

where $\text{Encode}(m, p)$ denotes the preparation of the message m for sending to p, such as encoding m into packets and finding p's address on the network, mp is the result of the encoding, and $\text{Transmit}(mp)$ represents the actual transmission of m until received by p including any lower level protocol (e.g. acknowledgements).

Most of the timing complexity is in the **receive** waiting time. A simple schema suffices for the client/server application:

$$T(\textbf{receive } m \textbf{ from } p) = T(\textbf{receive } m \textbf{ from } ?p)$$
$$= T(\text{Wait\_Receive}) + T(\text{Decode}(\text{data}))$$

where $Wait\_Receive$ accounts for any waiting time until a message is in the receiver's buffer. *data* is the transmitted encoding of the message and

---

[6]It is convenient to include transmission time as part of the **send**, since messages are buffered at the receiver end; communications is assumed to be perfectly reliable.

sender name, and Decode(data) is the processing involved in unpacking the message.

In the absence of any outside information, $T(\text{Wait\_Receive}) = [0, \infty]$ for the RPC server process. If the maximum interarrival time of RPC requests is known, the upper bound can be made tighter.

The client **receive's** admit to a more detailed analysis. The best case occurs when a client c sends a request to a free server, giving the minimum processing time through the server. The worst case happens when the server has $(n-1)$ unserviced client requests ahead of a given client c. Putting these together, we get

$$
\begin{aligned}
T(\text{Wait\_Receive}) = {} & T(\text{Decode}((\text{pname, input\_params}))) \\
& + T(\textbf{local\_call}(\text{pname, input\_params, results})) \\
& + T(\textbf{send}\ (\text{results})\ \textbf{to}\ c) \\
& + \text{n}[0, t_{max}(\text{Decode}) + t_{max}(\textbf{local\_call}) + t_{max}(\text{loop})] \\
& + [0, \sum_{client \neq c} t_{max}(\textbf{send})]
\end{aligned}
$$

One concrete example of a server implementation is developed to illustrate the practicality of the above schema. We assume that a message arrival from a client is announced through an interrupt on the server machine and that the message itself enters through an interface register r. The interrupt handler (IH) on the server will transfer a message in r to an n slot software buffer, one slot per potential client, that resides between IH and the server process (Fig. 1).

The code for the interrupt handler is:

```
IH : {Activated by message arrival interrupt}
       Disable_Interrupt_and_Save_State;
       next := (next + 1) mod n
       Buffer[next] := r;
       size := size + 1;
       Restore_State_with_Interrupt_Enabled;
```

The initial part of the **receive** in the server process will consist of a spin (busy wait) loop until at least one message is in the buffer, followed by a buffer transfer. This corresponds to the first part of a general implementation of **receive** m **from** $?p$, where the messages are handled on a first-come, first-served basis. The code for this portion is:

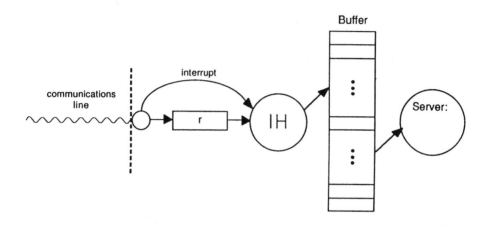

Figure 1 Server Implementation

receive m **from** $?p$:
        while size $= 0$ **do** {null}; {spin}
        data $:=$ Buffer[first];
        first $:=$ (first $+\ 1$) **mod** n;
        Disable_Interrupt;
        size $:=$ size $-\ 1$;
        Enable_Interrupt;
(Initially, next $=$ first $=$ size $= 0$)

The execution time of the statements following the spin loop are part of the $T(\text{Decode}(\text{data}))$ component of $T(\textbf{receive } m \textbf{ from } ?p)$.

We approach the analysis of general message passing using the same notions of *a priori* knowledge of the interarrival times of messages, as used for the study of general semaphores. Let $t_{max}(\Delta\text{send})$ be the maximum interarrival time of messages to a (blocked) receiver process. Knowledge of $t_{max}(\Delta\text{send})$ is obtained by specific analysis of sender processes and perhaps external input data rates. Then, using

$$T(\textbf{receive } m \textbf{ from } ?p) = T(\text{Wait\_Receive}) + T(\text{Decode}(\text{data})),$$

we get simply

$$T(\text{Wait\_Receive}) = [0, t_{max}(\Delta\text{send})] + T(\text{Receive}_{start})$$

where $T(\text{Receive}_{start})$ accounts for any overhead incurred at the time the message is received such as looping and interrupt_handling. We assume here that a receiver process buffers messages.[7]

A similar schema for $T(\textbf{receive } m \textbf{ from } p)$ can be defined in an identical manner. Here we assume $t_{max}(\Delta\text{send})$ is the maximum interarrival time to a receiver for messages from a *particular* process p. Also, Receive$_{start}$ would involve a lengthier computation than in the previous case since the sender name has to be matched with the receiver's designated process (p).

Fully synchronous message communications, as for example, specified in Hoare's CSP, can be treated in a similar manner.

RESOURCE SHARING, CONTENTIONS, AND INDETERMINACIES

The preceding analyses and schema would be sufficient if all resources were dedicated and used in a straightforward manner that admitted deterministic behavior prediction. However, it is often both necessary and convenient to share resources such as processors and memories, and it is common practice to use hardware that is nondeterministic in practice if not in theory, for example, caches, in order to improve average performance. In this section, we show how some resource contentions can be handled and also discuss some of the problems of hardware nondeterminism.

---

[7]Buffer overflow is ignored. The number of buffers affects the timing analysis in that it would limit the amount of interrupt handling contention in a realization.

First, consider resource contention caused by *processor sharing*. One form of sharing occurs when we relax the assumption that each process runs on its own dedicated machine. Several forms of "controlled" processor sharing are examined in [12], but in the absence of process interactions. If processes that share variables through critical sections are all allocated to the same processor, then the complexities of interaction vanish in many cases. Provided that context-switches among processes are disallowed while a process is in a critical section, explicit locking is not necessary; no waiting need occur at critical section entry and the indivisibility is guaranteed. On the other hand, other forms of interaction, such as semaphores and message passing, become more complex because busy-waiting is no longer always the best policy.

It should be noted that if a set of processes share a processor in an interleaved fashion, then the timing schema given earlier for parallel programs no longer hold. Instead, we would need an interleaved-based schema, perhaps like:

$$T(S_1\|...\|S_n) = \Sigma_{i=1}^n T(S_i) + f(n,...) \times T(process\_switch)$$

where $T(process\_switch)$ is the cost of a context or process switch and $f(n,...)$ is some complex function that yields the number of context-switches that might occur during execution of the system.[8] For those parts of a system that are *not* interruptable, the techniques for computing $T(S)$, presented earlier, can be used without change.

Yet another form of processor sharing is almost unavoidable, even when processors are dedicated to single processes. This occurs on interrupt-based hardware, where devices such as timers and input-output, require processor cycles in order to perform some part of their functions. The analysis presented in [12] contains the basic idea for the general case discussed below.

Let t be the cost of running a (sequential) program on a dedicated processor in the absence of interrupts, let k be the number of different interrupts that might occur (concurrently), let f_i be the frequency of

---

[8] Even this analysis may be oversimplified. For example, if t' is the cost of running all n processes on a single processor, t is the sum of the costs of each process, s is the time for a context switch, and we do simple round robin quantum-based scheduling with time quantum q, then $t' = t + (t/q)s = t(1 + s/q)$. Here $f(n,...) = t/q$ $= \sum_{i=1}^n t(S_i)/q$.

occurrence of interrupt i, let h_i be the interrupt-handling time for interrupt i, and let t' be the cost of running the program in the presence of interrupts. Then, assuming there is enough processor time to handle all the potential interrupts (i.e. $\Sigma_{i=1}^{k} (f_i \times h_i) < 1$), the relation between t and t' is:

$t' = t + t' \times \Sigma_{i=1}^{k} (f_i \times h_i)$

giving $t' = t/(1 - \Sigma_{i=1}^{k}(f_i \times h_i))$.

These results can be formulated to produce best and worst case time bounds relating the "pure" execution time $T(S)$ to the expanded window $T'(S)$ obtained when S is executed in the presence of interrupts. We let $F_i = [f_{i1}, f_{i2}]$ be for minimum and maximum frequency of interrupt i and $H_i = [h_{i1}, h_{i2}]$ be the execution time window for the handler associated with interrupt i. Then the desired expression is simply

$T'(S) = T(S)/(1 - \Sigma_{i=1}^{k}(F_i \times H_i))$

Processor sharing due to interrupts can be completely avoided if the functions performed by interrupt handlers are instead done by separate processors, such as input-output processors or timers, that communicate through shared memory including special registers. *Memory sharing* of this kind and the more general multiprocessor version assumed in an earlier section introduce serious contention problems when attempts are made to access the same storage units simultaneously. The contention can occur on a common bus that connects the memories to the processors or on more complex cross-bar switches or on multiport memory buses.

One simple model that appears attractive, but may not apply to all such memory sharing contentions, assumes that these interferences affect execution times linearly with the amount of concurrency. For example, suppose $S = S_1 \parallel S_2$ and $t(S_1) > t(S_2)$ for some execution. Then, as before, we have

$t(S) = \max(t(S_1), t(S_2)) + t(\parallel_2)$
$\qquad = t(S_1) + t(\parallel_2)$

The execution time with contention $t'(S)$ would be

$t'(S) = t(S) + c \times \text{Overlap}(S_1, S_2)$
$\qquad = t(S) + c \times t(S_2)$

for some constant c that depends on the particular hardware used. Using bounds (windows), we would expect:

$T'(S) = T(S) + c \times \min(T(S))$

where $c = [c_1, c_2]$, a constant range. This idea can be generalized to n

concurrent processes.

It may be possible to treat specific contentions that occur at a smaller granularity, as the following example illustrates. Consider once again the busy-wait version of broadcast control presented earlier. Each S_i terminates with the common code [$end := end + 1$], with the resulting potential for n-way contention on accessing the variable end. If this contention is handled with no additional interferences, for example, due to spinning on requests for end, then the worst case execution of a process S_i has the time

$$t(S_i) = t(S_i) + (n - 1) \, t([\text{end} := \text{end} + 1])$$

assuming the same speed for each processor's increment and add. None of the above includes contention effects on the times of $T \, (\|_n)$. For the busy-wait $T(\|_n)$ implementation, it would be possible to obtain one interleave of the end access by the controller between successive [$end := end + 1$] operations, because of the $end < n$ test. $t'(\|_n)$, the concurrency control cost with contention, would then be a linear function of n in the worse case if the controller's access had highest priority.

Another source of interference that affects timing is *memory refresh*. Typically, the main store of a machine consists of dynamic RAMs that must be restored periodically in order to maintain their content. This restoration or refresh normally has a higher priority in accessing memory than the CPU. A technique similar to that described above for handling interrupts can also be employed to factor in such memory refresh interferences.

Some other indeterminacies, for example, due to instruction and data caches or to translation buffers used in virtual memory systems seem even more difficult to handle. One approach is simply to eliminate them ("turn them off") or prohibit their use in systems for which guaranteed execution bounds are required, and pay the subsequent performance penalty. Another approach is to include their effects but at a large enough time granularity so that statistical fluctuations in behavior are both predictable and at an acceptable level. Contention handling on communications lines has not been studied in detail yet. We hope to be able to treat this important problem by either adopting some of the ideas mentioned in this section, by using deterministic collision handling methods with bounded delays, or by employing explicit collision avoidance techniques (for example, a slotted token ring).

SCHEMA VALIDATION:
EXPERIMENTS IN PROGRAM TIMING
A Timing Tool for Sequential C Programs

In order to test our timing schema ideas on real programs and systems, we implemented two versions of a timing tool for sequential C programs. We chose a subset of C, the GNU C compiler (non-optimizing option), and the MC68010-based SUN2/100U as the target language, compiler, and machine, respectively. The subset of C handled by the second version of our tool encompasses most parts of the language including data types such as arrays, pointers, and structures; the main exclusions are logical operators and those that require library calls.

Atomic Block Selection and Code Prediction. A basic decision in defining timing schema and predicting code is the *granularity* of an atomic block. We investigated two granularities: a small atomic block (SAB) in the first version of the tool and a large atomic block (LAB) in the second. The SAB system permitted an extreme test through all elements of language while LAB lent itself to tighter timing predictions.

In the SAB approach, atomic blocks correspond to the terminal symbols of the source language. The timing schema can then be defined in a straightforward way as in the example in the earlier section entitled "The Timing Schema Approach". Conceptually, *code prediction*, i.e. predicting the implementation of each atomic block, also may be easy if code generation follows the parsing structure.

However, many compilers generate code across atomic blocks by using the information of related atomic blocks to generate the code for one atomic block, and sometimes consolidate several atomic blocks into one. For example, in the GNU C compiler on the MC68010, the sequence of statements, a = b + c; d = d + a; can be compiled as follows:

```
a = b + c;    =====>    mov @b,d0
                        add @c,d0
                        mov d0,@a
d = d + a;    =====>    add d0,@d
```

where @a means the memory address of variable a, and
d0 means data register 0.

The first statement is compiled to three instructions without any optimizations. However, the second statement (which has the same structure as the first) is compiled to just one assembly instruction, because a is already in the register and d is both the destination and one of the operands.

One way to manage these complexities, that yields tighter code predictions, involves *parameterized* timing schema. Contextual information is produced during statement analysis, and passed to code prediction through parameters in the timing schema. As an example, a parameterized timing schema for an assignment statement $S :< var >=< exp >;$ may be

$$T(S) = T(var, var\_type) + T(=, var\_type, exp\_type) + T(exp, exp\_type)$$

where the parameters, *var_type* and *exp_type*, are determined in statement analysis. This notion was used in the first version of the tool.

Our second approach is to define atomic blocks as large as possible. The idea of *LAB* is to consider a straight-line block as an atomic block; for example, an assignment statement a = b + c; may be one atomic block. Several assignment statements could be combined to one atomic block, but control statements such as **if** should be decomposed into multiple blocks.

The benefit of *LAB* is that it can eliminate the problems caused by some compiler optimizations. There are some subtleties however that require further study. For example, an apparently straight-line block may be implemented with branching code: a simple multiplication may be done with a sequence of shifts, adds, and branches.

For the LAB version of the tool, every expression statement is an atomic block, and every control construct has one or more atomic blocks, generally associated with possible transfers of control. An example is the **while** statement; both the Boolean expression and the statement are defined as atomic blocks. Code prediction for an atomic block is achieved by looking up the compiled assembly code. An extended compiler generates markers between the codes of atomic blocks.

Target Machine Issues. The MC68010, and many other computers, have instructions with variable execution times that depend on operand values and machine status. In the tool, these execution times are described by time bounds (e.g. *shift*), only a worst case time (e.g.

multiply), or by treating the best and the worst case as different instructions (e.g. *conditional jump*).

Two machine interferences that could not be eliminated were the *clock interrupt* and *memory refresh*. Because we could not find any detailed quantitative data on the effects of memory refresh on program execution times, we made our own hardware measurements with an oscilloscope. The results were surprising (to us) in at least two ways. First, memory refresh is the main source of nondeterminism in the hardware. Second, the amount of nondeterminism and the effects of memory refresh are much larger than expected (i.e. published by the manufacturer), mainly due to bus arbitration costs. Our measurements showed that a worst case processor slowdown of 6.7% was possible (but very unlikely) due to memory refresh interference, that a minimum slowdown was 0% (also very unlikely), and that a frequent slowdown appeared to be 5% with considerable variation above and below.

Time services, which we needed in order to measure execution times, were initiated via a periodic interrupt provided by a timer chip. Let the clock interrupt period be p_{clock}, the interrupt handling time be t_{clock} and the measured execution time of program P be t_P^m, which is a multiple of p_{clock}. Then, the adjusted time t_P', the pure execution time of program P if there were no clock interrupts, is

$$t_P' = t_P^m - \frac{t_P^m}{p_{clock}} \cdot t_{clock} \quad .$$

Tool Design. The timing tool consists of three major components: preprocessor, language analyzer, and architecture analyzer. The preprocessor interprets user commands, prepares the working environment for the tool, and converts the internal time scale (clock cycles) into a real time scale (μsec). The language analyzer, the heart of our timing tool, is decomposed into five functional blocks:

1. Parser (modified GNU compiler): analyzes the input C program, statement by statement.

2. Procedure Times: manages the table of procedure names and their execution times.

3. Loop Bounds: interacts with a user to obtain loop bounds.

4. Time Schema: analyzes a statement into atomic blocks, and computes the execution time of the statement using the times of the atomic blocks computed in Code Prediction. The timing schema are applied here.

5. Code Prediction: predicts the exact code for a given atomic block by looking up the assembly code prepared by the preprocessor and computes the time of the block using instruction execution times provided by the architecture analyzer.

Figure 2 shows a binary search example using the *LAB* version of the tool. Time bounds are output at the end of each statement. In the middle of the figure, "1 4" is the user's loop bounds input, which can be derived from the knowledge that the number of data items is less than 15. The tool gives two predictions: one for the whole procedure time including control transfer and register savings, and the other for the procedure body only.

Experiments and Results. We compared measured times with the time bounds predicted by the timing tool for several different sample programs. Test data for the best/worst cases of a sample program were generated by tracing the shortest and longest execution path of the program. Our basic measurement technique is the control/test loop method, similar to that described in [3].

Three sets of experiments were made. First, each language construct was predicted, measured and validated. Next, we tested simple procedures whose execution paths are completely known. Finally, more complex procedures were tested and analyzed.

Some experimental results using the tool are given below. The numbers [min, max] refer to the best and worst case execution times, respectively, in microseconds. The predicted times are adjusted for memory refresh effects and the measured times are adjusted for clock interrupt interferences.

```
Script started on Fri Apr 27 15:02:11 1990
june.cs.washington.edu% newpretime -b binary_search bs.c
struct {
  int  key;
  int  value;
}  data[15];

binary_search(x)
{
  int fvalue, mid, up, low ;

  low = 0;
                                                [  16 , 16 ]
  up = 14;
                                                [  20 , 20 ]
  fvalue = -1 /* all data are positive */ ;
                                                [  20 , 20 ]
  while (low <= up)
                                    *** WHILE statement ***
                                    Input LOOP-BOUNDS [ low  up ]: 1 4
  {
    mid = (low + up) >> 1;
                                                [  52 , 52 ]
    if ( data[mid].key == x ) {  /*  found  */
      up = low - 1;
                                                [  40 , 40 ]
      fvalue = data[mid].value;
                                                [  72 , 72 ]
    }
                                                [ 112 , 112 ]
    else /* not found */
      if ( data[mid].key > x )  up = mid - 1;
                                                [  40 , 40 ]
      else                      low = mid + 1;
                                                [  40 , 40 ]
                                                [ 128 , 134 ]
                                                [ 206 , 222 ]
  }
                                                [ 258 , 274 ]
                                                [ 352 , 1340 ]
  return fvalue;
                                                [  26 , 26 ]
}
                                                [ 434 , 1422 ]
  *** Target procedure( binary_sea )
      Cycles = [ 478   ,  1466 ]
      Times  = [ 48.62  ,  149.13 ] (micro-sec)
  *** Target procedure( binary_sea ) body time
      Cycles = [ 434   ,  1422 ]
      Times  = [ 44.15  ,  144.65 ] (micro-sec)
june.cs.washington.edu% exit
june.cs.washington.edu%
script done on Fri Apr 27 15:02:52 1990
```

Figure 2: An Example Using the Timing Tool

Program	Predicted Times	Measured Times
a. Sum 10 elements of an array	[155.64, 166.17]	160.39
b. Binary search thru 15 element sorted array	[44.15, 154.76]	[47.0, 147.57]
c. Multiprocessor scheduler for a 5 processor system		
i) pure tool	[51.88, 4253.31]	[280.68, 3242.6]
ii) using path specifications	[256.55, 3356.34]	

The second experiment on the Multiprocessor scheduler program employs a more complicated user input whereby a user can specify a program path ("then" or "else") in an alternative ("if") statement. With this facility, many impossible paths can be eliminated implicitly. (Of course, like loop bounds, one must somehow verify that some possible paths are also not eliminated inadvertently.) The results are quite good: measurements are within predictions and fairly close to the predictions.

First Experiments for Parallel Programs on a Multiprocessor

A busy-wait implementation of the broadcast approach to initiating and terminating n processes was completed on a shared memory multiprocessor Sequent system. For a system
$$S = S_1 \,\|...\| \, S_n, \quad 2 \leq n \leq 17$$
of n non-interacting processes S_i each running on its own processor, we predicted execution times using the schema
$$T(S) = T(\|_n) + \max_i(T(S_i))$$
where $T(\|_n)$ is the cost of initiating and terminating the concurrency for n processes. $T(\|_n)$ was considered an atomic block. This required that we use some clever measurement techniques to obtain $T(\|_n)$, taking into account that the initial broadcast and final termination involved shared

variables, bus contentions, and maintenance of cache coherency. Measured execution times were then compared with predicted times based on the schema.

The controller and process code for the Sequent is essentially a literal translation of the β, ρ, ω, σ code (presented at the beginning of the section entitled "Process Initiation and Termination") into Sequent assembly language. Each C_i in the process code was either empty or consisted of a simple loop:

for j := 1 **to** N_i **do** loop_body;

$T(\|_n)$ is first determined using a software measurement technique, resulting in a range $T^M(\|_n)$. (A superscript M will denote a measured time.) $T^M(\|_n)$ is then employed in our schema in order to predict execution times $T(S)$. The predictions are compared against measured values $T^M(S)$ for validation purposes. The computation of $T^M(\|_n) = [t_{min}^M(\|_n), t_{max}^M(\|_n)]$ is computed as follows.

$t_{max}^M(\|_n)$ is a function of the number n of processes. For n processes $(2 \leq n \leq 17)$:

1. Let $N_i = N$, a constant, for all processes. This produces the worst case timing for $t^M(\|_n)$.

2. Run and measure $t_{max}^M(S)$.

3. Run and measure $t_{min}^M(S_1)$ by executing its C_1 segment alone.

4. Compute $t_{max}^M(\|_n)$ by subtracting $t_{min}^M(S_1)$ from $t_{max}^M(S)$.

$t_{min}^M(\|_n)$ is a constant and occurs when one process executes much longer than the remainder. To compute this time, measurements were made for a single process $(n = 1)$, where C_1 was empty. The minimum of these measurements was chosen as $t_{min}^M(\|_n)$.

It should be noted that each of these measured minimum and maximum costs is only an approximation to the true minimum and maximum. Nondeterministic features of the hardware such as the 16 byte instruction queue, 4 byte instruction prefetch, and storage refresh make precise predictions unrealistic. This approximate aspect was partially compensated for by using a "safe" prediction line for $t_{max}^M(\|_n)$. Other possible approaches to predicting $T(\|_n)$, such as counting instructions and machine cycles, or employing a digital oscilloscope, are not practical because of the inherent complexity of the Sequent system.

Figure 3 shows the data and results for the $T^M(\|_n)$ computation. $t^M_{min}(\|_n)$ and $t^M_{max}(\|_n)$ include measurements of nondeterministic parts of $T^M(S)$, e.g. the busy-waits in the process and controller segments. Consequently, our $t^M_{min}(\|_n)$ ($t^M_{max}(\|_n)$) may be larger (smaller) than a true best (worst) case measurement. Because of this, our predictions are based on a conservative analysis of the measurements: the *safe prediction line* in Figure 3, obtained by fitting the "closest" line on or above the data, is our predicted cost for $t^M_{max}(\|_n)$.

The *predicted* minimum and maximum in Figure 4 were computed by adding the concurrent cost in Figure 3 to the execution time of the C_i segment in the longest process. The single worker process execution times given in the figures refer to this execution time.

The *measured* times are the measured $T^M(S)$. The minimum and maximum were chosen from 100 measurements taken for each configuration. The data in the figures show that all the predictions both cover the real measurements and are reasonably close to the measurements. The experiments thus give us some confidence that the schema techniques work for the basic case of non-interacting processes on a multiprocessor.

The Sequent is a complex machine with apparently nondeterministic and unpredictable timing, due (at least) to caching, bus contention protocol, memory refresh, instruction queue, and instruction prefetch. Nevertheless, it proved possible to do some basic deterministic timing prediction using the schema approach. Further experiments with more complex interacting programs are planned.

CONCLUSIONS

We have presented our recent research results in specifying, predicting, and verifying the deterministic timing properties of software. These results include a more detailed development and analysis of timing schema for higher level language constructs, that permit the prediction of best and worst case execution times of sequential and concurrent programs; the timing schema define the *timing semantics* of a programming

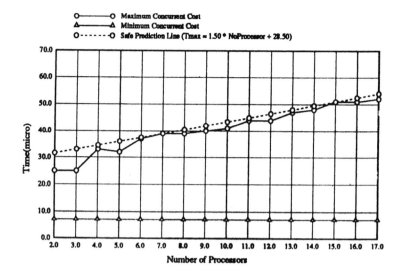

Figure 3: Concurrent Cost

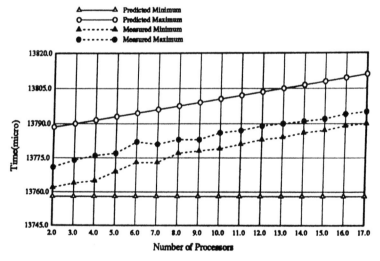

Single worker process execution time = [13751, 13757]

Figure 4: Predicted and Measured Results for $N_i = 5000$

language in a machine and system independent fashion. Several validation experiments that compare predicted and measured times on real machines were also performed. We have shown that our concepts and methodology extends from higher-level abstractions through some practical realizations, and offer substantial promise for meeting our goals.

A number of important research problems remain. One problem under current study is how to specify software requirements in a way that is compatible with our techniques for describing and predicting the timing of behavior of programs. More work is necessary at characterizing the features of modern computer hardware, so that deterministic hardware timing properties can be accurately obtained and so that hardware nondeterminacies can be handled. A search for better mechanisms for software fault tolerance and exception handling, that provide some predictability, is also under way. We have barely started using our methods for more interesting reasoning beyond program deadlines and performance; an appropriate logic for this task must be selected or created. Finally, the ideas should be further tested on some minimal but complete concurrent programming language, for which a complete timing semantics has been defined.

Acknowledgements

Contributions to this project have also been made by Rebecca Callison, Kevin Jeffay, Jihong Kim, and Chang Yun Park.

References

[1] Anderson, T., "The Performance of Spin Lock Alternatives for Shared-Memory Multiprocessors", *IEEE Trans. on Parallel and Distributed Computer Syst., 1*, 1, Jan. 1990, 6-16.

[2] H. Callison and A. Shaw, "Building a Real-Time Kernel: First Steps in Validating a Pure Process/Adt Model", Tech. Report #89-07-04, Dept. of Computer Science and Engineering, Univ. of Washington, July 1989. (A revised version is in publication in *Software: Practice and Experience.*)

[3] R. Clapp et al., "Toward Real-Time Performance Benchmarks for ADA", *Comm. ACM 29*, 8, Aug. 1986, 760-778.

[4] V. Haase, "Real-Time Behavior of Programs", *IEEE Transactions on Software Engineering, 7*, 5, Sept. 1981, 494-501.

[5] J. Kim and A. Shaw, "An Experiment on Predicting and Measuring the Deterministic Execution Times of Parallel Programs on a Multiprocessor", TR #90-09-01, Dept. of Computer Science and Engineering, University of Washington, Sept. 1990.

[6] A. Mok et al. "Evaluating Tight Execution Time Bounds of Programs by Annotations", *Proc. 6th IEEE Workshop on Real-Time Operating Systems and Software*, May 1989, Pittsburgh, pp. 74-80.

[7] M. Shaw, "A Formal System for Specifying and Verifying Program Performance", CMU-CS-79-129, Dept. of Computer Science, Carnegie-Mellon Univ., June, 1979.

[8] C. Park and A. Shaw, "A Source-Level Tool for Predicting Deterministic Execution Times of Programs", TR #89-09-12, Dept. of Computer Science and Engineering, University of Washington, Sept. 1989.

[9] ChangYun Park and Alan Shaw, "Experiments with a Program Timing Tool Based on Source-Level Timing Schema", *Proc. IEEE 11th Real-Time Systems Symposium*, IEEE Computer Society Press, Dec. 1990, pp. 72-81.

[10] P. Puschner and Ch. Koza, "Calculating the Maximum Execution Time of Real-Time Programs", *The Journal of Real-Time Systems, 1*, 2, Sept. 1989, 159-176.

[11] A. Shaw, "Real Time Systems = Processes + Abstract Data Types", *Proceedings of the EUROMICRO Workshop on Real-Time"*, IEEE Computer Society Press, June 1989, pp. 188-197.

[12] A. Shaw, "Reasoning About Time in Higher-Level Language Software", *IEEE Transactions on Software Engineering, 15*, 7, July 1989, 875-889.

[13] A. Shaw, "Deterministic Timing Schema for Parallel Programs", TR # 90-05-06, Dept. of Computer Science and Engineering, University of Washington, May 1990 (revised Sept. 1990). (A revised version will appear in *Proc. 5th Int. Parallel Processing Symp.*, IEEE Computer Society Press, May 1991.)

[14] A. Stoyenko, "A Real-Time Language with a Scheduability Analyzer", TR CSRI-206, Computer Systems Research Institute, University of Toronto, Dec. 1987, Ph.D. Thesis.

CHAPTER 10

FLEX : A Language for Programming Flexible Real-Time Systems

Kwei–Jay Lin
Jane W. S. Liu
Department of Computer Science
University of Illinois at Urbana–Champaign
Urbana, Illinois 61801

Kevin B. Kenny
Northrop Research and Technology Center
One Research Park
Palos Verdes Peninsula, CA 90732

Swaminathan Natarajan
Computer Science Department
Texas A&M University
College Station, Texas 77843

Abstract

Programs in hard real-time systems have stringent timing requirements. To ensure that the deadlines will always be met, real-time systems must be designed to have flexible performances so that they can handle variable system loads. We describe a language called FLEX which makes it possible to implement real-time systems which may respond to dynamic environments. This ability to write programs which are flexible in their execution time is facilitated by the constraint mechanism for expressing timing requirements, and the flexible performance structures like *imprecise computation* and *performance polymorphism*. We describe the rationale behind these primitives. We also present the implementation of timing constraint and the programming support tools.

INTRODUCTION

Programs in real-time systems [1] have stringent timing requirements. A *real-time computation* can be executed only after its *ready time*, must be completed by its *deadline*, and must satisfy certain temporal relationships with other computations in the system. Different from non-real-time computations, a real-time computation must satisfy both the *functional* and the *temporal* correctness criteria; failure to satisfy either one makes the result unacceptable. For a *soft* real-time computation, a slight delay in meeting the deadline may degrade the usefulness of a result. For a *hard* real-time computation, any result produced after the deadline is often considered totally useless. For safety critical applications, a missed deadline may even cause a system failure or disaster. Hard real-time computations are much more difficult to construct due to their strict timing requirements. A defense system for anti-missile attacks is an example of a hard real-time computation; a missed deadline could bring the destruction of the whole system.

Computations in real-time systems are usually triggered by external inputs or interval timers. The program specification [2] includes the times at, before or after which inputs and responses may occur, as well as the minimum and maximum time intervals that may elapse between events. To ensure that a program meets its specifications, a real-time programming system must be able to

- express different types of timing requirements,

- enforce timing requirements either at run time or pre-run time,

- check the feasibility of meeting timing requirements.

Given a real-time program and the timing constraints on it, the system must know how much time and resources the program needs in order to decide if the timing constraints can be satisfied. The problem is non-trivial since many factors may affect the execution time of a program. For example, many processors have operation pipelines which have different execution times depending on the number of branch operations executed. Factors like data-dependent execution path make compile-time analysis impossible. In fact, the problem is equivalent to the halting problem which means we may not tell if a program execution will terminate.

Even with a good performance prediction, deadlines can still be missed if the resources available to a computation vary. The available resources may vary in systems with a variable amount of resources like in many dynamically structured or fault-tolerant systems. For many applications, the program implemented must ensure that deadlines will be met even in the worst-case scenario. Many real-time systems therefore are configured with excessive resources so that computations have a high probability to finish on time. In addition to being expensive, these systems usually are very difficult to modify or extend.

We propose a different approach in building real-time systems. We suggest that real-time computations should be designed with flexible execution times. It is then up to the system to adjust the time and resources to be used by each computation so that all important deadlines are guaranteed to be met under all circumstances. One way to do this is to allow computations to return *imprecise* results. In many hard real-time applications, an approximate result before the deadline is much more desirable than an exact result after the deadline. Another way is to provide multiple versions of a computation, each has a different *performance* capability. Given a timing constraint on the computation, one of the versions is selected to produce the best possible result before the deadline. To implement the approach, we need some programming primitives to express the program structures and to make deadline-driven decisions.

In this paper, we present the design and the implementation of a real-time language called FLEX[3]. FLEX is a part of the Concord project [4] which investigates effective means for real-time programming in order to handle dynamic timing requirements. This paper describes how different types of timing requirements may be expressed in FLEX, how they may be enforced by the run-time system, and how the programming tools can help in making timing-related binding and scheduling decisions. In the next section, we review the issues in programming real-time systems. We next discuss the real-time constructs of FLEX. The timing primitives of FLEX and the implementation issues are discussed in detail. We then present a performance analysis tool which derives the expected execution time for a segment of the program from the actual measurement data. Finally, we discuss the concept and the programming primitives of imprecise computation and performance polymorphism which can be used to build flexible real-time programs.

REAL-TIME PROGRAMMING ISSUES

Most early real-time systems were written in assembler or other low level languages. Not only is it difficult to write these programs in the first place, but they are also not easily reusable or portable. Exhaustive trial-and-error testing is needed to establish that they meet the timing requirements. Many of today's real-time systems are developed using languages such as Ada[1] and Modula-2 which were designed to be general-purpose programming languages. The programmer writes a logically correct program, using mechanisms such as coroutines, priorities, interrupts and exception handling to control the execution timing behavior. Knowledge of the run-time environment is required to tailor the program to meet timing specifications, but this makes the program sensitive to hardware characteristics and system configurations.

In the past, a real-time system programmer's job is to write a program with an execution time which is shorter than the time allowed in the constraints. However, since it is difficult to predict a precise execution time, it may not be easy to build a dependable real-time system with tight timing constraints. Unfortunately, many next-generation real-time systems will have very strict and tight timing constraints. A different approach is not to expect a precise execution time from a computation, but to make the computation so flexible that it can meet a wide range of timing constraints. A computation can be designed to make the best use of whatever amount of time and resources available to it. It is then up to the system scheduler to determine the amount of time the computation should use. In this way, the computation is guaranteed to be always *temporally* correct, although it may sacrifice its *functional* correctness by producing less precise results. In many hard real-time systems, the requirement for functional correctness is not as strict as the requirement for temporal correctness. For these applications, the flexible timing performance approach is thus preferred.

To develop the next generation real-time systems, we also would like to use a programming language which has primitives for the direct ex-

---

[1] Ada is a registered trademark of the US government.

pression of timing constraints. The program specifies the deadlines for (part of) the computation and provides the codes to be executed. The run-time system, together with the system scheduler, must ensure that the constraints are met.

In summary, to implement a dependable real-time system, we need to have flexible program structures, primitives for specifying timing constraints, and facilities for predicting program performances. In this section, we review these issues and the past work in real-time system development.

Timing Constraints

A consistent theory of timing constraints has been presented by Allen [5] in his study of how to maintain knowledge about the temporal ordering of a set of actions using the temporal logic. He represents each action as taking place in an interval of time, and defines seven relations between intervals, that describe the synchronization of one event with respect to another. These relations correspond to intuitive notions such as "A takes place before B," "A and B begin and end at the same time," and "A takes place during the time that B does."

One of the first researchers to describe timing constraints in real-time systems is Dasarathy [2]. He constructed a language, called the Real-Time Requirements Language (RTRL). In his scheme, timing constraints could express the minimum or maximum time allowed between the occurrence of stimuli S, actions in the outside world, and responses R, the completion of the actions that a system takes. All four combinations $S - S$, $S - R$, $R - S$, and $R - R$ could be specified. Constraints on the time before a stimulus were constraints on the behavior of the outside world (a telephone user, in Dasarathy's system, since his intended application was in designing telephone switches). Constraints on the time before a response were interpreted as constraints on the amount of time that the system could use to process the corresponding stimuli. Note that Dasarathy's RTRL was a specification language, and not intended for automatic processing.

Another similar scheme was Jahanian's Real-Time Logic (RTL) [6]. In this scheme events and actions, corresponding roughly to Dasarathy's stimuli and responses, were identified. A mechanized inference procedure, the first of its kind, was presented to perform automatic reasoning about timing properties, and the events and responses could be associated by annotation with program constructs.

Predicting Program Performance

The converse of constraining the performance of programs is, of course, predicting their performance. The designer will want to verify before a real-time system goes into service that it has a high probability of meeting all its constraints.

One typical approach to determine the performance behavior of a program is to run it, either on the target hardware itself, or on some sort of simulator that models the hardware. The simulation or test run must be presented with data that are representative of the data that will be seen in actual service of the system. The problem with this approach, of course, is that the testing is limited, and generally cannot include the entire set of possible inputs. The worst case for the consumption of time or some other resource may not be uncovered in testing. Moreover, if a simulator is used, there may be some uncertainty that the simulator actually reflects the performance of the underlying hardware.

For this reason, it has generally been considered preferable to conduct analyses that examine some form of the program code and attempt to prove assertions about the program's performance behavior. Knuth [7] has done many elaborate analyses at the assembly language level. Less work was done in higher level languages [8], because the performance behavior of the individual language constructs was more difficult to characterize. Instead, analysis of algorithms in high level languages contented itself with results that expressed performance only in the "big-oh" sense.

An early research to attempt to characterize the performance of high-level programs was conducted by Leinbaugh [9]. This work characterized the time required by a higher-level construct in terms of its CPU time, time spent waiting to enter a critical section, time spent ready and waiting for a processor, time spent performing I/O, and time spent waiting at a synchronization point. Conservative bounds for all of these quantities were estimated. Stoyenko [10] adopted Leinbaugh's ideas into a programming system for Real-Time Euclid. Among its features was the ability to verify, a priori, that all resource and timing constraints would be satisfied. Rather than using Leinbaugh's conservative time bounds, their system attempted to find tighter bounds on execution time by an exhaustive search of all possible sequences of execution of processes. However, Stoyenko made the analysis easier by forbidding a good many programming constructs, including **while** loops (only counted loops were allowed), recursion, and recursive data structures such as linked lists. In this way, tight time bounds could be established for all programming constructs, at the expense of increased programming effort in coping with the limitations of working with the set of constructs remaining.

Mok and his group [11] have taken another approach to this *a priori* program analysis. The performance analyzer works on an abstraction (the interval partition) of the flow graph of the program, and the programmer supplies the worst-case number of iterations of each unbounded loop using a separate timing analysis language. Still more points on program performance analysis, from the static viewpoint, have been made by Puschner [12], who has refined the calculation of time required in **if** ...**then** ...**else** constructs, and Shaw [8], who has presented some rules for formal verification of programs' timing behavior.

Flexible Performances

The concepts of constraining performance characteristics, on the one hand, and calculating expected performance characteristics, on the other, together provide us with enough tools to implement basic real-time systems. They naturally give rise to the question, however, of how to deal with the situation where constraints cannot be met.

One possibility, of course, is to implement an exception mechanism which takes such actions as aborting low-priority tasks to provide more resources for high-priority ones. Such exception mechanism may be too rigid to meet the actual needs for real-time software, as observed by Bihari [13] in some of the issues:

- Many embedded systems have inertial properties that can smooth over temporary failures and overloads. Even deadlines that are asserted to be hard can occasionally be missed provided that the system has the opportunity to correct itself within some specified time period.

- Time constraints themselves can be changed by the system. In a vehicle control system, for instance, an appropriate action to over-load is not, "dump low priority tasks," but rather, "slow down and increase the following distance to the vehicle in front." A process control system might similarly relax its deadlines by decreasing gain in feedback-control loops.

- Changes in the environment of a system may not just change the quantities with which the system works, but require rapid, major changes to the control software, on the level of substituting entire algorithms.

All of these suggest that software in real-time systems should provide flexible performances. Computations in real-time systems can, for example, provide multiple algorithms and data structures, all of which perform the same function. Having the run time system able to select from among these versions or decide the amount of work to be performed, based on the performance constraints, should be a major aid in performing these complex functions effectively.

THE FLEX TIMING PRIMITIVES

The Concord project at the University of Illinois [4] is engaged in building a programming environment for large real-time systems, supporting explicit timing constraints, imprecise computations, and multiple implementations of a single computation, to support different configuration and timing constraints. This environment is built around the programming language FLEX, a derivative of C++.

In this section, we describe only the timing primitives of FLEX since the rest of FLEX primitives are essentially the same as C++. Like C++, at present time FLEX does not have any primitive for parallel or distributed computing. Future extension in this aspect is expected. We choose C++ as the base language for FLEX because it is a powerful object-oriented language with a good performance. Many real-time systems have physical devices which can be modeled naturally as objects. Software servers for each specific function can also be implemented as objects. Using the object-oriented paradigm, it is much easier to port a real-time program from one configuration to another, which is an important requirement for many real-time systems. It is also easier to optimize objects independently to improve their performances. Finally, objects can be enhanced with different capabilities using the class hierarchy, with different classes corresponding to different generations of a real-time system component.

Constraint Blocks

FLEX reasons about time and resources by specifying *constraints* and propagating information among them. Rather than doing a general propagation scheme in which new information may be propagated through long chains of constraints, it uses a disciplined scheme, where any change in execution state causes only those constraints immediately dependent on the change to be checked; no propagation of constraints is done. This discipline, which puts restrictions on the form of constraints, must be adopted in order to ensure that the execution time of the constraint mechanism will be predictable.

In FLEX, constraints on time and resources are described by a new construct, the *constraint block*. A constraint block identifies a constraint that must apply while a section of code is in execution, and takes the form:

$$[label:] \ (constraint; \ constraint; \ \ldots) \ [\leadsto \{\ldots\}] \ \{$$
$$\ldots \ statements \ \ldots$$
$$\}$$

This block specifies that the sequence of statements is to be executed, and asserts that all of the constraints will be satisfied during the execution of the block. Constraint blocks can be nested. The optional label is provided so that one constraint block can refer to another. The block of statements following the '$\leadsto$' is optional, and represents an exception procedure to be executed if any of the constraints fails. A constraint may be either a Boolean expression (which is treated as an assertion to be maintained throughout the block's lifetime) or a timing constraint, which describes a constraint on the time at which the block may begin or end its execution.

Associated with each constraint block is an interval of time representing the lifetime of the block. Another block may refer to the *start* and *finish* times of a given block by using the block's label, thus *A.start* represents the start time of block *A*, and *A.finish* represents the finish time

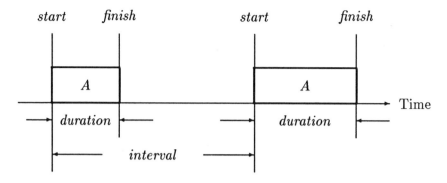

Figure 1: Timing attributes of constraint blocks

of *A*. The boundaries of a constraint block may be designated in terms of the relative time from the start of the block. *A.duration* represents the difference between the *start* and *finish* times of *A*, and *A.interval* represents the difference between the *start* time of one execution of block *A* and the *start* of the next time it is executed. Figure 1 shows all four of these timing attributes.

Timing constraints take one of the forms shown in Table 1. They can be classified by the following properties:

Start or Finish time. Constraints can refer either to the time that the computations represented by a constraint block begin, or to the time that they complete.

Absolute or Relative time. Absolute times represent the actual time of the start or finish event. Relative times represent the elapsed time from the start event to the event described.

Earliest or Latest time. Constraints can refer either to the earliest time at which an event may occur, or to the latest time at which it is permitted to occur.

The left-hand side of a timing constraint must refer to a timing attribute of the current block. The relational operator ($\geq$ or $\leq$) can be used to specify either the earliest or the latest time for executing the block. The right-hand side of a constraint can be a constant, or an expression involving the program variables and/or the timing attribute of

Table 1: Timing constraints in FLEX

	Absolute time		Relative time	
	Start	Finish	Start	Finish
Earliest	*start* $\geq t$	*finish* $\geq t$	*interval* $\geq t$	*duration* $\geq t$
Latest	*start* $\leq t$	*finish* $\leq t$	*interval* $\leq t$	*duration* $\leq t$

another constraint block. We can define a timing constraint relative to the execution of some other block. When one block refers to the attribute of another block that may be executed many times, the values always refer to the most recent activation of the block. We next show some examples of the timing constraints.

Example 1 (duration ≤ 1500)

This declaration specifies that the computations, whenever they begin, must take no more that time units of real time to complete.

Example 2 (start $\geq t_1$; finish $\leq t_2$; temperature < 110)

This constraint specifies that the computations must start at a time no earlier than t_1, and end at a time no later than t_2. During the computations, the contents of the **Constrained** variable *temperature* must be less than 110 at all times.

Example 3 A : (start $\geq B$.finish)

This constraint specifies that the computation, identified as block A, may not begin until some other computation, identified as block B, has completed.

Semantics of Timing Constraints

In **FLEX**, we assume that time is represented as a sequence of discrete, quantized *instants* t_0 t_1, ... An *event* is anything that can be identified with a specific instant; for the purposes of **FLEX**, the most significant events are the start and end of some computation. Instants are well ordered; for any two instants a and b, we assume that we know that a is earlier than b $(a < b)$, a is at the same time as b $(a = b)$, or a is later than b $(a > b)$. In situations such as can arise in distributed systems, where events may actually occur simultaneously, we assume that there is some unambiguous way to determine an 'earlier' or 'later' relationship between events. While FLEX does not specifically require that simultaneity be impossible, neither does it require that the underlying system support it.

Time Intervals. If an event has occurred in the past, we assume that we know precisely the time of its occurrence. Future events, however, are not known to the same degree of accuracy. We may know that an event is not allowed to occur until a certain time, or that it is not allowed to occur after a given time. We also always know that an event that has not occurred cannot occur before the current time *now*.

FLEX represents the interval of time within which an event is known to take place as a *time interval*. A time interval comprises two times, the earliest and latest time during which the event may occur. Time intervals thus have the same structure as the familiar intervals of numerical analysis. We define the union and intersection of intervals in the obvious manner. We define ⊥ to be the intersection of intervals that do not overlap.

It is important to note that a time interval represents the range of uncertainty about when an event occurs. It does not represent the duration of a continued process. Such a duration is described by an activation, or *act*, which is the period of time during which some process takes place. It comprises two times: the *start* time, at which the process begins, and the *finish* time, at which the process ends. Both of these times may be expressed as intervals in order to represent uncertainty about the actual times of these start and finish events.

Fault versus Wait. The timing constraints in FLEX come in two varieties: the 'earliest time' and 'latest time' constraints. If these are applied with dependencies among different blocks, there are two fundamental ways of implementing relations among the events. Let us say that block A may not start until block B has finished. We may view this as a requirement to delay the execution of block A as follows:

$$A : (start \geq B.finish) \ \{\ldots\}$$
$$\vdots$$
$$B : (1) \ \{\ldots\}$$

Alternatively, we may view the constraint as a deadline on block B, and require that B be completed before A starts, causing a timing fault if this constraint is violated:

$$A : (1) \ \{\ldots\}$$
$$\vdots$$
$$B : (finish \leq A.start) \ \{\ldots\}$$

Clearly these two constraints are synonymous in terms of temporal logic, but their run-time behaviors are very different. As a matter of programming style, we prefer to impose as few arbitrary deadlines as possible upon tasks. The former usage of causing a delay is to be preferred over the latter usage of imposing an additional deadline wherever possible.

Equality between Times. As we discussed earlier, FLEX does not depend on the possibility of simultaneous events. To implement true equality between the times of two events is inconsistent with this scheme.

Let us examine in more detail, though, what equality of times actually means. Rather than having it represent knowledge about the external world, it represents constraints which the FLEX system must satisfy. There are two ways to impose these constraints; they are analogous to the 'fault' and 'wait' semantics discussed above.

The first interpretation of an equality constraint is that it represents a synchronization point. When events A and B are constrained to occur 'at the same time', the first to arrive must be delayed until the second arrives. The programmer describes such a constraint in FLEX by the use of nested constraint blocks. Assume that operations A and B must begin at the same time. The FLEX notation to express this relationship will be:

```
A : (1) {                              B : (1) {
   A' : (start ≥ B.start) {               B' : (start ≥ A.start) {
      ⋮                                      ⋮
   }                                      }
}                                      }
```

Note that the constraints here are symmetrical; A bears the same relationship to B that B does to A. Let us examine what happens when we try to satisfy these constraints. Assume without loss of generality that the flow of control reaches A first. The constraint on block A is always satisfied, and so we attempt to enter block A'. The system finds that the current time is less than $B.start$ (remember that a future event is always known to occur after the current time), and therefore must delay execution until the flow of control reaches B.

When control reaches B, the execution proceeds into block B, since B's constraint is always satisfied. Now, however, $B.start$ is known. This information propagates to the process waiting at block A', and this process is allowed to proceed, finding that the current time is now at least $B.start$. Meanwhile, the process in block B attempts to enter block B', and finds that the current time is at least $A.start$; the entry to block B' therefore may proceed immediately.

Note that the naive implementation of synchronization points:

```
A : (start ≥ B.start) {                B : (start ≥ A.start) {
   ⋮                                      ⋮
}                                      }
```

may be erroneous. It is easy to verify the contention that this implementation results in deadlock on any system incapable of supporting simultaneous actions. Each process will be waiting for the other to begin, and neither will begin until the wait is complete.

The second interpretation of the equality constraint is that not only is there a synchronization point, but there is also a restriction on the amount of delay that is tolerable between the two events once the synchronization point is reached. Since **FLEX** does not assume that true

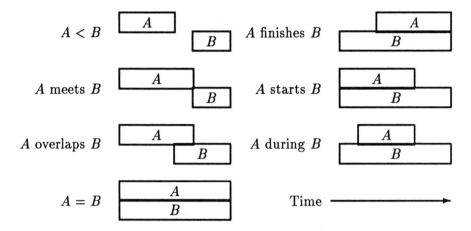

Figure 2: Relations between blocks

simultaneity is possible, we describe this constraint in terms of a tolerance, ε, and state that the two events must occur within ε time units of each other. Such a constraint is easy to add to the one above:

$A : (1)$ {
$\quad A' : (start \geq B.start;$
$\qquad start \leq B'.start + \varepsilon)$ {

$\qquad \vdots$

$\quad$ }
}

$B : (1)$ {
$\quad B' : (start \geq A.start;$
$\qquad start \leq A'.start + \varepsilon)$ {

$\qquad \vdots$

$\quad$ }
}

In keeping with the style of avoiding needless deadlines, this usage is to be disparaged unless some constraint in the physical world demands it. In any case, it appears that little if any benefit will accrue from this usage under most scheduling algorithms. Imposing the additional constraint will indeed ensure that A' and B' start within ε time units of each other. Nothing, however, prevents the system from preempting one or the other process immediately following entry into one or the other block. In other words, the additional constraint says nothing about the temporal relationship of the computations within the blocks. This relationship is better defined by constraints on the finish time of the blocks.

Allen [5] presents a temporal logic based on blocks and defines thirteen relations operating on pairs of intervals. Seven of these are shown in Figure 2; the remaining six are the inverse relations of the ones shown since equality is reflexive. With the timing primitives provided in FLEX, we can implement the timing relations as shown in Table 2. In all of these, the 'wait' and 'synchronization point' semantics are used, and no extraneous deadlines are introduced.

Overheads in Executing Constraint Blocks

To implement constraint blocks, we need system functions to maintain program context, to track constraints on variables, to limit execution time, and to delay execution. The complete structure of a constraint block is shown in Figure 3.

A scheme for maintaining timing correctness about programs should impose only an acceptable overhead at run time. Our scheme of disciplined constraints (with no new information ever causing constraints to be activated recursively) has constant time overheads to enter and to exit from a constraint block. For each constraint, the overhead required to establish and to revoke it is a linear function of the number of variables appearing in it. Our current implementation on a Sun 3/50 workstation takes roughly 9.5 ms to enter a constraint block, establish a nontemporal constraint involving two variables, revert the constraint, and exit the block. Nearly half of this time is spent in calls to the memory management routines `operator new` and `operator delete`; specialized memory management for the constraint data structures will be able to reduce this time substantially. Temporal constraints do not perform as well, needing about 15 ms to enter a constraint block, establish a two-variable temporal constraint, revert the constraint, and leave the block. Virtually all of the additional time is spent in the Unix[2] signal management routines `sigsetmask`, `sigblock`, and `setitimer`. An implementation of the constraint block using lightweight processes could no doubt do much better.

Detecting a failed constraint and invoking the exception handler requires time that is linear in the number of inner contexts that must be terminated before the fault can be delivered. Once again, this amount

---

[2]Unix is a registered trademark of AT&T Bell Laboratories.

Table 2: The timing relations in FLEX codes

Relation	Implementation in FLEX
$A < B$	$A : (1) \{ \dots \}$ $\vdots$ $B : (start \geq A.finish) \{ \dots \}$
$A = B$	$A : (finish \geq B'.finish) \{$ $\quad A' : (start \geq B.start) \{ \dots \}$ $\}$ $\vdots$ $B : (finish \geq A'.finish) \{$ $\quad B' : (start \geq A.start) \{ \dots\}$ $\}$
A meets B	$A : (finish \geq B.start) \{$ $\quad A' : (1) \{ \dots \}$ $\}$ $\vdots$ $B : (start \geq A'.finish) \{ \dots \}$
A overlaps B	$A : (finish \geq B.start) \{ \dots \}$ $\vdots$ $B : (start \geq A.start;$ $\quad finish \geq A.finish) \{ \dots \}$
A during B	$A : (start \geq B.start) \{ \dots \}$ $\vdots$ $B : (finish \geq A.finish) \{ \dots \}$
A starts B	$A : (1) \{$ $\quad A' : (start \geq B.start) \{ \dots \}$ $\}$ $\vdots$ $B : (finish \geq A.finish) \{$ $\quad B' : (start \geq A.start) \{ \dots \}$ $\}$
A finishes B	$A : (finish \geq B'.finish) \{$ $\quad A' : (start \geq B.start) \{ \dots \}$ $\}$ $\vdots$ $B : (finish \geq A'.finish) \{$ $\quad B' : (1) \{ \dots \}$ $\}$

```
Activation A;
{
  Context __C_n;                    // Establish context
  if (__C_n.save())
  {
    -- user's exception handler goes here --
  }
  else
  {
    -- declarations for non-temporal constraints --
    -- declarations for latest finish time --
    -- declarations for latest start time --
    -- code to delay until earliest start time --
    -- code to clean up latest start time structures --
    A.start = NOW ();     // Record the start time

    -- body of the constraint block --

    -- code to delay until earliest finish time --
    -- code to clean up latest finish time structures. --
    -- code to clean up non-temporal constraints --
  }
  A.finish = NOW (); // Record the finish time
}
```

Figure 3: Structure of a constraint block

of time is expected to be manageable, since we do not expect that constraint blocks will be deeply nested in actual programs. On the Sun 3/50, reverting a context requires about the same time as exiting it normally; the observed 5% difference is within the bounds of measurement error.

As can be seen from above, many of the overheads depend on the operating system supports. For applications where a very high resolution or a very low overhead is needed, hardware devices can be used to monitor and to trigger timing exceptions.

MEASURING PERFORMANCES

When implementing real-time systems, it is important to know the expected execution time and resource requirements of each task. These data are needed for scheduling tasks, and are also needed for selecting from among alternative methods of carrying out the same computation. Unfortunately, it is difficult to determine this time accurately in advance. Many analysis systems, for example those of Mok[11] and Stoyenko[10], ignore the uncertainties in time caused by such facilities as caches and paging systems, assuming a fixed time for each type of instruction. Despite their attempts at utmost reliability, the results generated in these systems are therefore at best approximate. Moreover, there is no good way to quantify how well the time computed by such a system reflects the actual time needed by a task.

One approach that can help with these problems is to measure the program in actual execution, rather than hypothesize about its time requirement *a priori*. The problem with measurement, though, is to relate the results of the measurement to some model of the program's behavior in a way that gives us confidence that the program will continue to behave as measured. The programmer's knowledge about an algorithm's performance is of value here. While programmers are notoriously bad at estimating run times, they frequently have a very good idea about the performance of their algorithms, at least from the 'big-oh' standpoint. What is lacking in their mental model is a good perspective of the time required for the individual operations of the program — exactly what measurements can provide.

We propose, therefore, a system that can measure the time required for a task under various conditions, and integrate these measured times into a parametric model supplied by the programmer. The measurement must require only insignificant time compared to the task being performed. Such a system will be able to:

- analyze program structures that are impossible for other systems, such as unbounded loops and recursive control structures,

- provide accurate timing information even on hardware whose timing behavior is difficult to model and analyze, and

- provide confidence in the timing model, by validating it statistically for goodness of fit.

In this section, we present a system facility that determines the execution times by measuring the program's execution. The system allows for dependency of the execution time on the input data. It allows the programmer to build a model of a task's timing behavior that incorporates knowledge about the expected timings, and gives a measure of statistical confidence that the model accurately represents the program's actual behavior.

Language Support

To support timing measurement and modeling, the FLEX language is augmented with a new directive, **#pragma measure**. This directive both directs the compiler to generate code to measure the time or resources consumed by a block of code and provides the parametric model for analyzing the measurement. The syntax for this directive is:

pragma-measure:

> **#pragma measure** *case resource* **defining** *parameters*
> **in** *expression* [*safety*]

case:

> **mean**
> **worst**

resource:

> **duration**
> **count**

parameters:

```
            identifier
            parameters , identifier
safety:
            safety number
```

The *case* identifies whether the model is expected to fit to the mean resource usage or to the worst case. Generally speaking, the system designer will use the mean case if the timing behavior of the block is expected to be deterministic (expecting, in other words, that variations in the measured time are caused by measurement errors) and the worst case if the timing behavior has a stochastic or unpredictable component.

The *resource* identifies which resource is to be measured. Ones that we have implemented are *duration,* which is the amount of real time that is consumed in the block, and *count,* which is the number of trips that are made through the top-level control structure in the block. While we have not experimented with other resources, it would be easy to implement resources modeling the amount of memory used by a program, the communications bandwidth that it consumes, the number of processors on a parallel-processing system that it uses, and so on.

The *expression* gives the model for the expected resource behavior, and the *parameters* are the parameters to the model. Their values are determined by the timing analyzer. Any variables, other than the parameters, that appear in the expression are *free* variables. The free variables are recorded by the measurement logic so that the timing analyzer can use their values in determining the best fit to the observed performance data.

The optional *safety* clause specifies a safety factor — a number by which to multiply the computed time when determining the time to allow for a computation. The safety factor allows the programmer to specify that the system should, for example, always provide at least ten percent more time than the worst case seen so far.

An example of the **#pragma measure** directive is seen in Figure 4. Here, the programmer has coded an insertion sort. The time taken by the sort on average (**mean duration**) is expected to be a quadratic function of the length of the list n. The programmer has specified that a safety factor of two is to be provided, that is, that the insertion sort should always be allowed to take double the average time that it has been

```
void isort (register int* x, register int n)
#pragma measure mean duration defining A, B, C
        in (A*n+B)*n+C safety 2
{
  for (register int i = 1; i <= n; ++i) {
    register int y = x [i];
    for (register int j = i-1; j >= 0 && y < x [j]; --j)
      x [j + 1] = x [j];
    x [j + 1] = y;
  }
}
```

Figure 4: An instrumented insertion sort

observed to take for any given list length. This safety factor reflects the programmer's knowledge that insertion sort, in the worst case, requires twice the amount of time that it does on average.

The Measurement Analysis

Once the program has been run, possibly a number of times, to collect the measurement data, a measurement analysis program is run. This program determines the best fit of the parameters to the observed run time. It produces a report that describes the values thus determined, and gives a confidence level (determined using the χ^2 statistic) for the model. The measurement analysis program also updates the file containing the model description with the observed values for the parameters.

The process of determining the model parameters given the observed time and resource data is a curve-fitting problem. There are a number of techniques for this problem in the literature; one excellent survey is Lawson and Hanson[14]. The problem of parameter estimation for #pragma measure, however, is a quite difficult one; many of the techniques are unsuitable. After trying a number of methods, we decide to use a modified Levenberg-Marquardt method [15]. There is a requirement in the algorithm for an approximate inversion of a matrix; this matrix will be rank deficient if the problem is underdetermined. The approximate inversion, in our implementation, is carried out using the singular value decomposition with careful editing of the singular values[16] to ensure adequate convergence and avoid delicate parameter cancellation. A more detailed discussion on the measurement analysis techniques can be found in [17].

For timing measurements to be useful, the clock used to obtain them must be accurate. In order to achieve this accuracy, there are several issues that must be addressed:

- **Granularity.** The clock must measure a time unit that is much shorter than the duration of the blocks of code being measured.

- **Overhead.** Reading the clock must be inexpensive, that is, it must take much less time than the function to be measured. Likewise, writing a measurement record must be inexpensive.

- **Atomicity.** Reading the clock, and writing the measurement record, must not suffer unpredictable delay and interruption. Many Unix systems fail to meet this constraint, as any system call (such as the `gettimeofday()` that reads the clock) causes the program to be returned to the ready queue, and possibly allows another program to be dispatched.

Confidence in the Analysis

Although we have discussed the level of statistical confidence on the program performance model derived from the measurement data, one may object to having only statistical confidence in the prediction. For this reason, let us examine the principal sources of error.

The first is that the user-supplied model may fail to describe reality. This is a problem with any scheme, whether based on measurements or on analysis of the program. With the schemes based on analysis, there is no way to validate the underlying assumptions, as they are embedded in the hardware model used by the analysis program. The measurement based scheme, though, gives statistics to quantify the goodness of fit. As a check to this assertion, we have tried analyzing the insertion sort program given the incorrect assertion that the time required is $An \ln n + B$. The confidence level corresponding to the calculated χ^2 statistic dropped from 0.999 to 10^{-13} — a clear indication that something was wrong with the model.

The other problem is that the observed data on which the model is based may not be realistic (in a worst-case scenario, the measurement cases may have failed to uncover the actual worst case). We address this problem by allowing the user to specify a safety factor, and thus allow for either a worst case that is known theoretically or simply a conservative margin of error. Developing techniques for verifying theoretically that the worst case has in fact been found, analogous to the techniques that verify that a set of test cases has exercised all of a program's code, is an important topic for future research.

Another objection to the use of measurement-based analysis tools is that the measurement process interferes with the timing behavior of the program being measured. We have found this interference to be negligible for the rather coarse-grained program units that we have studied – a measurement typically takes at most a few hundred microseconds to observe and record, for operations that take from milliseconds to seconds to complete. Of course, for measurements that must be extremely precise or fine-grained, this objection is relevant. We foresee, however, that any appropriate measurement technology can be integrated into our analysis scheme. If high-accuracy and fine-grained measurements are required, the measurement analyzer can be made to operate on the output of an in-circuit emulator or other hardware monitor.

Integrating Measurements with Program Analysis

No matter how well the measurement system performs, there will always be a place for formal analysis of programs; the confidence provided by formal analysis is too important to ignore. It may be, however, that there is some component of the program that is not amenable to the formal analysis, and that the designer is willing to accept the statistical confidence provided by the modeling system. We must then provide a means to integrate the two.

To see how the methods are integrated, let us first review how the program analysis systems work. They begin by partitioning the program into basic blocks. The time for each basic block is calculated. The time requirements are then combined to give the time requirements for successively higher-level blocks of code, using some representation of the program's control structure. The choice of representation varies —

Mok[11] uses an interval partition of the program's flow graph, while both Stoyenko[10] and Puschner[12] use the control flow constructs of the high level language.

It is easy to expand this sort of analysis to take measurements into account. A block of code whose running time is measured can be treated as a basic block for the purpose of analyzing its timing. In addition, a block of code that is constrained by the system to complete in a given length of time can be treated as a unit. There are then four means by which the running time of a block may be determined:

- The time may be determined by program analysis of the basic blocks.

- The timing of the code can be measured.

- The time for one iteration of a loop can be determined by one of these techniques, and the number of iterations can be measured (We provide a facility, '#pragma measure count,' for measuring the number of trips through a loop).

- The maximum time for the block may be specified by the programmer.

Given basic block times and loop counts determined from any of these sources, it is then a simple matter to combine them all into an overall estimate of time, by adding up the individual times for program constructs.

Resources other than time can be handled similarly. The rules for combining them under programming constructs, however, may be different. It is instructive to classify the resources according to these rules. We call the major resource classes *time-like* and *space-like* resources. A time-like resource, in general, models some sort of time, or another resource that, once consumed, is never reused. By contrast, a space-like resource models a physical object; once a task has completed using an object, another task can use it. Space-like resources include memory, disc space, processing elements, critical sections, and so on.

In order to combine the resource usage of two operations that use time-like and space-like resources, the only operations that we need consider are summation, taking a maximum, and multiplication by a constant factor. Table 3 shows how the two types of resource are combined

Table 3: Combining resource usage

Construct	Space-like	Time-like
$a;\ b$	$\max(c_a, c_b)$	$c_a + c_b$
loop a **end**	c_a	$n \cdot c_a$
if $(c) \rightarrow a$ **else** b	$\max(c_a, c_b, c_c)$	$\max(c_a, c_b) + c_c$
cobegin $a;\ b$ **coend**	$c_a + c_b$	$\max(c_a, c_b)$

Note: n represents the number of times that the loop will be executed.

under common programming language constructs. For example, consider the **if** statement:

$$\textbf{if } (c) \rightarrow a \textbf{ else } b \ .$$

The amount of time needed to execute this statement in the worst case is the worst-case amount of time needed to evaluate the condition c, plus the greater of the worst-case amounts of time needed to execute the two parts a and b. The amount of dynamically allocated storage is simply the greatest amount of storage required to execute a or b, or to evaluate the condition c.

Combining the resource usage in this way is similar to the methods of Shaw[8] or Puschner and Koza[12] for time-like resources, and the 'time-like' column in the table shows the same rules that appear in their work. The 'space-like' column is unique to our model.

IMPRECISE COMPUTATIONS

The timing constraint block structure in **FLEX** allows programmers to define totally dynamic timing constraints. In addition, the run-time mechanism guarantees that the timing constraints will always be followed, or else the program is aborted and the exception handler is invoked. However, the constraint mechanism has solved only half of the problem for real-time system programming. It has guaranteed only the *temporal* correctness but not the *functional* correctness. It is still up to the programmer to implement real-time programs which can guarantee an acceptable level of functional correctness whenever the system must terminate the computation to achieve its temporal correctness.

We have identified two program models which can be used to provide the functional correctness under different temporal requirements. The first of these is called *imprecise computation* which implements a computation as a refinement process so that results of improving qualities can be produced using increasing amount of time. The other model, to be discussed in the next section, is called *performance polymorphism* which implements a computation with multiple versions each with a different performance capability.

Result Correctness

In a real-time system, if a computation in progress has not completed when its deadline is reached, we have two alternatives: either we can discard the partial results from the computation, or we can attempt to utilize them in some fashion. If the partial results could possibly constitute useful approximations to the desired output, it is preferable not to discard them. We call this model of allowing incomplete computations to produce approximate results as *imprecise computation*. The notion of an imprecise result is a familiar one, and it has been adopted in many practical systems. For instance, the SIFT system [18] records partial results at the end of each iteration, and uses them for error checking in a replicated system. Another example of imprecise results being used in existing systems is the backup copy saved by many text editing programs, which is provided to the user if the editor program crashes during an editing session.

Traditionally, the correctness C_R of a result R from a computation is defined to be a step function of time. At the beginning of an execution, C_R has the value of zero. At the time of completion, C_R becomes one. In our model, we use the term *correctness* to mean the extent to which execution has progressed to produce an acceptable result. We assert that as computations proceed, they continually make progress towards the desired results. Using the definition, the correctness of a single procedure execution is no longer a step function of time. Rather, the correctness function is a continuous function $c(t)$ where $c(t_1) \leq c(t_2)$ for $t_1 < t_2$, and $c(T) = 1$ at the completion time T (Figure 5). In general, we may

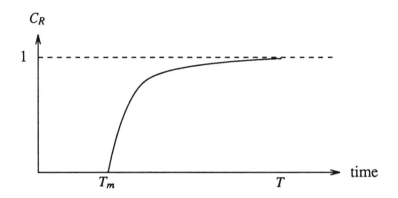

Figure 5: A continuous correctness function

have $c(t) = 0$ for $t < T_m$ for some $0 < T_m \leq T$. This allows us to model the situation where an imprecise result would be unacceptable if the computation has been terminated before the minimum time T_m.

An ideal $c(t)$ is a continuous function so that any extra amount of computation will improve the correctness more. In practice, the correctness function will usually be a sequence of step functions (Figure 6). Each step indicates the completion of another stage in the computation, such as a block of code. For example, consider the simplex method which is used in linear programming to optimize an objective function given certain linear constraints. It consists of a series of steps, with each step computing a new set of values for all the parameters so that the objective function is improved. Many numerical algorithms compute a better approximation to the final result iteratively. For instance, a program to evaluate a function using its Taylor series expansion may compute another term of the series on each iteration. If the Taylor expansion converges, the sum of the terms computed so far provides successively better approximations to the final result at the end of each iteration.

Basic Structures of Imprecise Computations

Many computations perform their operations in distinct stages or phases. After each stage of a computation, part of the problem is solved and an intermediate result, or *milestone*, is produced. In the milestone

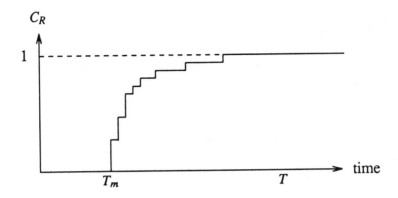

Figure 6: A staircase correctness function

method, some significant intermediate result produced before deadline may be returned as the result of the computation. The programmer may specify 'milestones' at which the current partial results are saved. When the deadline is reached, the computation is terminated and the best result from these milestones is returned.

The choice of milestones is left to the programmer. Depending on the characteristics of the application, any number of milestones may be specified. In the case of a computation consisting of a few discrete steps, the completion of each step may be a milestone. However, if a computation consists of a big number of smaller operations, such as adding a million numbers, the milestones may be defined after some collection of operations, such as adding every ten thousand numbers. Choosing more milestones may provide a more precise result when the computation has to be aborted, but at the expense of increased overhead for saving imprecise results.

Another structure of imprecise computation is called *sieve*. The motivation for the sieve structure is that not every step in a computation might be essential to obtain a result. In a computation consisting of series of steps, while some steps may perform operations crucial to obtaining an acceptable result, other operations may simply improve or verify the accuracy of results which have been produced. For instance, in image processing, while edge detection may be crucial to pattern recognition, edge enhancement serves only to improve the likelihood of an accurate recognition. If the deadline of the computation is earlier than the expected time of completion, we may choose to skip certain steps such as edge enhancement which are not vital to obtaining at least an approximate result. This is the central idea of the sieve technique which optionally omits some of the intermediate steps in a computation. The programmer specifies which part of the computation are 'sieves' so that they can be skipped if time available is not sufficient for a complete execution.

The shape of the correctness function does not affect whether sieves can be used. It may, however, affect the choice of which sieve to skip. If the steps are independent of each other, the flattest step (the least gain in correctness for the longest execution time) should be skipped. If the criticalness of each step is predefined, the selection of the sieve to skip may be based also on the relative significance of the different sieves. If some of the steps depend on previous steps, skipping a step will imply skipping all subsequent steps which depend on it. Therefore, we generally formulate as sieves those steps which perform incidental bookkeeping functions, or which merely improve the quality of the final result. For example, when inserting or deleting from an AVL tree, rebalancing the tree may be formulated as a sieve - if the tree is not rebalanced, it is still usable, though the search time may no longer be optimal. Similarly, in iterative numerical algorithms such as function evaluation using Taylor's series, and Newton-Raphson and Gauss-Siedel iteration for solving simultaneous equations, each iteration can be considered a sieve. Not performing some iterations will mean that the final result will be more approximate, but it may still be usable.

Once the program for an imprecise computation is constructed, we can find its correctness function by running some test data and monitoring their result qualities along the time line. Given the correctness function, we can decide how much time should be given to a computation in order to receive a result of acceptable quality for a given application. The system scheduling issues for imprecise computations have been studied extensively [19, 20].

PERFORMANCE POLYMORPHISM

Another approach to addressing the needs for flexible program performances is to implement multiple versions of a function that carries out a given computation. These versions all perform the same task, but differ only in the amount of time and resources they consume, the system configuration to which they are adapted, the precision of the results that they return, and similar performance criteria. The versions may be specialized for a particular machine architecture, a particular problem size, a particular optimization strategy, and so on. The multiple versions may be supplied by the programmer, as when different algorithms adapted to problems of different sizes are supplied. They may also be generated automatically, as when a program rewriting tool is used to adapt a sequential program to a vector or parallel machine.

For real-time programs, we present a model for specifying these multiple versions. We call this model *performance polymorphism,* because of its similarities to the conventional polymorphism where different functions carry out the same operation on different types of data [21]. The example we use is that of sorting on a parallel computer system. We have (at least) three different sorting techniques available: a fast insertion sort `isort`, a heap sort `hsort`, and a parallel merge sort `bsort`. The amount of time that these sorts take is $An^2 + Bn + C$, $Dn \log n + E$, and $F(n \log n)/p + G \log p + H$, respectively, where n is the number of elements to sort and p is the number of processing elements given to the parallel sort. We expect H, the overhead of starting the parallel sort, to be quite large. It may therefore be more effective to sort a short list of numbers on the local processor, without using the parallel sort. We also expect the constant factor in the time required for heap sort to be greater than that for insertion sort; it therefore may be more effective to choose the $O(n^2)$ insertion sort for extremely short lists.

To manage this information, a number of different items need to be taken into account. The programmer needs some way to specify the constraints on time and resources that are in effect, in order to determine when the choice of a version is feasible. In addition, a figure of merit for a given version may have to be defined, in order to choose the better of two feasible versions. The *binding* problem, the problem of determining the most appropriate version, must then be solved. Solving the binding problem demands information about the expected performance of versions of the program, so the system must be able to predict the performance of a version.

Language Support

In order to implement the model of performance polymorphism, we augment FLEX with a means to describe the candidates, their performance, and the objectives. In this section, we show the various primitives by simple examples.

We begin by providing a means to declare a performance polymorphic function, by allowing the keyword `perf_poly` to replace the function body in a function declaration.

Example 4 `void sort (int n, int* list) perf_poly;`

This example declares `sort` to be a performance polymorphic function accepting a integer n and a 'pointer to integer' `list`. Presumably, `sort` is a function that sorts a list of integers.

Next, we provide a way to give a candidate for a performance polymorphic function. We do this by adding an external definition to the language:

Example 5 `provide hsort for void sort (int, int*);`

This example supplies the function `hsort` as a candidate for the `sort` function defined above. The description of the types accepted and returned by the `sort` function must be supplied because `sort` may be polymorphic in the conventional sense as well; there may, for instance, be another `sort` function that sorts a list of floating-point numbers.

Finally, we need to add a description of the objective. We do this by extending the definition of a compound statement:

Example 6 `#pragma objective minimize duration`
`{ ... }`

The directive shown in this example requests that the system minimize the real time taken to perform the computations enclosed in the braces, subject to all constraints.

We now have the declaration of performance polymorphic functions, of the candidates for a function, and of the constraints that apply to an invocation of a function. The only other data needed to perform the binding step are the claims that describe the time and resource requirements for the candidates. One way to provide these claims is to use the measurement approach (with #pragma measure) as discussed earlier. Another source for timing data is a timing analyzer that examines the code of a function and gives its resource claims [11, 12].

Run-Time Binding

Given the information described above, late binding at run time is easy to describe. The binding algorithm simply loops through all the candidates, looking for feasibility, and selects the candidate with the greatest figure of merit. It is obviously somewhat expensive (the computation of the resource claims is a loop that is nested within the loop through the candidates), although it can be improved somewhat by caching the resource claims and feasibility information, assuming that a few configurations of the parameters account for most of the invocations. The way that the caching would operate is to record the configuration of the parameters for the last few calls to the function, and as the first part of the binding step, check whether the parameters supplied match a recent invocation. If so, the binding need not be recomputed; the system can simply reuse the binding that was used on the earlier invocation.

The advantage of run-time binding is its flexibility; it is required for cases where the relevant parameters cannot be determined at compile time. Such cases include data-dependent performance, where input data obtained at run time can affect the binding decision, fault-tolerant systems, where run-time binding may be needed to reconfigure around a system failure, and run-time allocation of time and resources. The disadvantage of run-time binding is the overhead involved in making the binding decision; we therefore prefer early binding in the cases that do not require late binding. We also recommend appropriate choice of granularity for performance polymorphic functions that will require late binding. Short functions that complete in only a few instruction times are not appropriate candidates, as the cost of choosing an inappropriate function is small compared to the cost of binding.

System Tools

A complete environment that supports performance polymorphism has been implemented. The environment provides the programmer the tools to specify and to conduct the performance measurements, and to decide the binding time. Figure 7 shows the overall structure of our system. Boxes represent the tools provided in the environment, and rounded boxes are the program and data files used as inputs or produced as outputs by the tools. The left subsystem has all the compilers. FLEX programs are processed by the FLEX compiler. The output of the FLEX compiler is a C++ program that is, in turn, processed by a C++ compiler to produce an object program. The object program contains the guarded commands needed to invoke performance polymorphic functions. In addition, it contains the code that enforces the constraints associated with the constraint blocks. It also contains the codes to measure the execution time and resource commitment required for the various versions of the performance polymorphic functions.

The lower right subsystem is the dynamic timing analyzer. It starts with the dynamic timing model which is produced by the FLEX compiler from `#pragma measure` directives supplied by the programmer. The model describes a parametric function whose parameters are to be determined by the actual timing data obtained by running the program. Determining these parameters is the role of the dynamic timing analyzer. It reads the model description and the actual time and resource measurement data obtained by running the program. It writes a file containing the parameters of the model. Subsequent runs of the FLEX program may use these parameter values to estimate the running times of performance polymorphic function versions in making binding decisions.

The static timing analyzer, at upper right, is a planned future subsystem. Its role is to determine the times and resource commitments required for high-level constructs. It can determine these times based on the measured times, based on examination of the object code, based on the constraint structure of the program, or any combination of these. The static analyzer will be capable of generating a description of the performance of the versions of a function. The description can be used in a subsequent compilation to optimize the early binding decisions.

CONCLUSIONS

We have described the time-related aspects of FLEX which is a language designed for real-time systems programming. FLEX uses timing constraint blocks to specify and to enforce timing requirements in real-

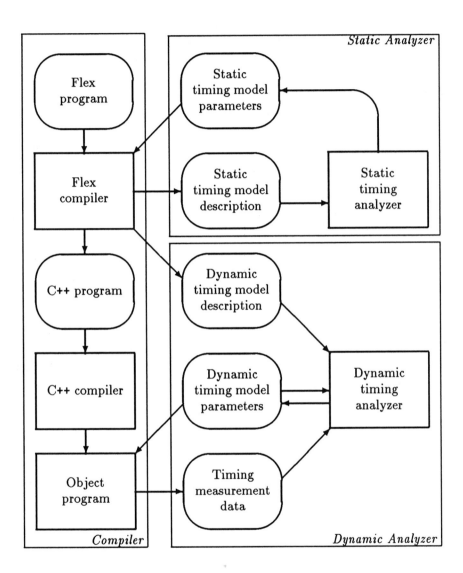

Figure 7: System supports for performance polymorphism

time programs. A measurement-based performance analyzer has been implemented for FLEX programs using user-defined performance functions. Moreover, to help computations meet timing constraints, FLEX programs can be implemented with flexible performance structures like imprecise computations and performance polymorphic functions. With these primitives and tools, we hope to make real-time programs easier to implement yet more dependable.

Currently, FLEX does not have any primitive for distributed or parallel programming. As most future real-time systems will be implemented on either multiprocessors or distributed systems, we need a good model for real-time parallel programs. One of such effort is the Real-Time Mentat system [22] which is a macro data-driven object-oriented language designed for parallel real-time systems. RT Mentat has adopted the constraint block structure in its actor definition and can easily provide the flexible program structures supported in FLEX.

We have introduced the basic structures of two flexible performance models: imprecise computation and performance polymorphism. Many real-time applications naturally fit into these models. However, there also exist many applications which do not fit into these models but can be modified to simulate the models. Moreover, we believe that there are many other models which can provide the flexibility in real-time performances. Much effort is still needed to identify these applications and to investigate the effectiveness of the new models.

Acknowledgements

This research was sponsored by the Office of Naval Research under grants N00014-87-K-0827 and N00014-89-J-1181, by the National Aeronautics and Space Administration under grant NASA-NAG-1-613, and by the National Science Foundation under grant CCR-89-11773.

References

[1] J. A. Stankovic, "Misconceptions about real-time computing," *IEEE Computer*, October 1988.

[2] B. Dasarathy, "Timing constraints of real-time systems: constructs for expressing them, methods for validating them," *IEEE Transactions on Software Engineering*, vol. SE-11, pp. 80–86, January 1985.

[3] K. Lin and S. Natarajan, "Expressing and maintaining timing constraints in FLEX," in *Proceedings of the Ninth Real-Time Systems Symposium*, (Huntsville, Ala.), pp. 96–105, December 1988.

[4] K. Lin, S. Natarajan, and J. W. Liu, "Concord: a system of imprecise computations," in *Proceedinngs of COMPSAC '87*, (Tokyo, Japan), IEEE, October 1987.

[5] J. F. Allen, "Maintaining knowledge about temporal intervals," *Communications of the ACM*, vol. 26, pp. 832–843, November 1983.

[6] F. Jahanian and A. K. Mok, "Safety analysis of timing properties in real-time systems," *IEEE Transactions on Software Engineering*, vol. SE-12, pp. 890–904, September 1986.

[7] D. E. Knuth, *Fundamental Algorithms*. Vol. 1 of *The Art of Computer Programming*, Reading, Massachusetts: Addison-Wesley, second ed., 1973.

[8] A. C. Shaw, "Reasoning about time in higher–level language software," *IEEE Transactions on Software Engineering*, vol. 15, pp. 875–889, July 1989.

[9] D. W. Leinbaugh, "Guaranteed response times in a hard real-time environment," *IEEE Transactions on Software Engineering*, vol. SE–6, pp. 85–91, January 1980.

[10] A. D. Stoyenko, "A schedulability analyzer for real-time Euclid," in *Proceedings of the Eighth Real-Time Systems Symposium*, (San Jose, Calif.), pp. 218–227, December 1987.

[11] A. K. Mok, P. Amerasinghe, M. Chen, and K. Tantisirivat, "Evaluating tight execution time bounds of programs by annotations," in *Proceedings of the Sixth IEEE Workshop on Real-Time Operating Systems and Software*, pp. 272–279, May 1989.

[12] P. Puschner and C. Koza, "Calculating the maximum execution time of real–time programs," *J. Real–Time Systems*, vol. 1, pp. 159–176, 1989.

[13] T. E. Bihari, "Current issues in the development of real-time control software," *Real-Time Systems Newsletter*, vol. 5, pp. 1–5, Winter 1989.

[14] C. L. Lawson and R. J. Hanson, *Solving Least Squares Problems*. Englewood Cliffs, New Jersey: Prentice–Hall, 1974.

[15] J. G. Moré, "The Levenberg–Marquardt algorithm: implementation and theory," in *Numerical Analysis: Proceedings of the Biennial Conference*, (G. A. Watson, ed.), (Dundee), pp. 105–116, Springer–Verlag, 1977. Lecture Notes in Mathematics 630.

[16] P. E. Gill and W. Murray, "Algorithms for the solution of the non-linear least-squares problem," *SIAM Journal of Numerical Analysis*, vol. 15, pp. 977–992, October 1978.

[17] K. B. Kenny and K. Lin, "A measurement-based performance analyzer for real-time programs," in *Proceedinngs of Int. Phoenix Conf. on Computers and Communications*, (Scottsdale, Arizona), IEEE, March 1991.

[18] J. Wensley, L. Lamport, J. Goldberg, M. Green, K. Levitt, P. Melliar-Smith, R. Shostak, and C. Weinstock, "Sift: design and analysis of a fault-tolerant computer for aircraft control," *Proceedings of IEEE*, vol. 66, pp. 1240–1255, October 1978.

[19] J. Chung, J. W. Liu, and K. Lin, "Scheduling periodic jobs that allow imprecise results," *IEEE Transactions on Computers*, pp. 1156–1174, September 1990.

[20] J. W. Liu, K. Lin, W. Shih, A. Yu, J. Chung, and W. Zhao, "Algorithms for scheduling imprecise computations," in *Proceedings of Third Workshop on Foundations of Real-Time Computing*, pp. 95–125, ONR, 1990.

[21] L. Cardelli and P. Wegner, "Understanding types, data abstractions, and polymorphism," *ACM Computing Surveys*, vol. 17, pp. 471–522, December 1985.

[22] A. Grimshaw, J. W. Liu, and A. Silberman, "Real-time mentat: a data-criven, object-oriented system," in *Proceedings of IEEE Globecom*, (Dallas, Texas), pp. 141–147, November 1989.

CHAPTER 11

REQUIREMENTS SPECIFICATION OF HARD REAL-TIME SYSTEMS: EXPERIENCE WITH A LANGUAGE AND A VERIFIER

Constance Heitmeyer and Bruce Labaw
Naval Research Laboratory
Washington, D.C. 20375

Abstract

An informal description is presented of the Modechart language and a mechanical verifier, both products of the University of Texas SARTOR project. Modechart specifications and timing assertions are provided for two real-time examples, the second a nontrivial function extracted from an existing avionics system. Based on NRL's experience with specifying and verifying these examples, Modechart and the verifier are evaluated, and recommendations for improvements and enhancements are presented. Topics for future research in real-time specification and verification are described.

INTRODUCTION

Hard real-time (HRT) computer systems must deliver results within specified time intervals or face catastrophe. To detect timing problems in HRT systems, current development practice depends on exhaustive testing of the software code and extensive simulation. Unfortunately, this expensive and time-consuming process often fails to uncover subtle timing and other software errors. To improve this situation, important new research in real-time computing is now in progress, largely in scheduling theory (e.g., [19], [20], [24]) and real-time programming languages and operating systems (e.g., [5], [7], [27]).

Although such research should significantly improve the quality of HRT software code, further research is needed in methods for specifying and verifying the requirements of HRT systems. Correct specifications of the requirements are critical: studies have shown that errors introduced during the requirements phase can cost as much as two hundred times more to correct than errors made later in the software life-cycle [3]. Unfortunately, most current software requirements documents for HRT systems are of poor quality, containing little precise guidance on the required timing behavior. Developers are usually forced to glean essential details from informal, natural language descriptions that are ambiguous, imprecise, and incomplete. Timing requirements are often missing. When they exist, they are usually embedded in premature design decisions.

To remedy this situation, we advocate a three-phased approach to developing HRT systems that emphasizes the requirements phase of the software life-cycle. With this approach,

- mathematically precise specifications of the timing, functional, and other system requirements are developed,
- machine-based verification tools are applied to the requirements specifications to improve self-consistency and to ensure compliance with critical timing and other properties, and
- a semiautomated procedure is used to develop an implementation from the specifications. This implementation must meet the timing and functional constraints imposed by the requirements specifications.

Such an approach should dramatically decrease the number of timing and functional errors in the system implementation. Formal requirements specifications should reduce errors by including rigorous definitions of the timing requirements and by removing ambiguous and unnecessary information. Computer-based verification should decrease errors by uncovering inconsistencies in the specifications and by demonstrating that the specifications satisfy critical timing properties. Finally, semiautomatic generation of an implementation should reduce the number of new errors introduced during the transition from requirements to software design and implementation.

Present work at the Naval Research Laboratory (NRL) is focused on the first two phases of this approach. Our interest is in methods and tools that help software developers specify, analyze, and verify the functional and timing requirements of HRT systems. A major goal is to assemble a software requirements toolset containing tools developed at NRL as well as promising tools developed elsewhere. Because most existing methods and tools for software specification focus on functional behavior, we especially seek tools for specifying and analyzing timing behavior. Of special interest are methods and tools that *scale up*, i.e., tools that are useful in specifying and verifying requirements of real-world, practical HRT software.

The planned NRL toolset contains four kinds of tools, namely, requirements generation tools, consistency checkers, verifiers of functional and timing properties, and tools that help build an executable version of the specification [10]. The language (or languages) supported by requirements generation tools should lead to formal, yet intuitive, specifications. The purpose of a consistency checker is to insure that the requirements specification does not contradict itself; without executing the specification, such a tool detects those parts of the specification that are inconsistent. Verifier tools provide formal proof that given assertions about functional behavior and timing can be derived from the specification; of special interest in the development of real-time software are proofs that certain critical events occur within specified time intervals. Tools that help translate a requirements specification into an executable version also have important benefits. An executable version can serve as a rapid prototype with which specifiers and future users can experiment to validate and refine the specifications. By running an executable version, users can ensure that the requirements specifications capture the intended external behavior. Further, an executable version can provide information useful in describing the timing constraints on certain critical functions; such constraints are crucial in reasoning about a system's timing behavior.

Although current commercial tools supporting HRT requirements specification and validation are few and limited in capability, the SARTOR project at the University of Texas (UT) has developed a number of promising experimental tools. One, a requirements generation tool, supports a graphical language called Modechart [16], [18] that is designed to specify a system's timing and functional requirements. A second, a mechanical verifier, provides formal proof that a specification satisfies critical timing properties [17], [26]. These prototype SARTOR tools are based on methods for specifying and analyzing timing properties that complement methods for specifying functional requirements invented in NRL's Software Cost Reduction (SCR) project [11], [12] and recently refined by NRL [1] and Queens University [28].

This chapter describes NRL's experience with the Modechart language and a prototype version of the verification tool [26]. Recently, we developed Modechart specifications for several example systems and then used SARTOR's verifier to prove the consistency of a set of Modechart specifications with selected timing assertions. This chapter introduces SARTOR and the Modechart language, presents two sets of Modechart specifications and associated timing assertions, and evaluates Modechart and the SARTOR verifier, identifying their contributions to real-time software technology and recommending improvements and enhancements. The chapter concludes with a summary of significant issues in real-time specification and verification that are topics for future research.

OVERVIEW OF SARTOR AND MODECHART

After describing how a specifier uses the SARTOR tools to build and prove properties about a requirements specification, this section provides a brief, informal summary of the Modechart language. For a more complete description of Modechart and a definition of its formal semantics, see [18].

SARTOR Toolset

Figure 1 shows the relationship among three tools in the SARTOR toolset. These are **chart**, which supports the generation of Modechart specifications; **trans**, which translates Modechart specifications into a form of first-order predicate logic called Real-Time Logic (RTL) [15]; and **verify**, which provides automated support for verifying timing assertions expressed in RTL. Each timing assertion is a *safety assertion*, i.e., a logical statement of the properties that must hold for the specifications to be considered correct. Such an assertion describes either the required temporal ordering of events (e.g., "No weapon can be released unless the Master Arm switch is on") or the required temporal distance between events (e.g., "The fire warning light is illuminated no more than 250 milliseconds after the software detects an engine temperature above the upper limit").

To develop, analyze, and verify a real-time requirements specification, the specifier first uses **chart** to express the requirements in the Modechart language and then applies **trans** to translate the Modechart specifications into RTL. Next, the specifier expresses the required timing properties in terms of RTL assertions. Finally, he applies **verify** to the specifications and each assertion to determine whether the assertion can be derived from the specifications. In particular, **verify** determines whether the assertion is valid, satisfiable, or not satisfiable. If the assertion is valid, then any legal implementation of the specifications is guaranteed to satisfy the assertion. If the assertion is satisfiable, then it is possible to find some implementations that satisfy the assertion, but certain implementations may not. If the assertion is not satisfiable, then the specifications are intrinsically incompatible with the assertion.

The specification and verification process outlined above is that ultimately envisioned by the SARTOR researchers. The current process, illustrated by the dashed line in Figure 1, is simpler. At present, the verifier operates directly on the Modechart specifications: no translation of the Modechart specifications to RTL is required. Further, the classes of timing properties that the current verifier can prove about Modechart specifications is limited.

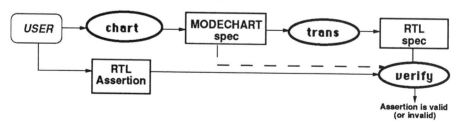

Figure 1: Specification and Verification with SARTOR

Modechart Specification Language

The historical roots of Modechart are Statechart [8], a graphical language based on concurrent finite state diagrams, and the concept of modes invented by NRL in the SCR project [12]. The formal semantics of Modechart are defined by an action/event model containing five constructs. One of these, the *mode* construct, describes control information that imposes structure on a system's operation. Each mode is either primitive, parallel, or serial. A *primitive* mode contains no other modes, i.e., has no children. A *parallel* mode contains one or more children that are said to be *in parallel*; if the system is in parallel mode M, then the system is simultaneously in all of M's children. A *serial* mode contains one or more child modes that are said to be *in series*; if the system is in a serial mode M, then the system is in exactly one of M's children. Given a serial mode M, exactly one of M's children is the *initial mode*, the mode entered when mode M is entered.

The other four constructs of the model are actions, events, state variables, and timing constraints. An *action* is an operation that is executed when a mode becomes active. A *state variable* describes the current state of a property or physical aspect of the system. An *event* is a point in time at which some state change occurs that is significant to the system's behavior. Several classes of events exist, including *external events*, e.g., the system operator sends an input to the system; *start* or *stop events*, which mark the starting and completion times of actions; *state variable transition events*, which mark a change in a state variable's value, and *mode entry* and *mode exit events*, which capture mode changes. In Modechart, a mode transition occurs when either a triggering condition or a timing constraint is satisfied. A *triggering condition* is an event occurrence and/or the truth of a predicate on modes or state variables (e.g., DAVAIL=*false*). Modechart uses deadlines and delays to specify timing constraints on mode transitions. A *deadline* is an upper bound on the time interval from mode entry to mode exit, a *delay* is a lower bound. Both Modechart and RTL assume a discrete model of time (i.e., represent time by the non-negative integers).

In Modechart, state variables and modes have important semantic differences, both in the time changes to them require and whether these changes are implicit or explicit. Because actions take nonzero time to complete, changing a state variable's value takes nonzero time. In contrast, a mode transition takes effect in zero time, i.e., the exit from the old mode and the entry into the new mode occur at the same time. Changing the value of a state variable requires the explicit invocation of an action. In contrast, a mode transition, e.g., mode entry, is implicit, occurring when a given triggering condition is satisfied or a delay or deadline has expired.

Expressing and Proving Timing Assertions in SARTOR

Timing assertions about a set of Modechart specifications are expressed in RTL using a special *occurrence function*, named @ [15]. This function, which has the form $@(\mathbf{E}, i) = j$, maps the ith occurrence of an event $\mathbf{E}$ to the time j that it occurred. The expression $@((M = b), i)$, where M is a mode and b is *true* (T) or *false* (F), represents the occurrence function for mode entry and mode exit events. The expression $@((M = T), i)$ represents the time of the ith entry into mode M, $@((M = F), i)$ the time of the ith exit from mode M.

Figure 2, which is based on [26], describes some timing properties that the SARTOR verifier can derive from a set of Modechart specifications. The verifier either determines whether a given formula is consistent with the specifications (Inner Universal, Outer Universal, All Universal, Reachability) or derives timing information from the specifications (Separation, Elapsed Time). In Figure 2, M_k represents the kth mode; c, c', and c'' are integer constants; and $t_{k,i}$ and $\hat{t}_{k,i}$ represent the times $@((M_k = T), i)$ and $@((M_k = F), i)$. An asterisk (*) next to the name of a timing property indicates that any $\leq$ in the corresponding formula may be replaced by a $<$.

NAME	TIMING PROPERTY
Inner Universal* Outer Universal* All Universal	Given M_1, M_2, M_3, M_4, $\forall i \exists j : \; t_{1,j} + c \leq t_{2,i} \; \wedge \; t_{2,i} + c' < t_{3,i} \; \wedge \; t_{3,i} + c'' \leq t_{4,j}$ $\forall j \exists i : \; t_{1,j} + c \leq t_{2,i} \; \wedge \; t_{2,i} + c' < t_{3,i} \; \wedge \; t_{3,i} + c'' \leq t_{4,j}$ $\forall i : \; t_{1,i} + c \leq t_{2,i} \; \wedge \; t_{2,i} + c' \leq t_{3,i} \; \wedge \; t_{3,i} + c'' \leq t_{4,i}$
Separation	Given M_1 and M_2, find c such that $\forall i : t_{1,i} + c < t_{1,i+1}$ ($t_{1,i} + c$ is a lower bound of $t_{1,i+1}$) $\forall i : t_{1,i} + c > t_{1,i+1}$ ($t_{1,i} + c$ is an upper bound of $t_{1,i+1}$) Alternatively, given M_1 and M_2, find c such that $\forall i \exists j : t_{1,i} + c < t_{2,j} \wedge (j > 1 \rightarrow t_{1,i} > t_{2,j-1})$ $(t_{1,i} + c$ is a lower bound of $t_{2,j})$ $\forall i \exists j : t_{1,i} + c > t_{2,j} \wedge t_{1,i} < t_{2,j}$ $(t_{1,i} + c$ is an upper bound of $t_{2,j})$
Reachability	Given $M_1, M_2, \ldots, M_K$ and $M'_1, M'_2, \ldots, M'_L$, *reachability* means $\exists d, i_1, \ldots, i_K :$ $d \in (\cap_{k=1}^{K} [t_{k,i_k}, \hat{t}_{k,i_k}]) \; \wedge \; \forall l, 1 \leq l \leq L, \forall j, d \notin [t_{l,j}, \hat{t}_{l,j}]$
Elapsed Time	Given M_k and set D of times the system is in M_k, $D = \{\hat{t}_{k,i} - t_{k,i} \mid i \in I^+\}$, find $d_{max} \in D : \forall d \in D, d_{max} \geq d$ (max. time in M_k) or find $d_{min} \in D : \forall d \in D, d_{min} \leq d$ (min. time in M_k)

Figure 2. Some Timing Properties Supported by the Verifier

TWO EXAMPLE MODECHART SPECIFICATIONS

To evaluate Modechart and the verifier, we generated several sets of Modechart specifications, two of which are presented in this section. Example 1 describes the required system behavior at a railway crossing. Its purpose is to suggest an alternative, designed for ease of change, to the specification presented in [17]. To evaluate Modechart and the current verifier on a more realistic example, we extracted the second example from the software requirements document of an existing avionics system, the Operational Flight Program (OFP) for the A-7E aircraft [12]. Example 2 has several features that make the specification nontrivial, i.e., a shared resource (the display) and several different environmental inputs and outputs. Prior to presenting the examples, we describe the top-level structure that we used to construct the Modechart specifications. The structure is designed to make the specifications easy to change.

Organizing Modechart Specifications for Ease of Change

A critical aspect of a requirements document, and one whose importance is often overlooked, is the document structure. Because the document specifying a system's requirements is likely to change, both during development and when subsequent versions of the system are built, the document should be organized for ease of change. Influenced by the structure of the A-7 requirements document [12] and Parnas' theory of software documentation [23], we have designed a methodology for organizing Modechart specifications based on ease of change. With this methodology, a HRT system is described as a top-level parallel mode with three children: an *input recognizer*, an *output generator*, and a *processor*. The input recognizer describes the required behavior of the input devices, i.e., translates the environmental variables of interest (such as characters typed by a human, continuous data from a sensor) into discrete input data items. The output generator describes the required behavior of the output devices, i.e., translates discrete output data items into the appropriate user-visible output (the display of sensor data, the firing of a missile, etc.). The processor component uses history (captured by the current set of modes) and input data items to initiate the appropriate output. In Modechart, external events represent environmental input variables, state variables represent input and output data items, and actions are used to produce user-visible output and to assign values to input and output data items.

Given this structure, we impose restrictions on how information is communicated among the three top-level modes. As in [12], the input recognizer in the sample Modechart specifications below uses only input data items to communicate with the processor component, while the processor component uses only output data items to communicate with the output generator. Future Modechart specifications could relax these restrictions somewhat. For example, a driver in the input recognizer might communicate directly with a driver in the output generator.

Organizing the requirements in this manner is based on separation of concerns. Each of the three top-level modes captures some well-defined aspect of the requirements and isolates it from the other requirements. In particular, the input recognizer encapsulates information about the relevant environmental input variables (i.e., their values, data types, etç.) and their relation to the input data items; it makes no assumptions about how the variables will be used. Similarly, the output generator only contains information about the environmental output variables and their relation to the output data items; it makes no assumptions about the input. Only the processor mode describes the required relation between the inputs and the outputs.

Example 1: Railroad Crossing

In this example, the system's purpose is to lower a gate at a railroad crossing when a train approaches and to keep the gate down as long as the train is in the crossing. We assume that trains only move in one direction and that two trains are always some minimum distance apart. The original Modechart specification of this example (see [17]) consists of two parallel modes. In contrast, the specification shown in Figure 3, called **RAILROAD CROSSING**, uses the three top-level modes described above. The input recognizer, called **TRAIN MONITOR**, uses modes to represent the system state relative to four external events, the detection of an incoming train and the train's position at three points relative to the railroad crossing, namely, 1/2 mile from the crossing, at the entrance to the crossing, and at the crossing exit. An input data item TRAIN with value **NEAR** signals that the train is 1/2 mile from the crossing. The output generator, called **GATE CONTROLLER**, describes the behavior of the output device that raises and lowers the crossing gate. Finally, the processor, called **COMPUTER**, uses the train's position relative to the crossing and the current mode to signal via an output data item, *GATE*, that the gate is to be lowered or raised.

Figure 3 presents the Modechart specifications for this example. In the figure, parallel modes are represented by thick lines, serial modes by thin lines, initial modes by oblongs, and all modes but initial modes by rectangles. State variable transition events are represented by the notation (**state-variable=value**). Figure 3 includes several delays and deadlines. The timing constraint, 'delay 300', on the transition in the Train Monitor from mode **NEAR** to mode **CROSSING** indicates that a train will enter the crossing at least 300 time units after it is 1/2 mile in front of the crossing. In the Gate Controller, the local constraint, 'deadline 50', on the transition from mode **START DOWN** to mode **DOWN** indicates that the action lowering the gate takes at most 50 time units to complete.

RAILROAD CROSSING

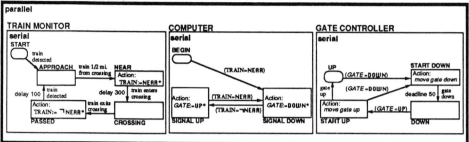

*Time to change state variable values is 50

Figure 3: Modechart Specifications for the Railroad Crossing Example

A timing assertion we would like to prove about the specifications is that the gate is down while a train is in the crossing. To express this assertion in RTL, we write

$$\forall i \exists j @((DOWN = T), j) \le @((CROSSING = T), i) \land$$
$$@((CROSSING = F), i) \le @((DOWN = F), j).$$

This expression states that every time interval during which the system is in **CROSSING** mode is contained in a time interval during which the system is in **DOWN** mode. Because mode transitions take zero time, the exit time for mode **DOWN** is equal to the entry time for mode **START UP** and the exit time for mode **CROSSING** is equal to the entry time for mode **PASSED**. We proved the above assertion using the Inner Universal formula (see Figure 2).[1] In addition, we proved a weaker assertion, namely, if the train is in the crossing, then the gate is down (**CROSSING → DOWN**). Because the verifier cannot prove formulas in the latter form, we proved that the negation of this assertion, **CROSSING ∧ ¬ DOWN**, defines an unreachable state. To generate the proof, we augmented the Modechart specifications with an *unsafe* state, a state that violates the assertion, and executed the verifier on the augmented specifications to determine whether the unsafe state was reachable (see Figure 2 for a definition of reachability). Because it was not, the assertion is considered proven.

---

[1] Because the current verifier cannot prove formulas that include the expression $@((mode = b), i)$, where b is false, we replaced $@((CROSSING=F), i)$ with $@((PASSED=T), i)$ and $@((DOWN=F), j)$ with $@((STARTUP=T), j)$.

Example 2: Pilot Data Entry and Display.

Figure 4 presents Modechart specifications for an OFP function that reads a character sequence (e.g., latitude or longitude) typed by the pilot and writes the sequence to a display panel. To initiate data entry, the pilot first presses the **DATA ENTRY** button. The software responds by turning on a keyboard light and clearing the display panel. Next, the pilot types a sequence of characters, which the software writes one character at a time to the display panel. Finally, the pilot presses the **ACCEPT** button to indicate that he has completed data entry. In response, the software turns off the keyboard light and clears the display panel.

PILOT DATA ENTRY AND DISPLAY*

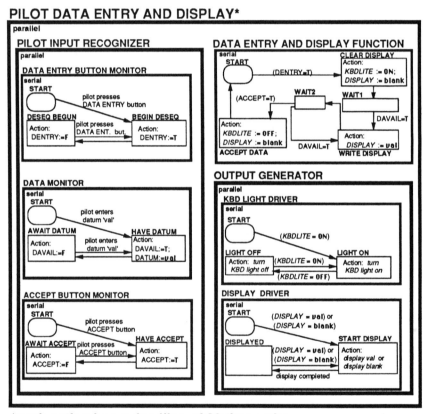

*each action has a deadline of 20 time units

Figure 4: Modechart Specifications of Pilot Entry and Display Example

To specify this example in Modechart, Figure 4 shows three top-level modes, called **PILOT INPUT RECOGNIZER, DATA ENTRY AND DISPLAY FUNC-TION**, and **OUTPUT GENERATOR**, that correspond to the input recognizer, the processor, and the output generator described above. The **PILOT INPUT REC-OGNIZER** consists of three input drivers, one for each of the three hardware devices that the pilot uses to communicate with the software, namely, the **DATA ENTRY** button, the **ACCEPT** button, and the alphanumeric keyboard. The **DATA ENTRY AND DISPLAY FUNCTION** specifies how the system responds (i.e., what outputs it produces) to a sequence of inputs. The software response depends on both the mode that the software is in as well as the input. Like the processor component of the Railroad Crossing example, the **DATA ENTRY AND DISPLAY FUNCTION** receives input via changes to input data items and produces output by changing output data items. The **OUTPUT GENERATOR** translates output data items into specific outputs (e.g., turn the keyboard light on). It consists of two drivers, one controlling the keyboard light, the other writing output to the display panel. In Figure 4, conditions on state variables (i.e., predicates that remain true for some nonzero time interval) are represented by the notation **state-variable**=*value*, and all unlabeled mode transitions occur at the time of action completion.

Using the current verifier, we proved two timing assertions about this set of Modechart specifications. One assertion is that a data character is displayed within some fixed time interval after it is entered. Specifically, if t is the time that the pilot entered the ith character, then the time at which the ith character appears on the display panel is less than or equal to $t + 200$. To express this assertion in RTL, we write

$$\forall i @((HAVEDATUM = T), i) \leq @((DISPLAYED = T), i) \land$$
$$@((DISPLAYED = T), i) \leq @((HAVEDATUM = T), i) + 200. \quad (1)$$

Unlike the proof in the railroad crossing example, where the timing assertion could be derived from the original Modechart specifications, proving this assertion required the addition of two constraints to the Modechart specifications. First, we needed to bound the pilot's input rate. Based on human performance limitations (humans can only type so fast), we defined a lower bound on the time interval between any two successive pilot key presses. Second, we needed to impose an order on the sequence of pilot inputs, since this assertion is only valid for some pilot input sequences. The specification of the **PILOT INPUT RECOGNIZER** in Figure 4 permits all possible pilot input sequences, even illegal ones. The assertion in (1) is true only when the pilot enters a legal sequence: a **DATA ENTRY** followed by one or more data characters followed by an **ACCEPT**.[2]

---

[2] In a complete specification of Example 2, the **DATA ENTRY AND DISPLAY**

Although we used the verifier's All Universal formula to prove (1), the proof only shows that the display is updated within some time period after the ith character is entered; both entry of a data character and entry of an **ACCEPT** could cause the display to be updated. One solution to this problem is to replace the **START DISPLAY** mode in the display driver specification with two modes: **START DISPLAY VAL** (displays a data value) and **START DISPLAY BLANK** (displays one or more blanks). Then, the timing assertion to be proven is

$$\forall i @((HAVEDATUM = T), i) \leq @((STARTDISPLAYVAL = F), i) \land$$
$$@((STARTDISPLAYVAL = F), i) \leq @((HAVEDATUM = T), i) + 200.$$

Because the current verifier cannot prove formulas containing the expression $@((\text{mode}=F), i)$, this assertion was rewritten in Modechart and proved using a reachability argument. (We note that a solution that replaces the **START DISPLAY** mode with two new modes is undesirable for ease of change reasons. The output driver specifications should not be influenced by the requirements of the verification process.)

The second timing assertion states that a minimum delay exists between the time that the last character of the character string is displayed and the time that a pilot press of the **ACCEPT** key is allowed. The rationale is that, before the pilot presses **ACCEPT**, he needs a minimum time to read and validate the string of characters that appear on the display. This assertion is expressed in RTL as[3]

$$\forall i \exists j @((HAVEDATUM = T), j) \leq @((HAVEACCEPT = T), i) \land$$
$$@((HAVEACCEPT = T), i) \leq @((HAVEDATUM = T), j + 1) \land$$
$$@((STARTDISPLAY = F), 2i+j-1) + 225 \leq$$
$$@((HAVEACCEPT = T), i) \quad (2)$$

If, in (2), complete pilot input sequences are required (i.e., every **DATA ENTRY** is paired with a unique **ACCEPT**) and if i is the number of character strings and j the total number of characters entered by the pilot, then $2i+j-1$ is the total number of pilot key presses. To prove (2), we needed to augment the two constraints above with a third constraint that defines an upper bound on the length of each character string and requires that an **ACCEPT** key press terminate

---

FUNCTION would also recognize illegal input sequences and generate appropriate responses (e.g., error messages).

[3] The formula's second clause is checked only if $@((\text{HAVEDATUM}= T), j + 1)$ is defined, i.e., only if the pilot has entered a character following the **ACCEPT**.

each character string. This proof used the verifier's Separation formula (see Figure 2).

The proofs of assertions (1) and (2) required that we extend the original Modechart specifications shown in Figure 4. Because the current verifier can only prove consistency between a set of Modechart specifications and a single RTL assertion, we generated Modechart specifications for all three constraints, adding them to the original Modechart specifications. (A technical issue about this approach is how to show consistency between the original and the extended Modechart specifications.) In developing the proofs of the assertions, an important consideration was whether the three constraints were requirements missing from the original specifications or whether they were simply logical statements needed to complete the verification process. We decided that two of the constraints should be added to the original specifications, in particular, the constraint describing human performance limitations and the constraint limiting the character string length and requiring termination of a character string by an **ACCEPT**. In contrast, the remaining constraint, which defines the legal pilot input sequences, was simply needed to complete the verification process: the statement that we wanted to prove concerns the system's response given legal pilot input. Hence, the statement of the assertion in (2) is incomplete. A complete statement includes (2) as a consequent and a description of legal pilot input as an antecedent.

CONTRIBUTIONS OF MODECHART AND THE VERIFIER

Modechart

The SARTOR research effort has contributed to real-time software technology by providing an integrated approach to the specification and verification of critical timing properties. A crucial aspect of SARTOR is the Modechart language. While specifications in logic-based languages, such as RTL, other first-order languages (e.g., [2], [9]), and temporal logics (e.g., CTL [4] and RTTL [21]), facilitate machine-based analysis and verification, humans find such specifications hard to produce and hard to understand (e.g., see [14]). In contrast, we found the graphical Modechart specifications highly readable and relatively easy to generate. Although complete graphical specifications of the requirements may be impractical for large systems, the readability of the Modechart specifications make them very useful during the process of constructing the requirements specifications.

A fundamental contribution of Modechart is the ease with which specifiers can use the language to understand and reason about a system's timing behavior. Specifiers can first use modes, actions, events, and state variables to define the parallelism and sequential behavior inherent in the application domain. We found that Modechart's hierarchical structure facilitated the construction of our specifications by allowing us to combine top-down and bottom-up approaches. Once the system's *functional behavior* is defined, then timing behavior can be added in terms of deadlines and delays.

Unlike temporal logics, such as CTL and RTTL, which are designed to specify the temporal ordering of events, Modechart and RTL are designed to specify both the temporal ordering of events and the temporal distance between events. In real-time systems, constraints on the temporal ordering of events are insufficient. In such systems, certain critical events (e.g., the firing of a weapon, an alert signaling the spill of a hazardous substance) need to occur within specified time intervals. Unlike languages based on temporal logic, Modechart and RTL provide a compact notation for defining the timing constraints imposed on critical events. These constraints are described in Modechart by delays and deadlines, in RTL by the occurrence function.

In addition to producing highly readable specifications that compactly express both temporal ordering and temporal distance, Modechart has additional benefits lacking in other specification languages. Unlike [12], which describes only the software requirements (represented in our specifications by the processor component), Modechart can describe the complete *system requirements*. The inclusion in Modechart of external events as well as action completions makes the specification of the complete system requirements possible. An additional benefit is Modechart's support for concurrency. In a HRT system, input devices, output devices, and computers need to operate concurrently, and their behavior needs to be synchronized. The parallel modes included in Modechart make the description of concurrency possible, while Modechart's state variables enable synchronization and communication among parallel modes. A third benefit is Modechart's support of nondeterminism. As Gabrielian has noted [6], in some parts of a specification, an event or condition may trigger a transition to more than one mode. If the actual requirements permit any one of the possible transitions, forcing a transition to exactly one mode is a premature design decision. Modechart's semantics allow the specifications to express such nondeterminism.

Verifier

We found the prototype verifier useful in improving the correctness and the completeness of our sample specifications. While human proofs of timing assertions are feasible, such proofs often contain errors, first, because proofs involving inequalities and substitutions are tedious, and, second, because humans may fail to provide complete proofs, especially for boundary cases. The verifier not only allowed us to detect such errors but also increased our overall understanding of the specifications, especially the interactions of individual components. However, while helpful, verification tools do not free the human from thinking about the logic of the specifications. They provide mechanical assistance for checking the logic. Our experience suggests that humans working with a mechanical verifier are more likely to find errors in the specifications' logic than humans doing manual verification alone.

Although it was designed to prove timing requirements, we discovered that the SARTOR verifier can also prove a class of functional properties. For example, to prove the assertion, "If the navigation mode is **AFLYUPDATE**, then the weapon mode is **BOC**," we can augment the Modechart specifications with an unsafe state, **AFLYUPDATE** $\land \neg$ **BOC**, and prove that this state is unreachable. However, the functional properties that the current verifier can prove are limited. It cannot, for example, prove functional properties that rely on data type definitions, since the tool does no type checking.

FURTHER DEVELOPMENT OF MODECHART AND THE VERIFIER

As noted above, the Modechart language and the SARTOR verifier are prototypes. In this section, we recommend some ways in which the SARTOR toolset could be more fully developed. One general comment about both Modechart and RTL concerns expressiveness. In some cases, a constraint was more easily expressed in one language than the other. For example, a Modechart specification of the legal pilot input sequences is straightforward, whereas a specification of the sequences in first-order predicate logic (such as RTL) is tedious and less intuitive, requiring considerable notation for bookkeeping purposes. In contrast, sometimes an assertion is more easily expressed in RTL. For example, given a set of Modechart specifications, defining timing constraints involving nonadjacent modes is easier and more natural in RTL than in Modechart. Further analysis is needed to identify other classes of constraints that are more easily expressed in one language than in the other.

Modechart

Passing Values. In Modechart, we found no formal way to capture a value which accompanies an external event. In the Pilot Data Entry and Display specifications, for example, suppose the pilot types the letter 'N'. The information to be communicated consists of two parts: the event E, where E represents the event 'new data available', and the value 'N'. Although Modechart provides notation for describing the event E, namely, ΩE, no notation exists for describing the value 'N'. For an example of a formal notation that describes both an external event and the value accompanying the event, see [13].

Shared Resources. We found the statement of certain timing assertions impossible if a given resource (e.g., a display device) was shared rather than dedicated. This problem arises from a lack of expressiveness in Modechart. To illustrate this, we consider Example 2. If the display driver is dedicated to the display of the character data, then the ith entry into the **HAVEDATUM** mode of the **DATA MONITOR** represents receipt of the ith datum and the $(2j + i - 1)$th entry into the **DISPLAYED** mode of the **DISPLAY DRIVER** corresponds to the user-visible display of the ith datum. However, if the display driver is shared, this correspondence no longer exists: the current version of Modechart provides no way to associate the ith entry into a mode with the jth time an associated action is completed by a shared resource.

Continuous Environmental State Variables. Currently, Modechart cannot describe continuous variables. While software can only handle discrete-valued variables, environmental variables that represent system inputs and outputs may be either continuous or discrete. An example of a continuous environmental variable is air pressure. Describing such a variable over time as a sequence of discrete samples, rather than as a continuous function of time, is a premature design decision. One possible solution that merits investigation is Parnas' concept of monitored and controlled variables [23].

Functionality. In generating sample Modechart specifications, we identified some cases in which Modechart's functionality was overly restricted. For example, Modechart prohibited the specifier from assigning timing constraints and triggering conditions to the same mode transition. In the **GATE CONTROLLER** specification in Figure 3, for example, both a deadline of 50 and a triggering condition ('gate down') are assigned to a single mode transition. The Modechart semantics forced the specifier to decompose this mode transition into two separate transitions, one governed by the deadline (or delay), the other by the triggering condition. In our view, assigning both timing constraints and triggering conditions to a single mode transition is more convenient (and less confusing). A second example of limited functionality was Modechart's treatment of *self-looping*, i.e., a transition from a mode back to itself. Even though specifiers find it very useful, Modechart prohibited self-looping for theoretical reasons: self-looping in modes with no associated action results in an infinite loop. In our view, self-looping should be allowed in Modechart as long as time in mode is nonzero.

Based on our suggestions, the UT researchers removed the two restrictions on functionality described above. In both cases, the enhanced functionality was achieved by changing Modechart's semantics. Another solution was to add 'syntactic sugar'. In most cases, we would argue against the addition of syntactic sugar, since it hides the semantics from the user.

Timing Constraints Involving Non-Adjacent Modes. Another problem we encountered in Modechart involves the expression of timing constraints involving non-adjacent modes, i.e., modes between which no mode transition exists. To express such timing constraints, we needed to create dummy modes. (We regard dummy modes as undesirable artifacts that add to the specifications' complexity.) This problem arises in conjunction with two kinds of timing constraints, those imposed by the system's physical environment and those caused by the performance limitations of the system's users. (Both kinds of constraints should be included in the requirements specifications.) In the railroad crossing system, for example, if t is the minimum time that a train requires to travel from a point 1/2 mile before the crossing to the crossing exit, Modechart provides no direct means for specifying the delay t. Because this constraint involves two nonadjacent modes, the only way to define t is to create a dummy mode. Similarly, in the Pilot Input and Display system, because the pilot can only type so fast, a lower bound can be defined on the time interval t between two consecutive key presses, say, the press of the **DATA ENTRY** button and entry of the first character. Because, in the Modechart specifications, two consecutive key presses can involve nonadjacent modes, expressing the delay t in Modechart is impossible without the use of dummy modes. (As stated above, RTL expresses such timing constraints easily.)

Verifier

User-Friendly Feedback. As Rushby has noted [25], determining whether an assertion is valid is only one of the useful functions that a verifier performs. In addition, a verifier should support an interactive human-computer dialogue that enhances human understanding of the specifications and that facilitates reasoning about them. The computer's side of the dialogue should provide feedback that is easy for the human to understand; the human's side should facilitate communication to the computer of the human's intentions. Because the goal of the SARTOR verification effort was to find an efficient decision procedure for verifying timing assertions, little attention has yet been paid to the verifier's user interface. Although the human's input to the verifier is a set of Modechart specifications, the verifier's feedback takes the form of the computation graphs used in the verifier's implementation. The result is an unfriendly user interface. To understand the verifier's feedback, the human is forced to translate his Modechart specification into the appropriate computational graph. An improved user interface is needed before the tool can be used in a production environment.

Bounds on Timing Variables. During the requirements phase of software development, complete knowledge about the system timing will be unavailable. However, in most cases, specifiers will have some limited information about timing (e.g., the time required by a given output device to complete an action, the interval between successive inputs, human performance times, etc.). In such cases, specifiers should be able to represent as a variable the time that the processor needs to perform an action (such as a computation). Then, using the known timing information and global timing assertions, the verifier should be able to derive bounds on such variables. These upper and lower bounds on processor times would have high utility for system designers, since they could supply values for the parameters of pre-runtime schedulers.

Points in Time Versus Nonzero Time Intervals. In most cases, we wished to prove that an assertion was true for a nonzero time interval rather than simply a point in time. As an example, consider the timing condition in Figure 2 called Reachability. Given two modes M_1 and M_2 that are not related serially, suppose that the system is in mode M_1 for some nonzero time interval $d = [t_1, t_2]$ and that it enters another mode M_2 at time t_2. Currently, the verifier may conclude that a state containing both modes M_1 and M_2 is reachable, even though the system spends zero time in that state. We recommend that the current timing properties supported by the verifier be reviewed to determine which, if any, should hold for zero length time intervals.

Overspecification of the Constraints. To prove the RTL assertion in (2) using the verifier, we needed to overspecify the requirement on legal pilot input and on the maximum length of the input character string. The actual requirement for legal pilot input sequences is that, if the final character string in the sequence is terminated by a key press, that key press must be an **ACCEPT**. In other words, the specification allows incomplete sequences. However, to prove (2) for legal input sequences, the verifier requires the final key press (i.e., the **ACCEPT**) to be present. Also, the verifier requires the limit on the character string length to be a constant. Such constraints force overspecification of the requirements and are thus artifacts required by the current verification process. We note that overspecification of the constraint was the result of specifying the constraint in Modechart. Specifying the constraint in RTL would have avoided the problem but was not an alternative due to limitations that the present verifier imposes on input formats (see below).

Limited Formula Repertoire. As noted above, the present verifier only supports a small number of RTL formulas. To prove the assertions presented in Section 2, we needed several additional formulas, such as (1) $A \rightarrow B$, where A and B are logical statements, and (2) $\forall i A \leq B \wedge B \leq A + n$, where n is a positive integer and $A = @((M_1 = T), i)$ and $B = @((M_2 = T), i)$ are occurrence functions with $M_1 \neq M_2$. The current verifier also restricts the form of the occurrence function, accepting only functions of the form $@((M = true), N)$, where N is a simple variable, not an expression (e.g., $2i + j - 1$). To handle the preceding formulas, we replaced each with an equivalent formula that the verifier supports. A future version of the verifier would be useful that proves formulas, such as the preceding examples, in their original form.

Limitations on Input Format. In some cases, we wanted to prove an assertion about a combination of Modechart specifications and one or more RTL assertions. For example, it is easier to describe certain timing constraints, for example, those that refer to nonadjacent modes, in RTL than in Modechart. (Note that such timing constraints, while defined in RTL, are part of the specifications rather than assertions to be proven about the specifications.) Currently, the verifier can only prove an assertion about a set of Modechart specifications. Enhancing the verifier to prove properties about a combination of Modechart specifications and RTL assertions would be useful.

RESEARCH IN HRT SPECIFICATION AND VERIFICATION

In our view, the Modechart language and the SARTOR verifier represent a significant advance in the state-of-the-art of specification and verification of HRT systems. A major advantage of Modechart specifications is their readability and the ease with which specifiers can use the language to reason about timing. Moreover, unlike temporal logics, Modechart specifications can compactly express both temporal distance and temporal ordering. The SARTOR verifier demonstrates the feasibility of machine-based proofs that Modechart specifications have certain specified timing properties.

Based on our experiments with the SARTOR tools, we have identified a number of high-level technical issues that are beyond the scope of the current SARTOR project. Below, we summarize some major topics for future research.

Uniform Approach to Functional and Timing Properties. The SARTOR toolset is designed to specify and verify only one aspect of the system requirements, namely, the timing requirements. Still needed is an approach to specification and verification that handles both functional AND timing requirements. As noted above, the SARTOR verifier can already prove a class of functional properties, e.g., that certain 'unsafe' states are unreachable [26]. However, a general-purpose verification tool is needed that can prove claims about both timing properties and a rich set of functional properties. Such a general-purpose tool could, for example, use data type definitions to determine whether certain assertions about functional behavior are valid.

A More General Timing Model. The current discrete-time model used in defining Modechart and RTL is appropriate for describing the processor component (i.e., the software model) of the system requirements, since the software runs on a digital computer. However, to describe the environmental inputs and outputs, a continuous time model is more appropriate. Further, the timing model that underlies Modechart and RTL is an idealization. A single master clock is assumed that makes no errors. In real software systems, more than one clock may be used, and each clock is imperfect. Defining a more general timing model for SARTOR would be useful.

Methodology for Requirements Specification and Verification. At each phase of the software life-cycle, specifications have different purposes and different properties. Because of its generality, Modechart can be used to construct specifications at many different levels of abstraction. Due to our focus on requirements, we seek a methodology for building and verifying *requirements* specifications in Modechart. Such specifications must have properties needed in a requirements document, e.g., design for ease of change, avoidance of premature design decisions, etc. This requirements methodology should also cover verification, providing guidance on the handling of various aspects of verification (e.g., should timing constraints be specified in Modechart or RTL, should given timing constraints augment the original specifications or are they part of the formulas to be verified, etc.). The top-level structure sketched in Section 2 is one step in the direction of a complete, comprehensive methodology for building and verifying Modechart requirements specifications. The principles developed in the SCR project (see [22], [23]) are a good starting point.

Methodology for Developing an Implementation. Although the current SARTOR methods allow us to specify, and prove properties about, required timing behavior, no guidance exists on how to derive an implementation from the specifications and how to prove that the implementation and critical timing and functional properties are consistent. Without such a methodology, the current methods and tools are incomplete. Such a methodology would extend the requirements methodology described above to later phases of software development.

An Effective, User-Friendly Toolset Interface. As noted above, tools, such as mechanical verifiers, can provide significant help in generating and improving the correctness of HRT specifications. Yet, tools that provide a powerful set of capabilities have significantly less utility if they have poor quality user interfaces. Unfortunately, the user interfaces of many existing CASE tools are ill thought-out and inadequately tested. Needed is research in interface design principles for tools supporting software specification and verification.

A Tool To Evaluate Scheduling Feasibility. In any real-time system, there will be contention for shared resources, such as I/O devices and processors. A problem is how to use the known timing information to determine that a schedule for assigning the resources is feasible. Because Modechart is not designed to handle resource contention, another tool would be useful that analyzes Modechart specifications and determines scheduling feasibility.

A final comment concerns the scaleability of Modechart. Little is known about the utility of Modechart, RTL, and the SARTOR verifier for building real-world systems. Our experiments suggest that Modechart's scaleability is limited: specifying large quantities of requirements data in graphical form is probably impractical. But this doesn't mean that Modechart isn't useful. In our view, more than a single approach to real-time requirements specification is needed. Because it produces highly readable, intuitive specifications of the required behavior, Modechart may be most appropriate during the process of building the requirements specification. In contrast, the tabular formats for requirements specification introduced in SCR (see [12], [28] for examples) are more appropriate in a reference document. These formats provide the reader with less intuition about the requirements than the graphical notation but do concisely and formally describe the large volume of requirements data associated with real-world, practical software. For these reasons, the toolset we are constructing supports both the Modechart and the SCR 'views' of the requirements data. Our future goal is to develop a single conceptual model that supports these two 'views'.

Acknowledgments. The authors are especially grateful to Paul Clements of UT and NRL for clarifying the Modechart semantics and helping us organize the Modechart specifications for ease of change. We also thank John Gannon of the University of Maryland for helping articulate the different roles that Modechart and the SCR tables might play in the requirements specification process and both Al Mok and Doug Stuart of UT for allowing us to experiment with the SARTOR tools and for their openness to our suggestions concerning further development. We also acknowledge Paul Clements, John Gannon, and Doug Stuart for comments on earlier drafts. Finally, we thank our NRL colleagues, Carolyn Brophy and Anne Rose, and our sponsor, CDR Van Fossen.

REFERENCES

[1] T. Alspaugh et al., "Software Requirements for the A-7 Aircraft," NRL report, Wash. DC (to be published).

[2] B. Auernheimer and R. Kemmerer, "RT-ASLAN: A Specification Language for Real-Time Systems," *IEEE Trans. Softw. Eng. SE-12*, 9, Sep. 1986.

[3] B.Boehm, *Software Engineering Economics,* Englewood Cliffs, NJ, Prentice-Hall, 1981.

[4] E.M. Clarke and O. Grumberg, "Research on Automatic Verification of Finite-State Concurrent Systems," *Ann. Rev. Comput. Sci. 2*, 269–90, 1987.

[5] M. Donner et al., "A Structuring Mechanism for a Real-Time Runtime System," *Proc., Real-Time Systems Symposium,* Santa Monica, CA, Dec. 5-7, 1989, 22-30.

[6] A. Gabrielian et al., "Specifying Real-Time Systems with *Extended* Hier-

archical Multi-State (HMS) Machines," Thomson-CSF, Inc., report 90-21, Jan. 1990.

[7] R. Gerber and I. Lee, "Communicating Shared Resources," A Model for Distributed Real-Time Systems," *Proc., Real-Time Systems Symposium,* Santa Monica, CA, Dec. 5-7, 1989, 68-78.

[8] D. Harel et al., "STATEMATE: A Working Environment for the Development of Complex Reactive Systems," *IEEE Trans. Softw. Eng. SE-16,* 4, Apr. 1990.

[9] C. Heitmeyer and J. McLean, "Abstract Requirements Specifications: A New Approach and Its Application, *IEEE Trans. Softw. Eng. SE-9,* 5, Sep. 1983, 580-589.

[10] C. Heitmeyer and B. Labaw, "Software Development for Hard Real-Time Systems," *Proc., Seventh IEEE Workshop on Real-Time Operating Systems and Software,* Charlottesville, VA, 10-11 May 1990.

[11] K.L. Heninger, "Specifying software requirements for complex systems: New techniques and their application," *IEEE Trans. Softw. Eng. SE-6,* 1, Jan. 1980.

[12] K.L. Heninger et al., "Software requirements for the A-7E aircraft," NRL Rep. 3876, Nov., 1978.

[13] R. Jacob, "A Specification Language for Direct Manipulation User Interfaces," *ACM Trans. on Graphics 5,* 4, 283-317, 1986.

[14] M.S. Jaffe and N.G. Leveson, "Completeness, Robustness, and Safety in Real-Time Software Requirements," Univ. of Calif., Irvine, TR 89-01.

[15] F. Jahanian and A. K. Mok, "Safety Analysis of Timing Properties in Real-Time Systems," *IEEE Trans. Softw. Eng. SE-12,* 9, Sep. 1986,

[16] F. Jahanian et al., "Semantics of Modechart in Real Time Logic," *Proc., 21st Hawaii Intern. Conf. on System Sciences,* Jan. 5-8, 1988.

[17] F. Jahanian and D.A. Stuart, "A Method for Verifying Properties of Modechart Specifications," *Proc., Real-Time Systems Symposium,* Huntsville, AL, Dec., 1988.

[18] F. Jahanian and A. K. Mok, "Modechart: A Specification Language for Real-Time Systems," *IEEE Trans. Softw. Eng.* (to appear).

[19] J. Lehoczky et al., "The Rate Monotonic Scheduling Algorithm: Exact Characterization and Average Case Behavior," *Proc., Real-Time Systems Symposium,* Santa Monica, CA, Dec. 5-7, 1989, 166-171.

[20] J.Y.-T. Leung and C.S. Wong, "Limiting the Number of Late Tasks with Error Constraint," *Proc., Real-Time Systems Symposium,* Orlando, FL, Dec. 5-7, 1990, 32-40.

[21] J.S. Ostroff, "Real-Time Temporal Logic Decision Procedures," *Proc., Real-*

Time Systems Symposium, Santa Monica, CA, Dec. 5-7, 1989, 92-101.

[22] D.L. Parnas and P.C. Clements, "A Rational Design Process: How and Why to Fake It," *IEEE Trans. on Software Eng. SE-12,,* Feb. 1986, 251-257.

[23] D.L. Parnas and J. Madey, "Functional Documentation for Computer Systems Engineering," TR 90-287, Queens Univ., Kingston, Ontario, Sept. 1990.

[24] K. Ramamritham et al., "Distributed Scheduling of Tasks with Deadlines and Resource Requirements," *IEEE Trans. on Parallel and Distributed Systems 1,* 2, April 1990.

[25] J. Rushby and F. von Henke, "Formal Verification of the Interactive Convergence Clock Synchronization Algorithm using EHDM," SRI-CSL 89-3, SRI International, Menlo Park, CA, Feb. 1989.

[26] D.A. Stuart, "Implementing a Verifier for Real-Time Systems," *Proc., Real-Time Systems Symposium,* Orlando, FL, Dec. 5-7, 1990, 62-71.

[27] H. Tokuda and N. Kimura, "ARTS: A Distributed Real-Time Kernel," *ACM Operating Systems Review, 23,* 3, July, 1989.

[28] A.J. van Schouwen, "The A-7 Requirements Model: Re-examination for Real-Time Systems and Application for Monitoring Systems," Queen's Univ., Kingston, Ontario, TR 90-276, May 1990.

Index

A

Ada 9X, 190
assertional reasoning, 40, 113

B

bisimulation, 103

C

C programming, 238
communicating shared
    resources, 87
complexity results, 112
concurrent systems, 58, 195
concurrency, 167
constrained expressions, 198
constraint blocks, 259

D

dataflow, 24
data-driven scheduling, 23
dining philosophers, 204
distributed agreement, 119

F

faux states, 9
FLEX language, 251
function-valued auxiliary
    variables, 39

H

hierarchival multi-state
    machines, 139

I

imprecise computation, 276
interleaving model, 7, 173, 199

L

linear history semantics, 175

M

MIMD machine, 169
message passing, 230
modal primitive recursive, 57
modality, 16
Modechart, 293
model checking, 157
multiprocessor
    programming, 243